The Little, Brown Guide to
Writing Research Papers

The Little, Brown Guide to Writing Research Papers

Second Edition

MICHAEL MEYER
University of Connecticut

Little, Brown and Company
Boston   Toronto

Library of Congress Cataloging in Publication Data
Meyer, Michael, 1945–
  The Little, Brown guide to writing research papers.

  Includes bibliographies and index.
  1. Report writing. I. Title. II. Title: Writing
research papers.
LB2369.M42   1985   808'.02   84-29002
ISBN 0-316 56917-8

Library of Congress Catalog Card No. 84-29002

ISBN 0-316-56917-8

9 8 7 6 5 4 3 2 1

ALP

Published simultaneously in Canada
by Little, Brown & Company (Canada) Limited

Printed in the United States of America

Credits

    Fig. 3-2 is from *Bibliographic Index*, 1979. Copyright © 1979, 1980 by The H. W. Wilson Company. Material reproduced by permission of the publisher.
    Fig. 3-3 is reprinted from *Subject Guide to Books in Print*, 1980–81, with permission of R. R. Bowker. Copyright © 1981 by Xerox Corporation.
    Fig. 3-4 is from *Essay and General Literature Index*, 1965–69. Copyright © 1970 by The H. W. Wilson Company. Material reproduced by permission of the publisher.
    Fig. 3-5 is from *Readers' Guide to Periodical Literature*, March 1970–February 1971. Copyright © 1970, 1971 by The H. W. Wilson Company. Material reproduced by permission of the publisher.
    Fig. 3-6 is from *New York Times Index*, 1972. Copyright © 1972 by The New York Times Company. Reprinted by permission.
    Figure 4-3 is from *Book Review Digest*. Copyright © 1979, 1980 by The H. W. Wilson Company. Material reproduced by permission of the publisher.
    Figure 6-1 from Martin Primack, "Land Clearing Under Nineteenth-Century Techniques: Some Preliminary Calculations," *Journal of Economic History* 22 (1962). Reprinted by permission of The Economic History Association and the author.
    Fig. 6-2 (carbon cycle) is from Charles K. Levy, *Elements of Biology*, 2nd ed. © 1978. Addison-Wesley, Reading, MA. Figure 21.3. Reprinted with permission.

Preface

The Little, Brown Guide to Writing Research Papers, Second Edition is designed for both freshman English courses and upper division students who must write research papers for courses in a variety of disciplines. This book should prove useful for anyone who needs a concise reference guide that offers accessible information and practical advice about using a library and writing a research paper. To make this book concise and manageable, I have assumed that students using it understand basic writing skills or have access to a handbook that addresses itself to such matters. I do not assume, however, any significant previous knowledge about using the library or putting together a research paper. My purpose is to add substantially to the information offered in the (necessarily) brief chapters on the research paper that appear in handbooks and rhetorics.

This text serves as a guide to writing a research paper from beginning to end. The first chapter discusses the purpose and value of the research paper assignment and provides an overview of the kind of work that goes into one. The remaining chapters develop a step-by-step approach to finding information and presenting it effectively. Chapter 2 explains how to narrow a broad subject to a manageable topic that can then be developed into a thesis. Chapter 3 offers a walking tour of the library to familiarize students with its basic organization and resources; this chapter also includes an extensive annotated list of general reference sources that helps students get started with their research. (The final chapter further emphasizes use of the library by supplying another extensive annotated list of important reference works by academic discipline.) Chapter 4 shows how to establish a working bibliography, how to evaluate relevant sources, and how to take accurate, useful notes. The process of organizing those notes is discussed in Chapter 5, which also explains how to incorporate and document the information and quotations from the notes. Chapter 6 provides specific, practical advice on writing the paper from the first draft to the final draft. Chapters 7 and 8 explain how books, journals, and a variety of other sources are documented in the paper. These samples follow the conventions used in the second edition of the *MLA Handbook for Writers of Research Papers*, (1984). Detailed discussions and numerous examples explain the Modern Language Association's new guidelines for listing works cited (Chapter 7) and parenthetical documentation (Chapter 8). In addition, Chapter 8 includes the following: 1) the new MLA guidelines for writing footnotes and endnotes, if either is required instead of parenthetical documentation; 2) a concise discussion of documentation in the sciences; and 3) a detailed treatment of the *Publication Manual of the American Psychological Association*, a format often used for psychology research papers. Chapter 9 consists of a sample research paper on a topic that students, regardless of their majors, should find interesting—the social significance of Horatio Alger's novels. Comments about the strategies and issues raised by the sample paper appear on facing pages. The entire book is made readily accessible for reference by a thorough table of contents and index.

In general, I have tried to make the book readable as well as informative. I enjoy research and writing, and my hope is that students will, too, when they see that libraries are remarkable resources and that writing can be a way to discover and clarify what they have to say about a topic. If students come to understand the relationships among reading, writing, and thinking, then the research paper is not simply an exercise in a course, but an important element in their education.

For reviewing early stages of the manuscript and offering many valuable suggestions, I am grateful to Sylvan Barnet, Tufts University; Richard S. Beal, Boston University; Michael C. Flanigan, Indiana University; and Richard S. Hootman and Gene H. Krupa, both of the University of Iowa. For answering scores of questions and generously sharing their time and resources, I am indebted to the librarians, particularly Amanda Harmon and Ann Ronchetti, at the J. Murrey Atkins Library, University of North Carolina at Charlotte. For the second edition, I am especially indebted to Eileen Thompson of New York City for her help with incorporating into the text the new MLA guidelines for documentation. I am also glad to have benefited from the bibliographical scrupulosity offered by Joel Myerson of the University of South Carolina.

At Little, Brown, I also have debts among friends. This book began as a conversation with Elizabeth Philipps—a good start if ever there was one—and developed under the intelligent and patient editorship of Charles H. Christensen. That solid beginning was preserved by a number of people at Little, Brown, including Joan Feinberg, Donna McCormick, Anne Fulchino, and Dana Norton. For their work on the second edition, I am especially grateful to Adrienne Weiss for keeping the details at bay, to Judy Maas for fine copyediting, and to Janice Friedman and Victoria Keirnan for skillfully shepherding the book through production. And once again I am indebted to the editorial diligence and thoughtfulness of Carolyn Potts.

For interruptions I am particularly indebted to my sons Timothy and Matthew, whose irresistible joy continually subverted my preoccupations. Most of all, however, I want to thank my wife, Patty, by acknowledging that if I were to express adequately my gratitude for her support, this would no longer be a short book.

Contents

8. REFERENCES   144

The Little, Brown Guide to
Writing Research Papers

The Research Paper Assignment 1

THE PURPOSE

Students sometimes think of the research paper as a seasonal labor-making invention designed to afflict undergraduates just before Thanksgiving recess or the spring break, a device to keep them from family, friends, and free time. There probably are instructors who engineer their courses this way, but most assign papers so that you will have plenty of time to investigate a topic and put it into written form. Ordinarily, the immediate purpose of such an assignment is to learn something about the topic and to present what you've learned effectively. Papers are evaluated, therefore, on the basis of what you have to say and how you say it.

Instructors in upper division courses expect students to know how to write research papers before signing up for the course, and generally they expect students to have learned those skills in an English composition course. Few teachers of economics, business, history, psychology, literature, anthropology, nursing, political science — you name the discipline — are willing to sacrifice the time to go over research writing techniques when they assign such a paper. That's why freshmen usually find themselves writing research papers. In a very real sense the assignment is a prerequisite to courses taken throughout your academic career, because it familiarizes you with the techniques and conventions (the usual practices and rules) of formal research. There is a lot to know about writing a research paper, but there is some comfort in recognizing that you'll use that information repeatedly. Moreover, the process of gathering the information provides you with a method that you can use from course to course.

THE PROCESS

Although the method is essentially a process of first shaping a topic, followed by collecting and reading the available evidence so that you can then write up your findings and conclusions, a number of specific skills, such as handling quoted material and providing adequate documentation, make up the process. These skills are usually emphasized in a composition course, but it is unrealistic to assume that either as a freshman or a senior you will remember them all. There can't be more than two or three people in existence who remember, for example, how to write a citation for an unsigned, translated article found in a collection of essays, with no publication date, edited by two authors (one Chinese, the other with a religious

1

title) who use pseudonyms. In the unlikely event that you were ever to come across such a bibliographical horror, you would understand the value of having access to a reference guide. There are, however, less desperate and exotic reasons for using a guide. The following list suggests the range of the skills necessary to keep in mind as you put together a research paper; some of them overlap and some could be subdivided, but the list should make reasonably clear what you will be expected to do and what this book can help you to do:

1. Choose a manageable topic.
2. Find relevant sources in the library (and elsewhere if necessary).
3. Read and evaluate a variety of sources.
4. Keep track of the sources consulted and where the information used can be found in them.
5. Develop a thesis — the point to be made about the chosen topic — and take detailed notes related to it.
6. Organize the gathered material into an outline that addresses itself to the thesis.
7. Write the first draft.
8. Revise.
9. Document the sources of information in the list of works cited and parenthetical references.
10. Type the final draft and proofread.

The rest of this book discusses these skills in the order listed above, which is the sequence you will most likely use as you work on the paper. These ten steps should serve you for any kind of research assignment, whether it is called a "term paper," "library paper," "source paper," "semester paper," or "investigative paper." The paper you've been assigned may be your first research project for a freshman course or your final senior seminar paper; it makes no difference because the method remains essentially the same.

THE VALUE

In addition to providing you with the basic writing and documentary skills that you will need throughout your academic career, the research paper also introduces you to possibilities for learning that go well beyond your course assignments. For all the anxiety, frustration, and hard work, in exchange you receive a valuable premium: the library will be yours. Composing a research paper is, in one sense, what an education is all about because you learn on your own. After all the grades are turned in, the credits given out, and the degrees conferred, what finally matters is not the departmentalized bits of information you take with you or the major you have declared. Instead, it is your ability to go on finding the information that you need to make sense out of a world that rarely presents itself to us in an orderly, classified, compartmentalized way, except perhaps in the library. The processes of finding similarities and differences, and of ordering experience into meaningful patterns, are habits of mind developed and cultivated in school so that you can have them for a lifetime, and an important element in these processes is research, because it allows you to go beyond your own experience by drawing upon other people's work.

Your ability to find and evaluate information will inevitably affect the quality of your chosen work and your personal life. Professionals continually must draw upon research for their work in areas such as business, economics, government, law, journalism, science, engineering, medicine, and the humanities. Although most people do not make their living as professional researchers exploring, say, the influences on a writer's work, or the cultural life of a small tribe in South America, just about everyone has experienced the need to use and interpret information gathered by professional writers and researchers: the parents whose fourteen-year-old daughter is spending thirty hours a week with her friends strolling through a shopping mall will need to learn more about contemporary adolescence; the dairy farmer who sees a nuclear power plant going up within a mile of his barns will find himself investigating the hazards of nuclear energy; the building contractor in a boom town will want to know if newcomers are likely to have the income to buy houses or rent apartments. In sum, what you learn as you invest work in this paper is going to pay dividends both in school and out.

Unfortunately some students forfeit those dividends by purchasing or borrowing someone else's paper. This sort of dishonesty is the Unpardonable Sin of student life. It is worth emphasizing the unacceptability of this kind of cheating because in recent years a number of term paper "services" have appeared that sell papers by mail through elaborate catalog advertisements. These companies stress that they offer time-saving information about research and writing so that students can write a more effective paper, but it is no secret that the complete papers they mail out for an exorbitant fee are designed to be handed in with the buyer's name on it. Quite apart from the moral issue of cheating, these papers are bad investments. Students who use them learn nothing from the assignment (though they may discover some unpleasant things about themselves) and find that they are in the same position as the proverbial poor and hungry islander who has been given a fish to eat instead of being taught how to catch fish. What is most valuable about an education — the independence and self-reliance that equip you for learning throughout your life — cannot be bought or borrowed. It's as simple as that.

Despite the benefits that accrue from writing a research paper, it can be a discouraging experience filled with drudgery and boredom if you resign yourself to a mechanical approach to the assignment. Putting together a research paper is not inherently deadly. In fact, tedious topics and dull papers are more often made than assigned. Although the formal qualities of research papers are quite conventional in their use of documented sources, there is room for creativity. You still bring to the paper your own ideas, personality, and writing style. In presenting and evaluating the materials researched you should be as evenhanded and objective as possible, but objectivity is not the same as anonymity. Inevitably, the paper you write will reflect your choices, perceptions, understandings, and values. You may not come up with anything surprisingly new in terms of information or insights, but the treatment of the topic is nevertheless *yours*. Unless the paper is allowed to serve simply as a refuge for undisturbed facts and quotations solemnly protected by a dutiful list of works cited, there will be ample evidence that you wrote it. Furthermore, a research paper can be as exciting as any other kind of writing. Even if your source on medieval agricultural techniques is written in a dull, laborious manner, that does not mean you must pay your respects to the source by duplicating its style; a citation will do. Use the writing skills you already have to convey the concern and curiosity that prompted you to choose the topic in the first place. Obviously, a good deal will depend on that choice, which is why shaping the topic is the first crucial step toward writing the paper and why the next chapter examines in detail the process of making a choice.

Shaping the Topic 2

PRELIMINARY CONSIDERATIONS

Before you start work on the paper, be certain that you understand what is expected of you. The length and nature of the paper will be affected by your instructor's guidelines and suggestions. Ask questions.

Length of the Paper

When faced with a research assignment, it is perfectly reasonable to want to know at the beginning when you are likely to be finished, and so it is natural that you or the person sitting next to you will muster the courage to ask, "How long should the paper be?" Most instructors suggest a specific number or range of pages, but if no mention is made of that, you should not hesitate to ask. That information is important because it will guide you in choosing a manageable topic and indicate how much space you will have to develop and discuss your topic.

The typical assigned length for a research paper is between 2,000 and 3,000 words. An average typed page contains 250 words; that means a ten-page paper (not counting title page, notes, and list of works cited) comes to approximately 2,500 words. This is a fairly standard length for a term paper since it provides enough space to propose a thesis, organize relevant material, and present a reasoned argument that supports your conclusions. The length, however, may vary considerably. It depends on the amount of time you have (anywhere from several weeks to the entire term) and your instructor's requirements. If the paper is shorter, you will have to narrow the topic further, and if it is longer you will have to be sure that you have enough resource materials available to avoid repetition or padding. In case your instructor responds to your question about length with the frequently heard admonition that "the paper should be long enough to cover the topic adequately," you will have to take into consideration the type of course the paper is for and what percentage of the course grade it constitutes. When writing a term paper in an upper division course for which the only other grade is a final examination, you can reasonably assume that the paper should represent an extended effort, perhaps as many as twenty or thirty pages of text. If, however, your paper is one of a number of grades in a composition course, then ten pages will probably suffice. Should you still be in doubt, the most sensible course of action before choosing a topic would be to ask your instructor to show you some acceptable student papers from previous courses. You will probably discover that these papers are of varying lengths because, as your instructor wryly said, "What's important is covering the topic adequately, not counting words." Nevertheless, those papers should guide you in what constitutes a reasonable range.

Types of Research Assignments

Unrestricted Topics

Research paper topics that are totally unrestricted are usually written only in composition courses, because the primary purpose is to have you learn the method of putting together a research paper rather than learning about a specific topic. In other kinds of courses, such complete freedom is rare. Obviously, a paper on communism in Italy since World War II would be irrelevant in a course on American folk art.

Having the choice to investigate and write about any topic you wish can be an exhilarating experience. If you already have a subject tucked away in the back of your mind that you are eager to pursue, you don't have to worry about starting from scratch. For some students, however, that free choice leaves them scratching their heads with nothing to say. The experience is something like having a tape recorder microphone thrust in your face and being told to speak. Even though you can say anything you want, what follows is often a confused stammering or silence. This momentary empty-headedness is fairly common, so don't worry about it. With so many potential choices before you, it doesn't matter where you begin just so long as you do begin.

A sensible place to start is with yourself, your own ideas and experiences. What do you care about? What have you thought of lately that you'd like to know more about? What bothers you? What delights you? You eat, go to school, consume products, wear clothes, hear music, and pay for entertainment. These topics can be developed if you jot down some thoughts about any one of them. You're subject to laws; you're affected by college rules and regulations; you can vote in the next election; you laugh and cry. What about your career goals? The point is this: if you reflect on who you are and what your concerns are, you can draw upon yourself as a resource for topics.

Another good place to start is with what is going on around you. Take a look at newspaper headlines. What issues, beliefs, opinions, assumptions, experiences, personalities, places, movements, and events are there that lend themselves to further investigation? A newspaper report about legislation designed to control television advertising pitches to children could be promising. You might ask yourself why such legislation is necessary. What is the problem with such advertising? How do children respond to it? Questions like these require research and readily lead to a manageable topic.

Another important source for topics is your work in other courses. Provided that you do not hand in the same paper for both courses, it makes good sense to develop insights and interests generated by the courses you are taking. A survey of American history may not require a research paper, but it could provide a host of potential topics ranging from the structure of Puritan family life to the impact of Henry Ford's "Tin Lizzies" on American living habits. Or you might ask your instructor in another course what subject matter will be emphasized on the final exam. You can then determine the feasibility of working up a research topic that will help you to prepare for the exam.

On the other hand, you might find yourself taking required courses from which you would prefer some relief rather than more involvement. Suppose you are interested in psychology but were unable to fit a psychology course into your schedule. A look through journals or standard reference works in the field might give you some ideas. A friend's textbook could be helpful too. *Psychology Today*, a popular magazine, is filled with articles on topics that are suitable for research papers. Even a quick glance through back issues yields articles that examine such subjects as the nature of rumors and how they stay alive; the characteristics of creative people; the pains — real and imagined — of hypochondriacs; and what problems the children of divorced parents have in common. These kinds of topics can be intriguing beginnings for research papers. Whatever the field, there are sources that can be used efficiently to suggest topics. (For a list of standard reference works in a variety of fields see Chapter 10.) Avoid trying to think of a topic in a vacuum. If you find yourself sitting alone in your room racking your brain for something to write about, go to the library and browse through magazines that interest you. This kind of reading material should eliminate some anxiety and offer the stimulation necessary to get started. And do remember that people can be resources, too, particularly your instructor and yourself.

Course-Related Topics

A course-related topic requires that you investigate a subject dealing with material covered in the course. You choose the specific topic from a frame of reference that either your instructor will supply or the course readings will suggest. If, for example, you have been studying nineteenth-century Western industrialization, you might be asked to write about the impact of any single invention — only mentioned in the course readings — on people's lives during the period. The frame of reference would be considerably broader, however, if you were instructed to write on some aspect of nineteenth-century industrialization about which you wanted to learn more. This reading could take you into any number of areas such as reform movements, literary representations of factory life, the scientific challenge to religion, or political economy.

When confronted with an assignment that requires you to relate your topic to the ideas and materials of the course, you can use that opportunity to direct the paper toward your own interests and experiences. A business major might have little interest in the narrative structure of *Huckleberry Finn* but could be intrigued by Mark Twain's get-rich-quick schemes and their effect on his writing. A nursing student might turn a general sociology assignment into an investigation of the changing attitudes of nurses toward doctors. Nearly everyone has spent time and money walking through elaborate indoor shopping malls; an examination of how and why malls have integrated community arts into the marketplace through exhibits and concerts is a topic that could be relevant to an art history course as well as an economics course. With a little imagination, almost any course-related topic can be handsomely tailored so that it will not wear thin as you research and write the paper.

Assigned Topics

An assigned topic gives you a specific subject to research and write about. Your instructor has, in effect, already done a considerable amount of work for you by shaping the subject into a workable topic that can be adequately covered in a prescribed number of pages and for which the library has sufficient sources. Instead of having to devise a topic related to a course of study on nineteenth-century industrialization, you are given the specific assignment of doing research on "The Impact of the Sewing Machine on Nineteenth-Century Fashion." Unless you confer with your instructor and secure permission to develop a related or different topic, make sure that you focus on the assigned topic. A paper that does not mention fashion but instead details the infamous "sweatshops," in which women and children toiled for long hours and low wages over sewing machines, would not fulfill the assignment no matter how interesting and well documented. On the other hand, it is easy to see how the plight of those exploited women and children might have suggested an appropriate change of direction for a course-related assignment that covered a broad area rather than a specific topic. But, again, if you are assigned a topic, you are expected to address yourself to it.

Although assigned topics limit the range of your choices, you still will have decisions to make that will produce a paper that is uniquely yours. That paper on the impact of the sewing machine on nineteenth-century fashion could, for example, focus entirely on children's clothes. An assigned topic such as "Sex Education in the Public Schools" will offer plenty of room for any number of approaches, and these approaches will be determined by what issues and arguments you deem most important. A paper on this subject could examine the students' perspective, or the parents', or the teachers'. It could argue for a particular point of view or simply account for the reasons why sex education is so controversial an issue. Good research topics frequently yield to a variety of approaches or points of view, which is one reason why they are worth researching.

Summary and Thesis Papers

A frequent source of confusion for students writing research papers is the handling of information that has been located and selected for inclusion in the paper. Should you simply present the information without comment or evaluation? Or should you express an opinion about the material gathered and argue a particular point of view?

The answers to these questions depend on the kind of paper that is assigned. If your instructor asks you to gather information about a subject without evaluating the information or arriving at a synthesis by resolving conflicting points of view, then you are writing a summary paper (also known as a report paper). The summary paper records what you have learned about a subject without assessing or analyzing the information. A paper that describes the various psychological readings of *Hamlet* without taking up the validity of such approaches or making a case for one reading over another is a summary paper. It simply reports the psychological interpretations of the play that the student has found. It provides information and leaves the process of evaluation up to the reader. Similarly, a paper that cites without comment the health hazards associated with cigarette smoking along with the tobacco industry's defense of smoking is a summary paper.

In contrast, the writer of a thesis paper is expected to evaluate and interpret the information gathered in order to draw reasoned conclusions that argue a point of view. Unlike the neutral summary paper, the thesis paper chooses up sides and argues for or against something. It goes beyond reportage to evaluations and conclusions. Those neutral descriptions of psychological readings of *Hamlet* become in the thesis paper the basis of your own interpretation of the play, which may accept or reject the perspectives the critics offer. A thesis paper on smoking could offer its point of view in its title: "Smoking Should Be Banned in Public Places." There is no question where the writer stands here.

Both the summary paper and thesis paper are valuable, but it is the thesis paper that is most often assigned, because it not only includes the skills needed to report facts and opinions accurately but goes beyond reportorial skills by requiring you to use that information to support your understanding and assessment of the material. In a sense, the responsibility shifts from the reader to the writer. You can't retreat behind a series of citations and insist that your readers make up their own minds; instead you are responsible for your own point of view and are evaluated on how successfully you have presented it. That's risky, and even though you might feel some initial anxiety about judging the work of "experts," it is satisfying to realize that what you have said is yours and that you said it only after careful study and reflection.

FROM SUBJECT TO THESIS

Once a broad subject is narrowed to a specific topic, a tentative thesis can be developed that describes your approach to the topic.

Exploratory Reading

When you begin the paper, you may have only a vague idea of what you want to write about. An interest in a broad subject such as international trade or child development could lead to a number of promising topics, but until you do some exploratory reading you may not have enough background information to see the kinds of topics that might be developed. The purpose of exploratory reading is to get an overview of a subject so that you can narrow your focus to a manageable topic. This introductory reading will alert you to potential topics that warrant the kind of intensive reading necessary for developing a research paper. Exploratory reading in general reference works, magazines, textbooks, or the subject headings in a card catalog will help you to determine if enough information is available for a particular topic and will provide you with the beginnings of a working bibliography.

Exploratory reading should be done quickly. Much of the background material you discover will not be used in your paper, so don't slow yourself down by taking detailed notes that you will very likely discard. If you find that your interest in international trade is focusing on Japanese automobile exports to the United States, it makes no sense to record information about American trade relations with the Soviet Union or Japanese exports of electronic equipment to the United States. Take brief notes to keep track of what you have read, but resist taking extensive notes until you are fairly certain that you have settled on a topic you want to explore in detail. Even if you had the time to take detailed notes on all your exploratory reading, those note cards can be more distracting than helpful when you are faced with having to choose a topic from so many possibilities. A paper on child development that finally focuses on the conflicting medical advice offered to the parents of thumb suckers will not be improved by a stack of note cards on the politics of Dr. Benjamin Spock.

Focusing the Topic

Choosing a topic is like choosing a roommate; it is essential to make sure that you can live with your choice. Given the amount of time that the assignment will require, you should try to find a topic that is compatible with your own interests. Even an assigned topic usually forces you to narrow your focus so that the topic can be adequately covered. An assigned paper on Hollywood war films is unmanageable unless it is narrowed to something like "Hollywood's Image of the Japanese Soldier, 1941–1945" or "Government Censorship of Hollywood Films During World War II." Depending on your own interests, the general assignment can be shaped into any number of topics dealing with such matters as popular actors, particular films, or typical plots. Once you are able to see the many elements that are related to a broad subject, focusing on the topic should represent an opportunity to explore something of interest to you rather than a chore. Figure 2-1 shows examples of how subjects can be narrowed to some of the elements within them, which can then lead to suitable topics. Although these narrowed topics do not by themselves suggest a thesis, a central idea that governs your approach to the topic, they represent at least the beginning of the process of developing a thesis around which you can organize the information you gather.

The amount of work and time required to complete the paper will be determined largely by how you define the topic at the beginning. The sooner you can develop a broad subject into a focused topic, the sooner you can shape your reading, note taking, and writing into a finished paper.

Unmanageable Topics

Several kinds of topics are almost guaranteed to be frustrating, troublesome, and, in some instances, impossible to complete. If you find your paper headed in the direction of any of the problems listed below, rethink what you are working on and take the necessary steps to avoid the problem. Often a slight change of direction or shift in emphasis can reshape the topic into a manageable one. If that does not work, then choose a

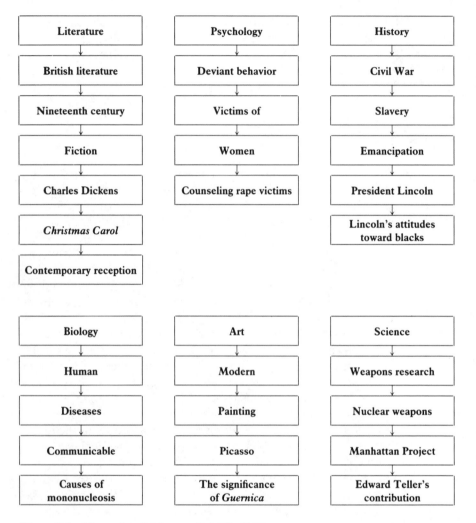

Figure 2-1 Narrowing Subjects to Suitable Topics

different topic. It is easier to abandon an unmanageable topic after several days of getting nowhere than it is several days before the paper is due.

Broad Topics

Topics that cover too much material represent the most common difficulty for students. Topics that require extensive treatment will not condense themselves into research papers. "American Literary Criticism on Shakespeare's Plays" or "The Impact of the European Discovery of America" would yield thousands of sources and years of reading. What is needed in both instances is a focus that limits the amount of research you have to do. The first might be narrowed to an investigation of mythic approaches to a particular Shakespearean play, while the second could be limited to a description of how the American Indians living along the Massachusetts coast were affected by English settlements in the seventeenth century.

Narrow Topics/Limited Sources

With topics that are too big you bite off more than you can chew, but with topics that are too narrow you chew more than you bite off. If your subject is too limited, you may find yourself hungry for sources that either do not exist or are unavailable in your library. Much has been written on the oppressiveness of life in North Korea, but a student majoring in physical education and recreation would be hard pressed to write a research paper about North Korean amusement parks. If such parks indeed exist, it is highly unlikely that there are more than a few sources available concerning them, and they might not be in English. Most instructors require that a student use at least ten sources from periodicals, books, or other appropriate materials so that the student will become familiar with the various kinds of resources available. For this reason current events are also sometimes difficult to research if the only materials at hand are from newspaper and magazine sources contemporary to you. When only two or three sources turn up after several hours in the library, it is usually best to try another topic.

Technical Topics

Any topic that requires your learning an entire discipline's worth of concepts and terms before writing the paper is going to overwhelm you (and perhaps your instructor). A rudimentary understanding of physics does not prepare you for an investigation of recent theories about subatomic particles, nor does English composition equip you to assess the function of structuralism in contemporary literary criticism. What is highly technical in a composition course may not be an upper division physics or literature course, but in general it is prudent to avoid a topic that you cannot adequately present and evaluate from the information gathered.

Single Source Topics

Topics that can be well researched from only one source are not acceptable. Even though you may consult twenty different articles and books on "Rules for Playing Backgammon," one source would have been sufficient.

Topics that describe processes ("How to . . .") are not for research papers. Similarly, those that simply recount a chronological sequence of events are also unacceptable, because such information can usually be drawn from one source. This is especially true of biographical topics that do little more than recount the facts of a person's life. "Fitzgerald in the 1920s" is a fascinating subject, but without a sharp focus it would be little more than a roller coaster ride of events that has been ridden many times by Fitzgerald's biographers.

Subjective Topics

Any topic that does not require you to go beyond your own opinions and experiences is not a research topic. Your opinion of how badly the course registration process is handled at your school might make an interesting essay, but in order for it to be a research paper you would need to look into how other schools organize registering their students for courses. You would then be able to write a research paper that either affirmed or qualified your opinion.

Controversial Topics

These are popular topics and for good reason: they often produce a variety of opinions and facts (and therefore many sources); they can be summarized and evaluated, and a reasoned conclusion may be argued. The danger here is that you may be personally drawn into an issue so much that you lose your ability to be objective. The closer you are to an issue the more wary you must be of your own assumptions and beliefs in order to avoid a lopsided paper. Resist the temptation to misrepresent or suppress evidence that challenges your point of view; instead make every effort to present opposing viewpoints as thoroughly and fairly as you would give those you support. If you remember that your task in writing the paper is not to settle an issue for all time, but to offer a well-researched, even-handed treatment of it, you should be able to present the material you find as honestly as your own views.

Clichéd Topics

Certain research paper subjects such as extrasensory perception, *The Catcher in the Rye*, and witchcraft have been done to death (mercy killing is among them). It is probably wise to eliminate the familiar topics you heard about in high school or in your college dormitory. Depending on the approach, they may be made fresh again, but too often such clichéd topics are painfully predictable and boring for your instructor. The arguments for and against the legalization of marijuana are probably about as fresh to your instructor as a composition assignment on "What I Did Last Summer" is to you. The more original and interesting your topic, the more likely you are to have an engaged reader and, for that matter, an engaged writer.

Developing a Thesis

Once you have done some exploratory reading and limited a broad subject to a focused topic, you can begin to develop a thesis. The central idea of your paper is the thesis. Usually a single sentence placed near the beginning of the paper, it sums up your own approach to the topic; it is your purpose for writing the paper, the point you want to make. The thesis statement helps both the writer and the reader, because it provides the rationale for what is included in the paper and sometimes even the order in which the information will appear. Any information that is not related to the thesis should be carefully scrutinized to determine if it should be eliminated.

After becoming familiar enough with the topic so that you can formulate your own approach, it is time to write up a working thesis. This preliminary thesis may be revised as you find additional information. Suppose you are asked to write a paper for a communications course and you have decided to focus your investigation on the subject of public television. Your exploratory reading might suggest a number of topics that could limit your investigations. Here are three:

1. Coverage of local news on public television
2. The audience for public television
3. Funding for public television

Any one of these potential topics can be explored further in order to determine what kinds of approaches would be interesting and fruitful. If you ask yourself some questions about a topic, you can usually develop a tentative thesis by attempting to answer the questions. The three topics listed above could, for example, yield these questions:

1. How does coverage of local news on public television compare with that on commercial television? Does public television have the resources to compete with commercial coverage?
2. Who watches public television? Is the programming aimed at a specific audience?
3. Who pays for public television? How does funding affect programming?

These are not the only questions that could be asked, but if they were, a thesis for each topic might look something like this:

1. Public television's coverage of local news is inadequate and will not improve until funding for local coverage is given a higher priority.
2. A survey of prime time programming reveals that public television is elitist and unresponsive to the tastes of most blue-collar workers.
3. Public television should sell commercial time to advertisers in order to expand the range of its programming.

The thesis is in the form of a declarative sentence, not a question. Each statement limits its respective topic and makes a central point that provides a researcher with a sense of direction for reading and note taking. The evidence examined and included in the paper is governed by how the central idea is defined, not simply by what information is available. While you are still recording information on your note cards it is wise to think of your thesis as a guide that will keep you from wandering aimlessly through a thicket of sources.

When you have carefully considered all your findings and are ready to write them up, your thesis may require a shift in direction. If you set out to prove one thing but end up discovering something else, then you may have to revise your thesis or even come up with an entirely new one. After finding out how much money is required for public television stations to cover local news, you might decide to change your thesis to reflect a different emphasis from what you started with: "Because most commercial television stations provide daily coverage of local news, public television should use its limited resources to concentrate on in-depth treatments of important local issues rather than daily reports of local events in the news." This revision represents a change in course, but that's all right, because that's where honest inquiry and the information gathered along the way directed the thesis.

An effective thesis statement limits and may indicate how you will approach the topic. If your thesis does not give you a firm sense of direction, then rethink what you want to do in the paper and write another one. A thesis such as "Walt Disney made great cartoons" may be true, but it is not very useful. Ask yourself some questions: What does "great" mean? Better yet: What specific qualities make Disney's cartoons "great"? Here is a more precise version that helps to organize the central idea: "Walt Disney's cartoons were innovative, because he introduced color, improved animation, and used more sophisticated plots." In the second version the word "great" (it might have been "interesting" or "important" or some other equally murky term) is transformed into three basic categories that explain why Disney's cartoons were innovative.

These three categories provide clear indications of what will be investigated and what will be included in the paper.

Note that a thesis sentence does not have to begin with phrases such as "The purpose of the paper is" or "In my opinion." If your thesis sentence makes a complete statement about your approach to the topic in clear, precise language, your intentions and conclusions will be evident without wordy introductions. Because clarity and precision are essential, you should also avoid using figurative language. To write that "Walt Disney was the Henry Ford of the cartoon industry" may be appropriate as a descriptive device at some later point in your paper, but such figurative language should not make its way into your thesis, because it does not provide a clear, specific statement that tells the reader that you are going to limit your discussion by demonstrating that Disney was innovative in his use of color, animation, and plots.

Before going to the library, make certain that you understand how a subject is narrowed to a topic, and then developed into a working thesis. Equipped with this understanding and a clear sense of the length and nature of the assignment, you are ready to begin working in the library.

3 Researching the Topic

FINDING YOUR WAY IN A COLLEGE LIBRARY

Libraries are intimidating. Maybe it's the quiet; perhaps it's the books. Whatever it is, many students feel slightly uneasy when they enter a college library for the first time. The shelves are so full and they feel so empty. You may react this way too, but after you learn how to tap the library's holdings, those books on the shelves will become one of the primary sources of your education instead of a source of anxiety. Libraries are guides, not tyrants; they are authoritative rather than authoritarian. Emerson shrewdly reminds us of this in a passage from his essay on "The American Scholar": "Meek young men grow up in libraries, believing it their duty to accept the views which Cicero, which Locke, which Bacon, have given; forgetful that Cicero, Locke, and Bacon were only young men in libraries when they wrote these books." Emerson wrote this nearly 150 years ago; the only revision required to make the passage relevant to the 1980s is to add that meek young women labor under the same misapprehension. The point is simple: those books are in the library not to intimidate or enslave you but to serve you.

Once you learn to use your college library efficiently, you will be able to use almost any other library, small or large. Because even small ones contain enormous amounts of information, they have to be well organized. Happily, just about all college libraries are organized along the same lines. It makes no difference whether your library is held up by Gothic arches or poured concrete and steel. It will nevertheless house some form of the following basic components:

Circulation Desk

The circulation desk is where books are checked out. When looking for a book that is not where it is supposed to be on the shelf, you can find out at the circulation desk if it is checked out, on reserve, or missing. Here you can also place a book on hold, renew books, and pay overdue fines. The library personnel at this desk circulate information as well as books. If they cannot answer your question, they will tell you who can.

Reference Area

The two major resources in the reference area are the reference books and the reference librarians. The reference books are there to provide information on any subjects and directions for further investigation. The reference collection does not circulate so that it is available to anyone who comes into the library; it consists of such books as almanacs, atlases, bibliographies, directories, dictionaries, encyclopedias, handbooks, and indexes to periodicals. The reference librarians are there to answer your questions and to show you how to use the library's resources. A good many research papers owe their success to the suggestions and leads offered by helpful reference librarians.

Card Catalog

The card catalog is an alphabetical index of all the books in the library. It tells you what books are in the library and where they are located. The card catalog is to research what a directory listing is to telephone calls: few connections are made without it. The alternative to using the card catalog is aimless wandering throughout the library, and some students have been known to grow old that way without ever becoming seniors. (This vital research tool is discussed in detail on pages 34–38.)

Stacks

The stacks are the sets of bookshelves that house the general collection of the library. Depending on the particular library, the stacks are either open or closed to readers. Open stacks allow you to browse through the collection and get your own books. Closed stacks, which are more likely to be encountered in very large libraries, prohibit readers from having direct contact with the shelved books. Instead, a call slip must be presented in order to have the book delivered to the reader. Closed stacks help to protect the condition and placement of books, but they are also a frustration for readers who like to poke around on their own.

Reserve Room

The reserve room houses those books temporarily removed from the stacks for use in a particular course. If an instructor judges a book to be an important part of a course reading list, then the instructor can have the book put on reserve for student use. Other readers may also use the book, but they can check it out only for a period of time allowed in the course, which is usually anywhere from a few hours to a few days. If you cannot find a particular book in the stacks and the circulation desk has no record of it, check the reserve room listings to see if it is there.

Current Periodicals

Current periodicals — both popular magazines and scholarly journals — are usually displayed alphabetically or by call number. Back issues of most periodicals are bound and kept in the stacks. Newspapers are also usually found nearby the current periodicals. Back issues of newspapers are most often kept on microforms.

Microforms

Microforms consist of many different types of materials photographed on film in reduced size. Back issues of newspapers and periodicals, as well as out-of-print books, are stored on microforms. Machines used for reading these microforms are usually kept close by the microform files. Although it is much easier to read the original materials than it is to read on a machine, some materials are available only in microform. Many libraries are increasing their use of microforms owing to restricted budgets and storage space.

Audiovisual Materials

Unless your school has a separate media center, audiovisual materials are probably kept in the library. These materials consist of records, tapes, films, slides, and other nonprint media. They may be included in the main card catalog or in a separate catalog listing only audiovisual materials.

Interlibrary Loans

If your library does not have what you need, you can sometimes borrow materials from other libraries through interlibrary loans. Check at the reference desk for information and assistance in placing a request. Keep in mind that it ordinarily takes several weeks to obtain materials through interlibrary loan services.

Other Services

Libraries, like the schools they serve, differ in size and facilities. Besides the basic components listed above, your college library may have separate sections for map collections; government documents (materials published by the U.S. Government Printing Office and other federal agencies); vertical files (pamphlets, brochures, clippings, or illustrations not suitable for shelving in the stacks); and special collections (rare books and other valuable materials). Each of these separate collections may have its own card catalog.

Many academic libraries offer computer searches in various fields. Using computer terminals that are linked to data base files, librarians can retrieve bibliographies on specific topics and, in some cases, copies of the sources themselves. This can be a quick way to collect information, but not all topics are covered by such data bases. Moreover, such services can be expensive. Check with your librarian to determine if a computer search is appropriate and feasible for your topic. Very likely you will learn that the information in these data base files is also available in printed form. Eventually, the usefulness of data base files will increase as the costs to users decrease, but for now computer searches are usually not practical for student research papers.

Your library may also offer conveniences that can make your research assignment easier. There may be private study carrels, a typing room, photocopying machines, change machines, and vending machines dispensing everything from pens to candy bars. Maps of the library, along with lists of services, can usually be obtained at the circulation or reference desk. Get one. If you spend five minutes looking it over, you'll have a good idea of what is in the library and where to find it. The sooner you are familiar with the layout of the library, the sooner you will feel comfortable enough to get to work. In a library, familiarity breeds information.

FINDING BASIC REFERENCE WORKS

General reference works are a useful starting point for your exploratory reading. They provide two kinds of information: (1) a broad overview of a subject, the sort of information you would find in an encyclopedia or biographical dictionary, and (2) lists of books and articles found in bibliographies that contain in-depth information about the subject. The second category will require you to go beyond the general reference source to the book or article for more detailed information. Equipped with an overview and bibliographic leads you will be able to see what potential topics might be explored in further detail. The following list of general reference works is hardly exhaustive, but it does list those sources that are likely to be the most useful in the preliminary stages of shaping a topic for a research paper. Brief annotations are supplied when the titles are not self-explanatory.

Dictionaries

Abridged Dictionaries

Before you begin exploratory reading on a subject, it is worth remembering that dictionaries are concise, efficient sources of information. When you come across a word you don't know, use a dictionary. Besides providing information about the spelling, pronunciation, syllabication, origin, meaning, and grammatical functions of words, many dictionaries also offer information about people, places, and things. You should own a good desk dictionary. Abridged dictionaries — much less complete than larger unabridged dictionaries — are reasonably priced and serve most student needs. Always make an effort to use the most up-to-date edition, since dictionaries reflect changes in language. Several or all of the following widely recommended dictionaries can be examined in your college library or bookstore. Listed alphabetically, each one has its own distinctive features:

> *The American Heritage Dictionary of the English Lanugage.* 2nd college ed. Boston: Houghton, 1982.
> *Funk & Wagnalls Standard College Dictionary.* New updated ed. New York: Funk, 1980.
> *The Random House College Dictionary.* Rev. ed. New York: Random, 1975.
> *Webster's New Collegiate Dictionary.* 9th ed. Springfield: Merriam, 1983.
> *Webster's New World Dictionary of the American Language.* 2nd college ed. Cleveland: Collins, 1978.

For a valuable detailed guide to these and many other kinds of dictionaries (unabridged, usage, synonyms, antonyms, etymologies, homonyms, rhymes, crosswords, spellings, punctuation, abbreviations, foreign terms, and so on), see Kenneth F. Kister's *Dictionary Buying Book: A Consumer Guide to General English-Language Wordbooks in Print* (New York: Bowker, 1977). Regardless of which desk dictionary you use, be sure to read the introduction to it so that you can interpret accurately the information presented in the word entries. If you are not aware, for example, that *Webster's New Collegiate Dictionary* lists geographical and biographical names in appendixes rather than with the main alphabetical listing, you may waste time going to another source. Or, to take another example, some dictionaries do not list very many scientific or technical terms, while others do. That would be an important piece of information for a science major. Know what you are getting into; use Kister's buying guide and the information provided in the introductions to the dictionaries to determine which ones meet your particular needs.

Unabridged Dictionaries

Unless you like the physical exercise, don't use unabridged dictionaries if you are simply looking up the spelling of a word. These are large dictionaries with thousands more entries than a typical desk dictionary such as *The Random House College Dictionary*, which lists more than 70,000 entries. Unabridged dictionaries also provide much more information about each word by incorporating word histories and quotations illustrating word usage.

> *The Oxford English Dictionary.* 13 vols. plus supplements. New York: Oxford UP, 1933, 1972, 1977. More than 500,000 entries provide a history of the development of the English language since the year 1150 by citing dates and quotations indicating when and how English words have been used. This well-known work is often referred to as the *OED*.
>
> *Random House Dictionary of the English Language.* New York: Random, 1966. Although not as large as some other unabridged dictionaries, it contains some 260,000 entries that are especially up-to-date.
>
> *Webster's Third New International Dictionary of the English Language.* Springfield: Merriam, 1961. When first published, this dictionary generated controversy because it showed how words are used rather than prescribing how they should be used. Some readers who think that its standards are too lax prefer the usage levels prescribed in the second edition of *Webster's New International Dictionary of the English Language.* Although the second edition is still useful, it is weak on new scientific and technical terms.

Special Dictionaries

SYNONYMS AND ANTONYMS

These dictionaries help you to find the right word when the one you have in mind won't quite do. Synonyms are words that have the same or nearly the same meanings. Antonyms are words that are opposite in meaning.

> *The Doubleday Roget's Thesaurus in Dictionary Form.* Garden City: Doubleday, 1977.
>
> Hayakawa, S. I., et al. *Funk & Wagnalls Modern Guide to Synonyms and Related Words.* New York: Funk, 1968.

March's Thesaurus and Dictionary of the English Language. Garden City: Doubleday, 1968.

Roget's International Thesaurus. 3rd ed. New York: Crowell, 1962.

Webster's Collegiate Thesaurus. Springfield: Merriam, 1976.

Webster's New Dictionary of Synonyms: A Dictionary of Discriminated Synonyms, with Antonyms and Analogous and Contrasted Words. 2nd ed. Springfield: Merriam, 1968.

Webster's Synonyms, Antonyms, and Homonyms. New York: Barnes, 1974. Homonyms are words that sound alike but have different meanings and, usually, different spellings (e.g., *bear* and *bare*).

AMERICAN ENGLISH

Among the books containing words and phrases that originated in America or are strongly associated with America, the following are regarded as important:

Craigie, William A., and James R. Hulbert. *Dictionary of American English on Historical Principles.* 4 vols. Chicago: U of Chicago P, 1936–1944.

Mathews, Mitford M. *A Dictionary of Americanisms on Historical Principles.* 2 vols. Chicago: U of Chicago P, 1951.

Mencken, Henry L. *The American Language: An Inquiry into the Development of English in the United States.* 4th ed. plus supplements. New York: Knopf, 1936, 1945–1948.

Thornton, Richard H. *An American Glossary: Being an Attempt to Illustrate Certain Americanisms upon Historical Principles.* 1912; rpt. in 3 vols. New York: Ungar, 1962.

USAGE

Usage books discuss the use and misuse of troublesome words and phrases. You may find that they disagree on what is "correct" or not, but you will at least be able to make an informed choice about when to use "shall" and "will" or "like" and "as."

Bryant, Margaret M., ed. *Current American Usage.* New York: Funk, 1962.

Copperud, Roy H. *American Usage: The Consensus.* New York: Van Nostrand, 1970. This book compares a number of dictionaries of usage and conventional dictionaries in an effort to arrive at some agreement on common usage problems.

Evans, Bergen, and Cornelia Evans. *A Dictionary of Contemporary American Usage.* New York: Random, 1957.

Follett, Wilson. *Modern American Usage: A Guide.* Edited and compiled by Jacques Barzun in collaboration with others. New York: Hill, 1966.

Fowler, Henry W. *Dictionary of Modern English Usage.* Englewood Cliffs: Prentice, 1974.

Morris, William, and Mary Morris. *Harper Dictionary of Contemporary Usage.* New York: Harper, 1975.

MISCELLANEOUS

There are many kinds of dictionaries to be found in the reference area of a college library. The following representative list includes specialized dictionaries on abbreviations, symbols, pronunciation, quotations, foreign words and phrases, slang, and rhymes.

Acronyms, Initialisms, & Abbreviations Dictionary: A Guide to Alphabetic Designations, Contractions, Initialisms, Abbreviations, and Similar Appellations. 5th ed. Detroit: Gale, 1976. Supplements are published annually.

Dreyfuss, Henry. *Symbol Sourcebook: An Authoritative Guide to International Graphic Symbols.* New York: McGraw, 1972. Includes a wide variety of subjects (map symbols, medical symbols, and so on).

Lass, Abraham H., and Betty Lass. *Dictionary of Pronunciation.* New York: Quadrangle, 1976. A guide to frequently mispronounced words.

Oxford Dictionary of Quotations. 2nd ed. London: Oxford UP, 1953. An index of more than 300 pages makes the entries very accessible.

Pei, Mario A., and Salvatore Ramondino. *Dictionary of Foreign Terms.* New York: Delacorte, 1974. Foreign words and phrases likely to be encountered in English.

Wentworth, Harold, and Stuart B. Flexner. *Dictionary of American Slang.* 2nd supplemented ed. New York: Crowell, 1975. Includes the language of everyone from pickpockets to politicians.

Wood, Clement. *Wood's Unabridged Rhyming Dictionary.* New York: World, 1943.

For specialized dictionaries in individual fields such as literature, business, philosophy, psychology, and education, see the bibliographies in Chapter 10.

Encyclopedias

General encyclopedias are designed to cover all branches of knowledge. Hence, an encyclopedia will probably be helpful in providing an overview and brief bibliography of the subject you are investigating, and that makes an encyclopedia a sensible place to begin when writing a research paper. For the most up-to-date information, find the most recent editions available.

> *Collier's Encyclopedia.* 24 vols. New York: Macmillan, 1984. Used in high schools and colleges, these volumes are easy to read, but the articles are generally briefer and less detailed than the *Britannica* or *Americana.* See also the annual *Collier's Encyclopedia Year Book.*
>
> *Encyclopedia Americana.* 30 vols. New York: Americana, 1984. Especially useful for its emphasis on science and mathematics as well as for information on American cities, towns, and people. See also *The Americana Annual.*
>
> *The New Columbia Encyclopedia.* New York: Columbia UP, 1975. An excellent one-volume desk encyclopedia for quick reference.
>
> *The New Encyclopaedia Britannica.* 15th ed., 30 vols. Chicago: Encyclopaedia Britannica, 1979. In 1974 the *Britannica* was completely restructured into three parts: The *Propaedia* (a one-volume outline of knowledge and a guide to the set), the *Micropaedia* (ten volumes of short factual articles), and the *Macropaedia* (nineteen volumes of lengthy in-depth articles). The 15th edition is sometimes difficult to use because of its complex organization. Some readers prefer earlier editions than the 15th since the indexing of those editions makes the information more readily accessible. Nevertheless, *Britannica* has been consistently regarded as scholarly and authoritative in all its editions, and it is worth taking the time to learn how to use the 15th edition. See also *Britannica Book of the Year.*

Specialized encyclopedias devoted to a particular field (e.g., *Encyclopedia of Education*) are listed in the bibliographies in Chapter 10.

Biographical Reference Works

If a full-length biography of a person is either unavailable or more than you require, you should consult biographical reference works. Dictionaries and encyclopedias also offer biographical information on thousands of people, both living and dead, but these sources ordinarily include only the most famous people. The chances are that one of the following biographical sources will even tell you something about the professor for whom you are writing your research paper (or see the *Directory of American Scholars*). The following works give basic biographical information such as dates, nationality, and occupation, and some provide lengthy essays about individuals. The list is divided into three categories: (1) American, (2) British, and (3) International.

American

Dictionary of American Biography. 11 vols. New York: Scribner's, 1974. Lengthy articles on significant Americans no longer living. The latest supplement was published in 1977. A shorter version of *DAB* is available; see *Concise Dictionary of American Biography.* 2nd ed. New York: Scribner's, 1977.

Encyclopedia of American Biography. Eds. John Garraty and Jerome L. Sternstein. New York: Harper, 1974. Includes living persons. Brief but useful sketches.

National Cyclopaedia of American Biography. 71 vols. Clifton: White, 1978. An ongoing project including deceased and living persons; comprehensive in scope.

Notable American Women 1607–1950. 3 vols. Cambridge: Harvard UP, 1971. An important supplement to the *DAB.* For distinguished women who died between 1951 and 1975, see *Notable American Women: The Modern Period.* Cambridge: Harvard UP, 1981.

Van Doren, Charles L., and Robert McHenry. *Webster's American Biographies.* Springfield: Merriam, 1975.

Who's Who Among Black Americans. 2nd ed. Northbrook: Who's Who Among Black Americans, 1978. Includes living persons.

Who's Who in America. Chicago: Marquis, 1899 to date. Regarded as the standard dictionary of contemporary biography. Basic information on prominent people: birth date, education, occupation, achievements, and, usually, address. There are also regional who's whos for the East, Midwest, South and Southwest, and the West. See also *Who Was Who in America,* 6 vols. (Chicago: Marquis, 1976) for biographical sketches removed from *Who's Who in America* owing to the person's death; also gives date of death.

Who's Who of American Women. Chicago: Marquis, 1958 to date. Unlike *Notable American Women,* this source lists living American women.

British

Dictionary of National Biography, 21 vols. London: Oxford UP, 1938. An essential source for notable inhabitants of Great Britain (and colonies) who are no longer living. Covers earliest history; seven supplements update the set to 1960.

Who's Who. London: Black, 1849 to date. An annual covering prominent people in Great Britain and the Commonwealth nations. *Who Was Who,* 6 vols. (London: Black, 1920 to date) reprints biographies from *Who's Who* of persons no longer living.

International

Chambers Biographical Dictionary. Rev. ed. New York: St. Martin's, 1969. Wide coverage; some contemporary figures included.

Current Biography. New York: Wilson, 1940 to date. Published monthly, this book describes people in the news from all fields. Includes photographs, pronunciation of names when needed, and bibliography of sources. Cumulated annually as *Current Biography Yearbook.*

Encyclopedia of World Biography. 12 vols. New York: McGraw, 1973. Easy-to-read entries describing 5,000 famous people throughout history. Illustrations and bibliographies.

Index to Women of the World. Ed. Norma Ireland. Westwood: Faxon, 1970. Information on where to find biographical materials and pictures of about 13,000 women.

International Who's Who. London: Europa, 1935 to date. Published annually, this source lists important people in the arts, literature, science, and government.

The New York Times Biographical Service. New York: Arno, 1970 to date. Published monthly. Reproductions of biographical materials (obituaries, news stories, and features) that have appeared in *The New York Times.*

Webster's Biographical Dictionary. Rev. ed. Springfield: Merriam, 1974. Includes brief sketches and pronunciation of names.

Two indexes to biographical materials are especially helpful because they each draw upon an enormous number of sources and will save you time.

Biographical Dictionaries Master Index. 3 vols. Detroit: Gale, 1976 to date. A guide to more than fifty biographical dictionaries and who's whos for living persons.

Biography Index. New York: Wilson, 1947 to date. Published quarterly. Indexes current books and more than 16,000 periodicals and professional journals that have biographical material on persons living and dead.

In case you do not find the biographical information you need in the selected sources listed above, consult Robert B. Slocum's *Biographical Dictionaries and Related Works* (Detroit: Gale, 1967). This listing, along with its supplements (1972, 1976), contains some 12,000 items; the book's subtitle is as thorough as the work itself: *An International Bibliography of*

Collective Biographies, Bio-Bibliographies, Collections of Epitaphs, Selected Genealogical Works, Dictionaries of Anonyms and Pseudonyms, Historical and Specialized Dictionaries, Biographical Materials in Government Manuals, Bibliographies of Biography, Biographical Indexes, and Selected Portrait Catalogs.

A Selected List of Who's Whos by Nation and Profession

Generally, these lists are by country or profession. Below is a representative list, but check with the reference librarian for a country or a profession not on this list.

Who's Who Among Japanese Writers
Who's Who and Where in Women's Studies
Who's Who in African Literature
Who's Who in American Art
Who's Who in American Education
Who's Who in American Jewry
Who's Who in American Law
Who's Who in American Politics
Who's Who in Canada
Who's Who in Communist China
Who's Who in Computers and Data Processing
Who's Who in Consulting
Who's Who in Ecology
Who's Who in Engineering
Who's Who in France
Who's Who in Germany
Who's Who in Government
Who's Who in Health Care
Who's Who in Italy
Who's Who in Japan
Who's Who in Journalism
Who's Who in Latin America
Who's Who in Opera
Who's Who in Religion
Who's Who in Saudi Arabia
Who's Who in Soviet Science and Technology
Who's Who in the Arab World
Who's Who in the Theatre
Who's Who in Vietnam
Who's Who of Children's Literature

Almanacs and Yearbooks

Almanacs and yearbooks are filled with up-to-date answers to all kinds of questions. Whether you are looking for the record for packing students into a phone booth or for your congressman's address, you are likely to find the information in one of the following sources. Both almanacs and yearbooks provide figures, charts, tables, and statistics. Encyclopedic yearbooks such as *Britannica Book of the Year* (for others see the encyclopedia listings cited above) provide articles as well as facts that constitute a record of events for the previous year.

> *Annual Register of World Events.* Various publishers from 1758 to date. Summarized events of the year in various fields for the British Commonwealth and other parts of the world.
> *Europa Year Book.* London: Europa, 1959 to date. Information on government, trade, religion, etc., for Europe and other countries.
> *Facts on File.* New York: Facts on File, 1940 to date. Weekly news digests ranging from world affairs to sports; bound annually.
> *Guinness Book of World Records.* New York: Sterling, 1955 to date. Annual records on just about everything. A joy to rummage through.
> *Information Please Almanac.* New York: Simon, 1947 to date. Miscellaneous information topically arranged with a subject index.
> Kane, Joseph N. *Famous First Facts: A Record of First Happenings, Discoveries and Inventions in the United States.* 3rd ed. New York: Wilson, 1964.
> *Statesman's Year-Book.* New York: St. Martin's, 1864 to date. Statistical and historical information on governments of the world.
> *World Almanac and Book of Facts.* New York: Newspaper Enterprises Assoc., 1868 to date. Comprehensive and well indexed.

Atlases and Gazetteers

An atlas is a bound collection of maps. A gazetteer is a geographical dictionary listing place names with information about location, geographical features, history, and statistics.

> *Atlas of the Universe.* Chicago: Rand, 1970. Photographs and maps charting space.
> *Britannica Atlas: Geography Edition.* Chicago: Encyclopaedia Britannica, 1974.
> *Columbia Lippincott Gazetteer of the World.* New York: Columbia UP, 1962. Not revised since 1952, this source is not up-to-date, but it is still useful.

National Geographic Atlas of the World. 4th ed. Washington: National
Geographic Soc., 1975.
The Times Atlas of the World: Comprehensive. 5th ed. London: Times
Newspapers, 1975. Maps plus an index-gazetteer of 200,000 place
names.
Webster's New Geographical Dictionary. Rev. ed. Springfield: Merriam,
1972. Includes information on pronunciation.

FINDING BOOKS

Classification Systems

In order to find books in a library, you must know how they are organized
on the shelves. Librarians keep track of books by assigning them call
numbers. A call number, consisting of letters and numbers, is placed on
the spine of every book. Each book has its own call number, which
corresponds to the call number found on the catalog cards for that book.
Once you have the book's call number — its address — you will quickly
be able to find it on the shelf.

Libraries use two classification systems to catalog books: the Dewey
Decimal and the Library of Congress. Since some libraries use both systems and all libraries use one of these systems, it is necessary to know
how they can help you to find a book.

The Dewey Decimal System

This sytem is named after its founder (Melvil Dewey) and the system used
(divisions of ten). Dewey classified all knowledge into ten general groups
and assigned a three-digit number to each group:

000–099 General Works
100–199 Philosophy
200–299 Religion
300–399 Social Sciences
400–499 Language
500–599 Pure Science
600–699 Technology (Applied Sciences)
700–799 The Arts
800–899 Literature
900–999 General Geography and History

These general groups are further subdivided by tens. Here, for example,
is the subdivision for literature (800–899):

800–809 General Works
810–819 American Literature
820–829 English Literature
830–839 German Literature
840–849 French Literature
850–859 Italian Literature
860–869 Spanish Literature
870–879 Latin Literature
880–889 Greek and Classical Literature
890–899 Literature of Other Languages

These subdivisions are then further divided. They follow logical patterns. American Literature (810–819) and British Literature (820–829) look like this:

810 American Literature (General)	820 English Literature (General)
811 Poetry	821 Poetry
812 Drama	822 Drama
813 Fiction	823 Fiction
814 Essays	824 Essays
815 Speeches	825 Speeches
816 Letters	826 Letters
817 Satire and Humor	827 Satire and Humor
818 Miscellany	828 Miscellany
819 Minor Related Literature	829 Minor Related Literature

Not all subdivisions correspond this tidily, but these two clearly demonstrate that the system has a recognizable order to it. It is not necessary for you to know the detailed techniques of card cataloging, but it is important to be able to read a call number from the card catalog so that you can find the book on the shelf.

The complete call number consists of (1) the classification number for the book, which appears as the first line of the call number, and (2) the author number below it. The author number gives you the location of the book. Here, for example, is the call number for a book by Christopher Lasch entitled *The Culture of Narcissism: American Life in an Age of Diminishing Expectations*.

309.17
L341c

The classification number (309.17) tells you that the book is classified in the social sciences, the 300 range. The 09 number indicates that it deals with social situations and conditions, and the .17 tells you that the book focuses on the United States. The author number (L341c) consists of (1) the first initial of the author's last name, (2) a code number assigned to the author's name, and (3) the first letter or letters of the title (excluding words such as "a" or "the"). Although you will find many books on the shelves classified in the social sciences as 309.17, only Lasch's, *The Culture of Narcissism*, has the author number L341c. Without the author number, you do not have the book's complete address, and that would be the equivalent of trying to find someone in a huge apartment building without the apartment number.

The Library of Congress System

Many larger libraries now use the Library of Congress system because it offers a more concise method of classifying specialized and expanding fields such as the sciences. Unlike the Dewey Decimal, which divides all knowledge into ten basic categories, the Library of Congress system uses twenty-one categories, indicated by a letter rather than a number:

A	General Works
B	Philosophy, Psychology, Religion
C	History and Auxiliary Sciences
D	History and Topography (except North and South America)
E–F	History: North and South America
G	Geography and Anthropology
H	Social Sciences: Economics, Sociology, Statistics
J	Political Science
K	Law
L	Education
M	Music
N	Fine Arts: Architecture, Painting, Sculpture
P	Language and Literature
Q	Science
R	Medicine
S	Agriculture
T	Technology
U	Military Science
V	Naval Science
Z	Bibliography and Library Science

These categories are further subdivided by adding another letter. Science, designated by the letter Q, is narrowed to mathematics by adding the letter A. Hence QA is the classification for mathematics. Here are some of the principal subdivisions for H (social sciences):

HA   Statistics
HB   Economic Theory
HC   Economic History
HD   Agriculture and Industry
HN   Social History and Conditions
HQ   Family. Marriage. Woman
HS   Societies: Secret, Benevolent, etc. Clubs
HT   Communities. Classes. Races
HX   Socialism. Communism. Anarchism

Numbers (between 1 and 9999) are added to these classifications to indicate additional subdivisions. The call number for Lasch's *The Culture of Narcissism* is, compared with the Dewey Decimal system, totally different in the Library of Congress system:

Dewey Decimal	*Library of Congress*
309.17	HN
L341c	65
	L33
	1978

The letter H indicates the general category for the social sciences. HN narrows the general category to the subject of social history. Below that, the number 65 indicates that the social history discussed in the book is limited to the United States after 1945. The L33 is an author number and 1978 is the date of publication.

It is helpful to think of a call number as an inverted pyramid. When you read the call number you start out with the most general kind of information concerning the subject matter of the book and move toward the specific point where you will find the book.

The Card Catalog

All the books in the library are listed in the card catalog on three-by-five cards, which are kept in drawers arranged in alphabetical order. Most books are listed on at least three separate cards by the author's name, the title, and the subject. These three different kinds of cards make it easy to find a book, though you may have little or no bibliographical information about the book. Should you know only the author's name, you will find the title listed on the author card (also known as the main entry card), and if you know only the title, you'll learn the author's name on the title card. The subject card is useful, since it allows you to find books for which you have no bibliographical information. Figure 3-1 shows three

Author Card

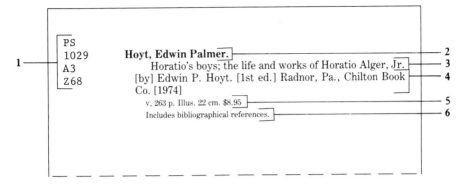

1 —

PS
1029
A3
Z68

2 — **Hoyt, Edwin Palmer.**
3 —   Horatio's boys; the life and works of Horatio Alger, Jr.
4 —   [by] Edwin P. Hoyt. [1st ed.] Radnor, Pa., Chilton Book
  Co. [1974]
5 —   v, 263 p. Illus. 22 cm. $8.95
6 —   Includes bibliographical references.

Title Card

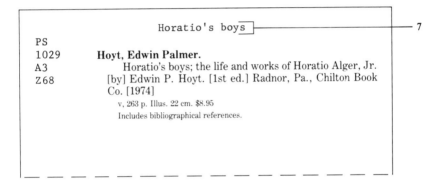

7 —   Horatio's boys

PS
1029
A3
Z68

Hoyt, Edwin Palmer.
   Horatio's boys; the life and works of Horatio Alger, Jr.
   [by] Edwin P. Hoyt. [1st ed.] Radnor, Pa., Chilton Book
  Co. [1974]
   v, 263 p. Illus. 22 cm. $8.95
   Includes bibliographical references.

Subject Card

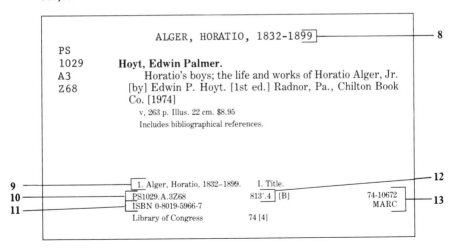

8 —   ALGER, HORATIO, 1832-1899

PS
1029
A3
Z68

Hoyt, Edwin Palmer.
   Horatio's boys; the life and works of Horatio Alger, Jr.
   [by] Edwin P. Hoyt. [1st ed.] Radnor, Pa., Chilton Book
  Co. [1974]
   v, 263 p. Illus. 22 cm. $8.95
   Includes bibliographical references.

12 —
9 —   1. Alger, Horatio, 1832–1899.   I. Title.
10 —   PS1029.A.3Z68   813'.4 [B]   74-10672
11 —   ISBN 0-8019-5966-7   MARC   — 13
   Library of Congress   74 [4]

Figure 3-1 Author, Title, and Subject Cards

catalog cards for the same book listed by author, title, and subject. Each card has the same information on it except that the title card has the book's title typed in at the top, and the subject card has it typed in the subject heading.

1. *Call number:* The call number, in this example a Library of Congress classification, always appears in the upper left-hand corner of the card, and you will need the complete call number to find the book in the stacks. Be alert for location symbols above the call number such as "Ref" (for reference) or "Spec Coll" (for special collections). Those books will be in locations other than the stacks, so consult a guide to your library to find them.

2. *Author's name:* Last name, first name, then middle name. This information is sometimes followed by years indicating the author's birth and death, if deceased.

3. *Title:* The complete title includes the subtitle, which follows the semicolon. The title on the card is written differently from the way it is written for your list of works cited and notes. You will use a colon where there is a semicolon and capitalize all the words of the title except articles, prepositions, and conjunctions, unless they are the first or last words, or they follow a colon or a semicolon. Hence, the complete title is written this way: *Horatio's Boys: The Life and Works of Horatio Alger.* Subtitles are important because they often provide a succinct description of the book. Underline the title to indicate italics.

4. *Publication information:* This listing gives the edition of the book; if there is more than one edition try to get the latest one since the information will be more up-to-date. The place of publication is followed by the publishing company and date of publication.

5. *Collation:* This information describes the book: (1) there are 263 pages (the "v" is a Roman numeral indicating five pages of front matter such as a table of contents); (2) there are illustrations; (3) the book is 22 centimeters high; and (4) the price is $8.95.

6. *Bibliography note:* An indication that the book can be used as a source for other works on the subject.

7. *Book title:* Typed at the top in black ink, this listing transforms the author card into a title card. The title card will be found in the card catalog under *Horatio's Boys,* not Hoyt, the author's name.

8. *Subject heading:* Notice that the subject heading, unlike the title card, is usually typed in capital letters (often in red ink). By looking under

the subject (here, Alger) you would find Hoyt's book even if you didn't know it existed.

9. *Tracings:* These indicate the subject headings under which the book will be found in the catalog.

Numbers 10–13 refer to information used by librarians:

10. *Library of Congress call number.*
11. *International standard book number.*
12. *Dewey Decimal call number.*
13. *Cataloging information.*

Cross-Reference Cards

In addition to the author, title, and subject cards there are also cross-reference cards. "See" and "see also" are the two kinds of cross-reference cards. The "see" cards let you know that there is another subject heading to look up when the one you have checked yields nothing. If, for example, you look under POP ART, you might find a card directing you to see ART, MODERN — 20th CENTURY — U.S. A "see also" card indicates additional headings under which related materials can be found. For ART, MODERN — 20th CENTURY — U.S., you might encounter a "see also" card for the artist WARHOL, ANDY. Cross-reference cards can provide many useful leads, particularly when you are in the early stages of narrowing a broad subject to a manageable topic.

The Alphabetic Arrangement of the Card Catalog

Keep the following points in mind when you look for information in the card catalog:

1. There are two methods of organizing card catalogs. Some libraries use a *dictionary catalog* while others use a *divided catalog*. In the more common dictionary catalog, the author, title, and subject cards are all filed together in alphabetical order. In a divided catalog, however, there are separate catalogs for authors, for titles, and for subjects (sometimes authors and titles are combined in a divided catalog, leaving the subject cards in a separate catalog). Find out which method your library uses.

2. Most libraries alphabetize the cards word-by-word rather than letter-by-letter. Unless you know which method your library uses you may

incorrectly assume that the material you are looking for is not listed in the catalog. In the following examples, notice how the order of items shifts in each system.

Word-by-Word	*Letter-by-Letter*
New Albany	New Albany
New England	Newark
New York	Newborn
Newark	New England
Newborn	Newgate
Newgate	New York

3. Abbreviations and numbers are filed as if they were spelled out: U.S. is filed as United States; Dr. as Doctor; St. as Saint; *15 American Authors* as *Fifteen American Authors.*

4. Names that begin with M', Mc, or Mac are all filed as though spelled Mac.

5. Books are alphabetized without regard to articles such as "a," "an," or "the" at the beginning of the title; hence *The Native Muse* is filed under N, not T.

6. When the same word is used for a person, place, and title the cards appear in that order:

> West, Nathanael, 1902–1940
> WEST AFRICA
> The west gate (a novel)

7. Works by an author are filed *before* works *about* the author.

8. Subject entries are subdivided in alphabetical or chronological order.

Alphabetical	EDUCATION — HISTORY
	EDUCATION — PSYCHOLOGY
	EDUCATION — TESTING
Chronological	EDUCATION — U.S. — COLONIAL PERIOD
	EDUCATION — U.S. — 19th CENTURY
	EDUCATION — U.S. — 20th CENTURY

Computer Catalogs

Some libraries use computer catalogs to save space and money. Computer catalogs use the same classification systems as the card catalog, but instead of the cards being stored in file drawers they are stored in bound computer printouts or on microforms. Your library will have a guide for the system it uses.

Bibliographies and Book Catalogs

The card catalog lists only those books in the library, but your research may require you to find more materials than your library has. If you have access to other libraries, or if your librarian can borrow a book for you through an interlibrary loan system, you may decide to look further rather than restricting your research to periodicals or changing your topic. To find books not in the card catalog you can consult bibliographies and book catalogs.

Bibliographies

Bibliographies for specific disciplines such as business, literature, or women's studies are listed in Chapter 10. There you will find useful reference works such as the *Business Periodical Index*, a *Bibliography of Bibliographies in American Literature*, and *The Women's Movement in the Seventies: An International English Language-Bibliography*.

For a general reference bibliography see the *Bibliographic Index: A Cumulative Bibliography of Bibliographies* (New York: Wilson, 1937 to date), which lists by subject current bibliographies that are published separately or as sections in books and periodicals. An entry for witchcraft is shown in Figure 3-2. Listed under the subject heading for witchcraft are two articles and one book that include bibliographic information on the subject. Notice too that the "see also" heading lets you know that more information is listed under the subject heading of voodooism. Once you consult the list of abbreviations and explanation of the entries provided in the *Bibliographic Index*, it is a simple matter to decipher them. In order to make sense of the entries for this source and others, you will probably need to examine the sample entries for each reference work you use, until you are familiar with the various conventions employed by them.

WITCHCRAFT
Jules-Rosette, B. Veil of objectivity; prophecy, divination, and social inquiry. Am Anthropol 80:569-70 S '78
Spanos, N. P. Witchcraft in histories of psychiatry; a critical analysis and an alternative conceptualization. Psychol Bull 85:435-9 Mr '78
Valiente, Doreen. Witchcraft for tomorrow. St Martins press '78 p 195-200
See also
Voodooism

Figure 3-2   From *Bibliographic Index*, 1979

Book Catalogs

There are a number of book catalogs that supplement your library's card catalog. Among the most useful are these:

Subject Guide to Books in Print. New York: Bowker, 1957 to date. Published annually, this guide lists books currently available from most American publishers. Subject headings are alphabetized and can be used for finding books the way subject cards are used in the

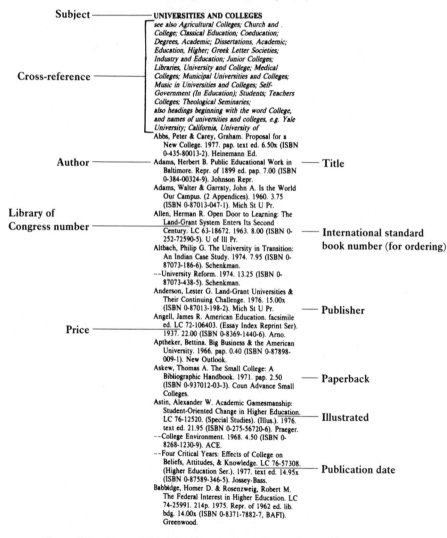

Figure 3-3   From *Subject Guide to Books in Print, 1980–1981*

card catalog. Figure 3-3 shows a portion of an entry about universities and colleges; the entire entry goes on for thirty-five columns. This subject heading is a broad one but there are many helpful cross-references for more specific subjects.

Books in Print. New York: Bowker, 1948 to date. Published annually, there are four volumes listing books currently available from American publishers. Two of the four volumes list books alphabetically by author while the remaining two list by title. These volumes, like the *Subject Guide,* provide the author, title, publisher, date of publication, and the price of the book, along with the complete addresses of the publishers.

Paperbound Books in Print. New York: Bowker, 1955 to date. Some books are published only in paperback form, and this guide lists paperbacks by author, title, and subject.

Cumulative Book Index. New York: Wilson, 1898 to date. Lists nearly all English language books by author, title, and subject.

In addition to the above sources supplied by publishers, you should also be aware that many countries make available catalogs listing books in their national libraries. In the United States, the *National Union Catalog* consists of hundreds of volumes listing books in the Library of Congress and other American libraries. These lists could be particularly useful for interlibrary loan materials, if you need them. Ask your reference librarian to explain your library's holdings.

Chapters in Books

Sometimes parts of books — individual chapters — can be relevant to your topic. A book may not appear in bibliographies about the topic because it might have only one essay related to the topic. To find chapters within books that are related to your topic use the *Essay and General Literature Index* (New York: Wilson, 1900 to date), which indexes essays and articles in books. In the sample entry shown in Figure 3-4, for example, the last item under the subject heading of Horatio Alger tells you that an essay by R. Weiss called "Horatio Alger, Jr., and the Response to Industrialism" appears on pages 304–316 in a book edited by F. C. Jaher entitled *The Age of Industrialism in America.* After locating this information by looking for Alger in the alphabetized subject headings, you will then find bibliographical information about Weiss's book in a list of the books indexed at the back of that particular volume of *Essay and General Literature Index.* Without this index, there would be no way of knowing that an article on Alger appeared in *The Age of Industrialism in America.*

Alger, Horatio
About
Cawelti, J. G. From rags to respectability:
Horatio Alger
In Cawelti, J. G. Apostles of the self-
made man p101-23
Nye, R. B. The juvenile approach to Amer-
ican culture, 1870-1930
In Mid-America Conference on Litera-
ture, History, Popular Culture and
Folklore, Purdue University. New
voices in American studies p67-84
Weiss, R. Horatio Alger, Jr., and the
response to industrialism
In Jaher, F. C. ed. The age of indus-
trialism in America p304-16

Figure 3-4   From *Essay and General Literature Index, 1965–1969*

FINDING PERIODICALS

Periodical literature, in its broadest definition, includes popular magazines, scholarly and technical journals, and newspapers. These sources
are particularly useful if you need information that is current or sharply
focused. If you were to write a paper on a recent and controversial election
in your state for the U.S. Senate, you would probably encounter no books
on the subject, but you would discover many reports in newspapers and,
very likely, some articles in popular magazines such as *Time* and *News-
week*. If the election was about a year or more ago, you might also discover
articles in political science journals. When choosing among a number of
articles on the same topic, keep in mind that newspaper stories and popular magazines are useful for general overviews while journal articles that
appear in professional publications are usually more detailed, technical,
and reliable; but they are also often more difficult to follow. Be sure you
have a strong overview of a subject before going to journals so that you
are not lost in the details and subtleties that often characterize professional
articles.

Indexes to Magazines and Journals

Articles in magazines, journals, and newspapers are not listed in the card
catalog, but they do appear in periodical indexes. For periodical indexes
to specific disciplines (e.g., *Art Index, Business Periodical Index*), see the
listings by discipline in Chapter 10. The most useful general index is:

Readers' Guide to Periodical Literature. New York: Wilson, 1900 to date.
Published semimonthly, this guide indexes articles by author and
subject in more than 150 popular magazines in a variety of fields.

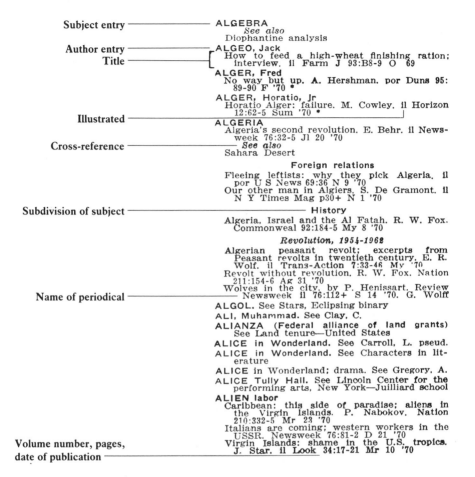

Subject entry	**ALGEBRA** *See also* Diophantine analysis
Author entry Title	**ALGEO, Jack** How to feed a high-wheat finishing ration; interview. il Farm J 93:B8-9 O '69
	ALGER, Fred No way but up. A. Hershman. por Duns 95: 89-90 F '70 *
	ALGER, Horatio, Jr Horatio Alger: failure. M. Cowley. il Horizon 12:62-5 Sum '70 *
Illustrated	**ALGERIA** Algeria's second revolution. E. Behr. il News- week 76:32-5 Jl 20 '70
Cross-reference	*See also* Sahara Desert
	Foreign relations Fleeing leftists: why they pick Algeria. il por U S News 69:36 N 9 '70 Our other man in Algiers. S. De Gramont. il N Y Times Mag p30+ N 1 '70
Subdivision of subject	**History** Algeria, Israel and the Al Fatah. R. W. Fox. Commonweal 92:184-5 My 8 '70
	Revolution, 1954-1962 Algerian peasant revolt; excerpts from Peasant revolts in twentieth century. E. R. Wolf. il Trans-Action 7:33-46 My '70 Revolt without revolution. R. W. Fox. Nation 211:154-6 Ag 31 '70 Wolves in the city, by P. Henissart. Review
Name of periodical	Newsweek il 76:112+ S 14 '70. G. Wolff
	ALGOL. See Stars, Eclipsing binary
	ALI, Muhammad. See Clay, C.
	ALIANZA (Federal alliance of land grants) See Land tenure—United States
	ALICE in Wonderland. See Carroll, L. pseud.
	ALICE in Wonderland. See Characters in lit- erature
	ALICE in Wonderland; drama. See Gregory, A.
	ALICE Tully Hall. See Lincoln Center for the performing arts, New York—Juilliard school
	ALIEN labor Caribbean: this side of paradise; aliens in the Virgin Islands. P. Nabokov. Nation 210:332-5 Mr 23 '70 Italians are coming; western workers in the USSR. Newsweek 76:81-2 D 21 '70
Volume number, pages, date of publication	Virgin Islands: shame in the U.S. tropics. J. Star. il Look 34:17-21 Mr 10 '70

Figure 3-5   From *Readers' Guide to Periodical Literature*

Hence it is especially useful for current events. Bound volumes collect the semimonthly entries and incorporate all entries in one alphabetical listing. Figure 3-5 shows a sample entry from the March 1970 through February 1971 volume (it is worth remembering that the indexes published by the H. W. Wilson Company use the same form of abbreviated entries).

Several other widely used periodical indexes also list articles by author and subject:

Poole's Index to Periodical Literature, 1802–1891. Boston: Houghton, 1891. An index, by subject, of nineteenth-century magazine articles including book reviews in the United States and England. A supplement covers the years 1892–1907.

Nineteenth Century Readers' Guide to Periodical Literature, 1890–1899. New York: Wilson, 1944. An author/subject index to articles published during the 1890s.

British Humanities Index. London: Library Assoc., 1962 to date. An index, by subject, of British periodicals in the humanities, including some in the social sciences.

Humanities Index. New York: Wilson, 1974 to date. Especially strong in literature, philosophy, and history. This guide, like the *Social Sciences Index* (see below), indexes by author and subject, and both indexes include many more scholarly journals than the *Readers' Guide to Periodical Literature.* For material on the humanities from 1907 to 1965, consult the *International Index;* for 1965–1974, consult the *Social Sciences and Humanities Index.*

Social Sciences Index. New York: Wilson, 1974 to date. From 1907 to 1965 material now covered in *Social Sciences Index* was combined with the *Humanities Index* and called the *International Index.* From 1965 to 1974 the combined indexes were called the *Social Sciences and Humanities Index.* Since their separation in 1974 the *Social Sciences Index* lists scholarly articles in areas such as geography, law, medical science, psychology, and sociology.

Popular Periodicals Index. Camden: Bottorff, 1973 to date. A useful supplement to the *Readers' Guide* for popular magazines not listed there.

General Science Index. New York: Wilson, 1978 to date. A listing of scholarly, but not overly technical, science periodicals.

Indexes to Newspapers

Newspaper indexes provide information about news stories, editorials, feature articles, and other materials. The following indexes are especially important and available in most college libraries. Keep in mind that other newspapers may have indexing services, such as *The Wall Street Journal.* By using one of the following indexes you can learn the approximate dates for coverage of events that appear in other newspapers for which there are no indexes.

Milner, Anita C. *Newspaper Indexes: A Location and Subject Guide for Researchers.* Metuchen: Scarecrow, 1977. Lists by state and county unpublished indexes located in libraries, historical societies, and newspaper files.

Newspaper Index. Wooster: Bell, 1972 to date. Subject and author indexes to four major American newspapers: the *Washington Post, Chicago Tribune, Los Angeles Times,* and *New Orleans Times-Picayune.* Since 1975, each index has been published separately.

The New York Times Index. New York: New York Times, 1913 to date. Entries provide detailed information about location and content of materials. Less complete indexes to *The New York Times* are available for the years 1851–1912. Many libraries have the entire run of the newspaper on microfilm. Figure 3-6 shows a sample entry from 1972.

The Times Index, London: Times, 1906 to date. Subject indexes to the *London Times,* the *Times Literary Supplement,* the *Times Educational Supplement,* and the *Times Higher Education Supplement.*

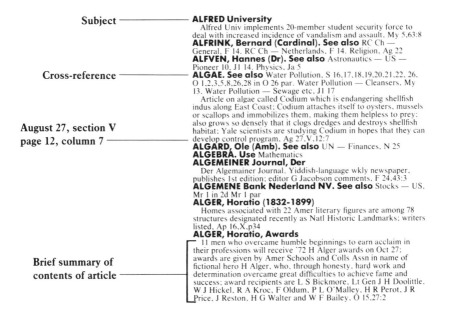

Subject — **ALFRED University**
Alfred Univ implements 20-member student security force to deal with increased incidence of vandalism and assault. My 5,63:8
ALFRINK, Bernard (Cardinal). See also RC Ch — General, F 14. RC Ch — Netherlands, F 14. Religion, Ag 22
ALFVEN, Hannes (Dr). See also Astronautics — US — Pioneer 10, Jl 14. Physics, Ja 5

Cross-reference — **ALGAE. See also** Water Pollution, S 16,17,18,19,20,21,22, 26, O 1,2,3,5,8,26,28 in O 26 par. Water Pollution — Cleansers, My 13. Water Pollution — Sewage etc, Jl 17
Article on algae called Codium which is endangering shellfish indus along East Coast; Codium attaches itself to oysters, mussels or scallops and immobilizes them, making them helpless to prey;

August 27, section V
page 12, column 7 — also grows so densely that it clogs dredges and destroys shellfish habitat; Yale scientists are studying Codium in hopes that they can develop control program. Ag 27,V,12:7
ALGARD, Ole (Amb). See also UN — Finances, N 25
ALGEBRA. Use Mathematics
ALGEMEINER Journal, Der
Der Algemainer Journal. Yiddish-language wkly newspaper, publishes 1st edition; editor G Jacobson comments. F 24,43:3
ALGEMENE Bank Nederland NV. See also Stocks — US. Mr 1 in 2d Mr 1 par
ALGER, Horatio (1832-1899)
Homes associated with 22 Amer literary figures are among 78 structures designated recently as Natl Historic Landmarks; writers listed, Ap 16,X,p34
ALGER, Horatio, Awards

Brief summary of
contents of article — 11 men who overcame humble beginnings to earn acclaim in their professions will receive '72 H Alger awards on Oct 27; awards are given by Amer Schools and Colls Assn in name of fictional hero H Alger, who, through honesty, hard work and determination overcame great difficulties to achieve fame and success; award recipients are L S Bickmore, Lt Gen J H Doolittle, W J Hickel, R A Kroc, F Oldum, P L O'Malley, H R Perot, J R Price, J Reston, H G Walter and W F Bailey. O 15,27:2

Figure 3-6   From *The New York Times Index*

Lists of Magazines, Journals, and Newspapers

The following lists provide publication information about periodicals and, in many instances, where you can locate them in other libraries, which is especially helpful if you need to request an interlibrary loan.

Ayer Directory of Publications. Philadelphia: Ayer, 1880 to date. A geographical listing of periodicals published in the United States and Canada.

Magazines for Libraries. 3rd ed. New York: Bowker, 1978. An annotated list of magazines and journals arranged by subject area.

Standard Periodical Directory. New York: Oxbridge, 1964 to date. An annual listing by subject of about 53,000 periodicals (except newspapers) published in the United States and Canada.

Ulrich's International Periodicals Directory: A Classified Guide to Current Periodicals, Foreign and Domestic. 17th ed., 2 vols. New York: Bowker, 1977. Classified by subject (e.g., education, literature, etc.), this listing of about 60,000 periodicals provides detailed publication information and where they are indexed.

Union List of Serials in Libraries of the United States and Canada. 3rd ed., 5 vols. New York: Wilson, 1965. This list of more than 150,000 titles helps you to locate libraries that have a particular periodical you might need and also indicates which issues a particular library has. It is supplemented by *New Serial Titles*, a listing of titles published after 1949.

FINDING GOVERNMENT DOCUMENTS

Government publications may be sponsored by local, state, or national offices. They are useful because they offer everything from bibliographies and congressional hearings to analytic research reports and practical advice for consumers. Some libraries have separate sections where these numerous materials are cataloged while others keep them in reference areas. Ask the reference librarian where and how they are cataloged in your library. The following reference works are helpful guides and lists of government publications:

Boyd, Anne Morris, and Rae E. Rips. *United States Government Publications.* 3rd ed. New York: Wilson, 1949. An overview of government publications and how to locate them.

Jackson, Ellen. *Subject Guide to Major United States Government Publications.* Chicago: ALA, 1968. Includes both the early and relatively recent important publications.

Leidy, W. Philip. *A Popular Guide to Government Publications.* 3rd ed. New York: Columbia UP, 1968. A listing of publications, organized by subject, that appeared from 1961 to 1966.

Monthly Catalog of United States Government Publications. Washington: GPO, 1895 to date. A monthly listing of all government publications with a comprehensive subject index.

Monthly Checklist of State Publications. Washington: GPO, 1910 to date. Lists all state publications received by the Library of Congress.

Pohle, Linda C. *A Guide to Popular Government Publications.* Littleton: Libraries Unlimited, 1972. Supplements Leidy (see above) for publications appearing between 1967 and 1971.

Schmeckebier, Laurence F., and Roy B. Eastin. *Government Publications and Their Use.* 2nd ed. Washington: Brookings Institution, 1969. Provides useful information about government publishing practices, what is published, and where to obtain the publications.

FINDING NONPRINT MATERIALS

Although books and periodical articles will most likely constitute the bulk of the sources for your research paper, you may also find useful information in nonprint materials such as films, slides, phonograph records, tape recordings, television and radio programs, lectures, public speeches, and interviews. If you are having a rocky time reading and writing a paper on Shakespeare's *The Tempest,* you'll find it easier to read the play if you listen along with a recording. Other audiovisual materials can help you to develop an overview of material so that when you get to in-depth reading and note taking you will have a better idea of the context and be better able to understand the material. Suppose, for example, you are assigned a research paper on Martin Luther King's role in the civil rights movement of the early 1960s. Your library (or audiovisual center) probably has some recordings of his speeches and perhaps some films or filmstrips of his activities. An hour or two with that material could provide a sense of the man and his ability to inspire crowds that might be difficult to appreciate from only the printed page. In short, remember that information can be found in a variety of forms, many of which, but not all, are in the library. Libraries are sources of learning, but they do not confine learning.

Perhaps it is worth emphasizing here that the most important sources of nonprint information in the library are the people who sit behind the reference desk. The reference librarians are there to answer your questions and they are well equipped to do so. To get the best answers from them it is important to ask questions that can be answered specifically. If, for example, you want to know which recordings of Beethoven's Ninth Symphony are regarded as superior by music critics, you would not ask "What does the library have on Beethoven?" The more specific you are — the more you can identify what it is you want to learn — the more helpful the librarian can be. In this case, the question is not so much about Beethoven as it is about the critics' assessments of the various recordings of one of his symphonies. The more you can ask specific questions, the better able the librarian will be to help you. Don't be shy about asking questions, but don't expect the librarians to do all the work for you. They won't hesitate to explain that it is their job to answer the question but your job to come up with one — which is to say that you are expected to have put at least some thought into what it is you want to learn. Having done that, you've got yourself a friend.

Using 4
the Sources

Once you have determined which sources are likely to have the information you need for your topic, your task will be to record where the information comes from, evaluate its usefulness, and take accurate notes. (General reference sources are discussed and listed in Chapter 3; for a selected list of important reference books and journals in various disciplines, see Chapter 10.) Keeping close track of the sources you use and taking careful notes of your reading will make organizing and writing the paper much easier than it would be if you had to waste time looking up sources again because you neglected to cite a page number or weren't certain where a quotation was supposed to end. This chapter explains how to establish a working bibliography and a list of works cited, how to evaluate your sources, and how to take effective notes on your reading. Before you begin, however, you may find it useful to familiarize yourself with the list of "Abbreviations for Reference Words" on pages 194–197, which lists terms that you are likely to encounter in your reading. These terms will also be useful to you in taking efficient notes.

ESTABLISHING THE BIBLIOGRAPHY

The bibliography is a list of sources of information for your topic. There are two kinds of bibliographies for research papers: a working bibliography and a "final bibliography," or list of works cited. The *working bibliography* is a preliminary list of books, articles, and other materials that you think might be useful for investigating the topic. This list is established by consulting the card catalog and other sources such as periodical indexes. Books often include bibliographical sources that may appear at the end of each chapter or at the end of the book. The notes to journal articles are also good sources for citations to other studies related to the topic. The more recent the book or article is, the more up-to-date the bibliographical information will be. If you find a recently published, well-documented scholarly book that includes an extensive bibliography or list of works cited, you may find that you will be able to limit your search for additional relevant sources to the past several years since the book already lists the best sources, which could save you considerable time in the reference area.

As you examine these books and articles, eliminating some while finding additional leads in others, the working bibliography will revise itself, depending on how you shape the topic. The *final bibliography*, which is actually a list of works cited, appears at the end of the completed paper. It is the typed, alphabetized list of sources used for the research. The list of works cited usually consists of fewer items than the working bibliography since it contains only those materials that were found to be useful. (A sample list of works cited for a student paper appears on pages 236–239.)

Preparing the Bibliography Cards

To prepare a working bibliography, list each title separately on a three-by-five card. Cards are preferable to notebook paper because, like the rubber band that keeps them together, the cards are flexible: they are easy to carry around and can be categorized in several ways. If the titles are arranged by call number, you will spend considerably less time walking through the stacks from floor to floor. You can simply pick up at one time all the materials located in the same section of the library. Also, the cards can later be alphabetized by author (and by title when no author is given) so that you can type your final bibliography from them even if cards were deleted or added along the way. Also, they will be legible because, unlike notebook paper, there will be no messy deletions or cramped additions in the margins.

List only those titles that seem likely to be relevant to your topic. Remember that your job is not to compile an exhaustive working bibliography but to find material related to the specific topic you are investigating. If your topic is a relatively limited and recent one — the critical reception of a novel published last year, for example — then your working bibliography may be exhaustive, but most topics will require you to sharpen your focus so that you won't be faced with an overwhelming number of sources. Your working bibliography will also indicate whether or not you can find an adequate number and variety of sources. Should you find no articles in periodicals and you know your instructor expects you to use articles as well as books, you will know early on that you'll have to reshape the topic.

The information on the card should appear in a standard bibliographical form (more about that in a moment) and include the data you will need for the list of works cited. This procedure will simplify typing the list of works cited and ensure that you'll have the information when you need it. Each bibliography card for a book or article should include the following basic information:

Book	*Article*
1. Author or editor	1. Author
2. Title (including subtitle)	2. Title of the article (including subtitle)

Book	*Article*

3. Publication data:
   Place
   Publisher
   Date
	3. Publication data:
	   Name of the periodical
	   Volume number
	   Date of the issue
	   Page numbers

Figure 4-1 shows a sample card for a book. This bibliography card is a record of the information listed in the card catalog entry for the book (see Figure 3-1, page 35). In addition to the bibliographic information for the book, the entry on this student's card includes the library call number in the upper left-hand corner. Although the call number will not be included in the list of works cited, it makes sense to list it on the card so that the book can be readily located in the stacks. (If periodicals are arranged by call number in your library, rather than alphabetically, record the call number for the periodical on your bibliography cards for articles.) Notice that at the bottom of the card there is a notation written by the student to check the bibliography at the end of the book for more sources. This information was included on the card catalog. Some students prefer to list on the card only the call number, author, and title when they first begin looking for relevant books. If you are going to examine many books, some of which may be only marginally related to your topic and which you will ultimately not use for the paper, you can save time by not recording all

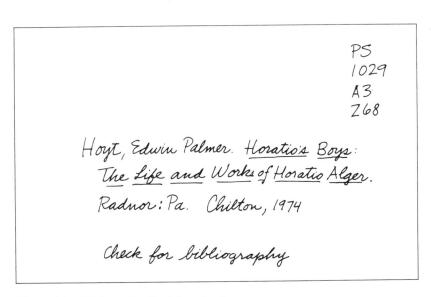

Figure 4-1   Bibliography Card for a Book

the publication data until after you have located the book and determined that you will use it. Suppose, for example, your topic is Harriet Beecher Stowe's treatment of abolitionists in *Uncle Tom's Cabin* and you came across Nina Baym's *Women's Fiction: A Guide to Novels by and About Women in America, 1820–1870.* The title covers the dates for *Uncle Tom's Cabin,* but after examining the book you'll find that there is nothing relevant to the topic. But again, if you are making cards up for only ten or fifteen book titles, it is probably best to record all the information in the form you will need for the final bibliography.

Figure 4-2 shows a sample card for a periodical. This bibliography card is a record of the information listed in *Readers' Guide to Periodical Literature* (see Figure 3-5, page 43). To find this periodical you will need all the information listed in the *Readers' Guide;* hence, you cannot get by with recording only the call number, author, and title, as you might for a book. Observe also that the student's note at the bottom of the card raises a question that might make its way into the paper. The more questions and ideas you jot down as you go along the more you will have to say when you begin to organize and write the paper.

Standard Bibliographical Forms

Before you begin to record information on the bibliography cards, look over the standard bibliographical forms listed in Chapter 7. There you will find models for books, journals, magazines, newspapers, nonprint

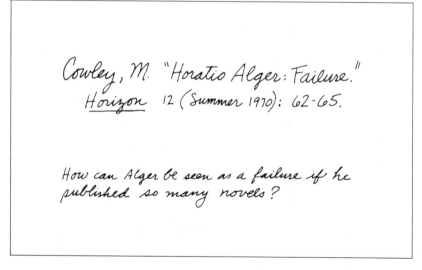

Cowley, M. "Horatio Alger: Failure."
Horizon 12 (Summer 1970): 62-65.

How can Alger be seen as a failure if he
published so many novels?

Figure 4-2 Bibliography Card for a Periodical

materials, and so on. You will also find examples of how to record editors, translators, editions, volumes, and a variety of other items. These models indicate what information you will need and how to arrange it for your list of works cited. By consulting the models as you write up the bibliography cards, you will avoid inadvertently overlooking information that will be needed for writing parenthetical references and your list of works cited. If you get all the required information down on the bibliography card, you won't be faced with having to make frantic last-minute searches in the library when you type up your paper.

EVALUATING SOURCES

As you locate the sources listed on your bibliography cards, you have to determine whether or not the sources are relevant and reliable.

Finding Relevant Sources

Remember that the sources in your working bibliography represent books and articles that you will consult for information but that may not have to be read from beginning to end. Some sources will be more useful than others; part of your job is to choose those that are the most relevant. If your topic is a manageable one, you should be able to limit what you actually read closely and take notes on in detail. Knowing a few simple strategies for finding relevant information will help you to cover a lot of ground and to dig deeply too.

Articles

Once you have located an article on the basis of a title that suggests the contents will be potentially useful, it is a fairly easy matter to assess its relevance. A typical journal article runs about ten to twenty pages in length and can be quickly skimmed for its major points. Begin by reading the article's first and last paragraphs for its purpose and conclusions. If it still looks promising, skim the paragraphs in between to see if the kind of detailed discussion you are looking for is there. This process should take only five minutes or so compared with an hour's worth of close reading. Save the close reading for the materials that yield the sort of detailed information you will want for your notes.

Books

Because of their length, books are more difficult than articles to skim efficiently. To determine if a book is relevant to your topic, pay careful attention to its complete title, the index, the table of contents, and any introductory material.

THE TITLE

The title of a book is especially important in the preliminary stages of compiling relevant works for your working bibliography. Unless you have the complete title (the main title and the subtitle), you may spend unnecessary time tracking down a work that sounds promising but which has nothing to do with your topic. Suppose, for example, that you are writing a paper for a sociology course on the difficulties of single parents raising children and managing careers and you come across the title *Fathers and Children*. This book, by Michael Paul Rogin, looks promising until its subtitle is considered: the complete title is *Fathers and Children: Andrew Jackson and the Subjugation of the American Indian*. Of course, you wouldn't make this mistake if you read the full title on the title card, but to save space sometimes subtitles are not included in bibliographies. Authors tend to title books the way many people name their children: a lot of time and thought goes into a main title that is not at all apparent to a stranger. Subtitles, like last names, give us a fuller identification. Catchy titles can sometimes be elusive. Consider this one by William B. Ober: *Boswell's Clap and Other Essays*. The remedy is the subtitle: *Medical Analyses of Literary Men's Afflictions*. Should a reader be looking for material on James Boswell's biography of Dr. Samuel Johnson, this book can safely be left on the shelf. Whenever you don't have a subtitle for a book, check to see if it has one by consulting the card catalog, the book itself, or, if necessary, another bibliography.

THE INDEX

Most biographies, histories, critical studies, and other serious nonfiction books include an index. The index is the quickest way inside a book, and it should be the first place you look for a specific topic. Arranged alphabetically, it lists the topics discussed in the text together with the page numbers where they can be found. A detailed index will often have topics subdivided and cross-referenced to related entries. In the time that it takes to flip through the pages of an entire book searching for a particular topic that may or may not be there, you can efficiently survey a score of books by examining their indexes. A student interested in American theater during the middle of the nineteenth century might find promising a title such as *Society and Culture in America, 1830–1860*. Here is the entry under "theater" in the index:

theater, 146–57; acting style, 150–1; audience, 147–8, 156; buildings, 146–7; concert tours, 128–9, 133; economics of, 147–8; European, 147ff., 156; frontiersman theme, 152–3; historical plays, 152; Indian themes, 152, 212, 217; melodrama, 156–7; minstrel shows, 134; morality, 155–7; Negroes, 233; "popular" vs. "serious," 147–8, 157; reform plays, 155–6; relevance, social, 148; satire, social, 154–5; touring, 146–7; urban themes, 153–4; "Yankee plays," 153; *see also* names of playwrights

This index entry informs you that "theater" is discussed on pages 146–157. Moreover, the entry indicates what specific theater topics are within those pages and elsewhere. The cross-reference is helpful if you have a particular playwright in mind. Indexes are valuable retrieval systems for information in books.

TABLE OF CONTENTS

The chapters of a book are listed in the table of contents, which gives you a sense of the general topics covered in the book. Some are very detailed (such as the one for this book), while others simply indicate broad categories of information. For books that have no index, the table of contents will be especially important, and so will be your ability to skim quickly, as you would an article, the contents of a chapter that looks promising.

INTRODUCTORY MATERIAL

Many books begin with a preface and/or an introduction that explains the scope of the subject matter and the author's approach to it. For a book about a single person, issue, or event, reading the introductory material may be more useful than looking through the index. A student focusing on the controversies associated with the assassination of John F. Kennedy will find almost any book devoted to theories about the assassination useful. In such a case it will already be evident that the book is relevant to the topic; what will have to be determined is how it differs from other studies.

Finding Reliable Sources

Besides finding sources that are relevant you must determine which sources are reliable. Keep in mind that the inclusion in an article or book of an assertion that has been proven wrong does not mean that the work has been removed from the library: don't believe everything you read. A significant part of your research assignment involves your ability to evaluate relevant materials, which will generally fall into two categories: primary and secondary sources.

Primary sources consist of materials that are the original sources of information for your topic. The primary sources for a paper on Virginia Woolf, for example, would be her novels, essays, letters, and any other writings by her. *Secondary sources* consist of comments and interpretations about primary materials. Biographies and critical commentaries in articles and books about Woolf's writings constitute secondary materials. Most student research papers include both primary and secondary sources. A familiarity with the primary sources of your topic will allow you to assess the accuracy and value of your secondary sources. If after having read *The Scarlet Letter* for a paper on Hawthorne's use of Puritan history you see a secondary source that describes the tone of the book as hilariously funny, you'll know enough to ignore it. If you had not read the novel, however, you might have accepted that description of the book's tone at face value. In short, commentaries and interpretations about people, events, works of art, statistics, or scientific data are secondary sources that should be evaluated on the basis of how well they describe and elucidate the primary sources they seek to explain.

Below are some questions to consider for determining the reliability of your secondary sources.

What Do You Know About the Author?

Information about a book's author often appears at the beginning or end of the volume. Most college libraries routinely discard the dust jackets that accompany books when they are cataloged, but if yours does not or if you are using a public library, check the dust jacket for the author's background and credentials. If the author has written other books on the subject or has an academic affiliation or appropriate experience related to the subject, then you can probably assume the study is reasonably authoritative. This hardly means that the book is infallible, but it does mean that you can take it seriously. For articles in periodicals, look for brief descriptions of the author; in journals they are usually located in the table of contents under "contributors." If no information is given by the book or periodical, see if the person's name appears in any of the citations from your other sources. Certainly one way to determine the value of an author's work is to learn if other people writing on the subject have found it useful. You can also check appropriate biographical dictionaries in particular fields such as *Who's Who in Journalism* or the *Directory of American Scholars*. Always make an effort to use a variety of sources: don't use ten books and articles by the same author, even if that person is an authority. Get other opinions too.

What Is the Nature of the Source?

The publication of information does not ensure its accuracy, completeness, or reliability. Common sense will tell you that many publications are not researched and written to present all the available information on a topic in the interest of arriving at the whole truth. Indeed, much is published to convey a particular point of view rather than to disseminate information. Do not expect a report sponsored by the American tobacco industry to say that cigarette smoking is harmful to your health. Nor should you look to an organization of pacifists or the National Rifle Association for the last word on gun-control laws. You could find useful information from any of these sources, but it is wise to remember where it comes from so that you can provide a more balanced perspective. Periodicals also have their particular points of view. A quick look at the treatment of social-welfare programs in the liberal *New Republic* compared with that in the conservative *National Review* makes this clear.

Is the Source a Scholarly or Popular Treatment?

Reliability can also be measured by the quality of evidence offered. Sources that are documented and based on solid information rather than on only the author's impressions and opinions are generally more reliable than the kinds of articles you might find in popular magazines. Whenever appropriate and possible, it is best to use sources that reflect a scholarly approach based on primary sources rather than a popularization of the topic. If you are writing a paper on international relations between the United States and the Soviet Union, you will find more authoritative information in a respected journal such as *Foreign Affairs* than you will in the Sunday supplement to your local newspaper. Also, books published by university presses and recognizable commercial presses are preferable to books published by their authors or by obscure organizations.

When writing about a famous person, be especially aware of popular biographies that uncritically put their subject's best foot forward. These are the books you'll find languishing in the stacks because no one ever seems to check them out. Be wary of them even if they are all that seem to be immediately available. They often read like extended eulogies rather than providing a reader with very much information and a perspective on their subject. Students will sometimes use them out of desperation, but the results are usually desperate too. Suppose you were investigating the scandals linked to the administration of President Harding during the early 1920s and came across this title by Thomas H. Russell: *The Illustrious Life of Warren G. Harding*. This biography was published in 1923, the year Harding died in office; it is therefore a memorial volume and unlikely to be critical. If the title didn't give you pause, then a quick glance at the dedication lets you know that you needn't look any further for information about the political scandals associated with Harding's administration:

> Dedicated
> to the young people of America, to whom the
> life of Warren Gamaliel Harding furnishes
> a high ideal of American citizenship
> and an inspiration for striving
> after and attaining the
> true success that
> is based on
> service.

This kind of instant book — stir and add your own occasion — is increasingly common today. Airplane crashes, natural disasters, bizarre political events, or the untimely death of a prominent person are only a few of the occasions for these books, and they usually generate more sales than they do information. Don't be satisfied with popular or sensational treatments of a subject.

Is the Source Up-to-Date?

Recent sources are usually based on previous scholarship as well as on new information and ideas not available to earlier researchers. An up-to-date source often provides an overview of previous studies through its citations, notes, and list of works cited. Using these supplements can save you time as well as give you a perspective on the subject. The use of recent information is especially important in rapidly changing areas such as the sciences. In the past several years, for example, scientific data obtained from space probes have radically changed astronomers' ideas about Saturn's rings. Observations published prior to 1980 are now either incomplete or inaccurate. Any research paper about Saturn's rings would have to take those recent studies into account. Not all topics, however, demand the latest sources. Some things are done well and done only once. Many literary and historical studies written years ago can still be useful, but in areas such as the sciences and technology, it is wise to get the most recently published work.

What Do Reviews Indicate About the Source?

Even if you determine that the author of an up-to-date source is an authority who has published many books on the subject with a reputable press, you may still be uncertain of the value or uniqueness of the work you have just examined. If the subject area is new to you, it would not be surprising if you felt unequipped to make that kind of evaluation. What may be completely new and intriguing to you could be assessed very differently by people who have spent years studying a subject. That is why book reviews are so useful. They are usually both descriptive and evaluative, they can help you determine if you will find the book relevant to your topic, and they often compare the book with related works. One of the most useful sources of reviews is the *Book Review Digest* (New York: Wilson, 1905 to date), which indexes and excerpts reviews published in about seventy-five major periodicals. Figure 4-3 shows a sample entry from the 1979 volume and lists reviews of Christopher Lasch's *The Culture of Narcissism*. To find reviews of this book you would look under the author's name.

The *Book Review Digest* offers both a brief description of the book and opinions about it. You may decide from the excerpts alone to eliminate the book or to use it; it is not always necessary to look up the reviews themselves. Because the *Book Review Digest* tends to list books of relatively general interest, you should consult the indexes below for highly specialized studies reviewed only in learned journals. These indexes do not, however, excerpt reviews, they simply list them:

Book Review Index. Detroit: Gale, 1965 to date. This index locates reviews in some 300 periodicals. Entries are alphabetized by the author reviewed and include the book's title, date and place of publication of the review, and the reviewer's name.

Index to Book Reviews in the Humanities. Williamstown: Thomson, 1960 to date. This index, like the *Book Review Index*, includes many more periodicals than *Book Review Digest*. It is especially strong in literature and the arts.

In addition to the general indexes listed above, there are more specialized indexes to locate book reviews in particular fields. For those such as the *Index to Book Reviews in Historical Periodicals* (Metuchen: Scarecrow, 1972 to date), check the reference works listed by discipline in Chapter 10. Keep in mind that when you look for a book published, for example, in 1980, the reviews for that book may appear in a 1981 or 1982 index as well as in a 1980 one. Reviews, especially in academic journals, sometimes take a year or two or even three to get into print.

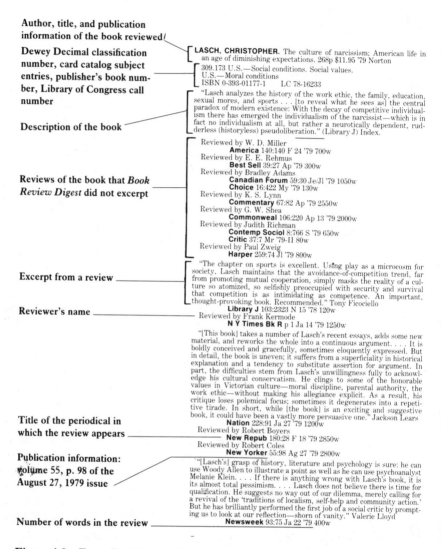

Author, title, and publication information of the book reviewed

Dewey Decimal classification number, card catalog subject entries, publisher's book number, Library of Congress call number

Description of the book

Reviews of the book that *Book Review Digest* did not excerpt

Excerpt from a review

Reviewer's name

Title of the periodical in which the review appears

Publication information: volume 55, p. 98 of the August 27, 1979 issue

Number of words in the review

LASCH, CHRISTOPHER. The culture of narcissism; American life in an age of diminishing expectations. 268p $11.95 '79 Norton

309.173 U.S.—Social conditions. Social values.
U.S.—Moral conditions
ISBN 0-393-01177-1   LC 78-16233

"Lasch analyzes the history of the work ethic, the family, education, sexual mores, and sports . . . [to reveal what he sees as] the central paradox of modern existence: With the decay of competitive individualism there has emerged the individualism of the narcissist—which is in fact no individualism at all, but rather a neurotically dependent, rudderless (historyless) pseudoliberation." (Library J) Index.

Reviewed by W. D. Miller
    America 140:140 F 24 '79 700w
Reviewed by E. E. Rehmus
    Best Sell 39:27 Ap '79 300w
Reviewed by Bradley Adams
    Canadian Forum 59:30 Je/Jl '79 1050w
    Choice 16:422 My '79 130w
Reviewed by K. S. Lynn
    Commentary 67:82 Ap '79 2550w
Reviewed by G. W. Shea
    Commonweal 106:220 Ap 13 '79 2000w
Reviewed by Judith Richman
    Contemp Sociol 8:766 S '79 650w
    Critic 37:7 Mr '79-Il 80w
Reviewed by Paul Zweig
    Harper 259:74 Jl '79 800w

"The chapter on sports is excellent. Using play as a microcosm for society, Lasch maintains that the avoidance-of-competition trend, far from promoting mutual cooperation, simply masks the reality of a culture so atomized, so selfishly preoccupied with security and survival that competition is as intimidating as competence. An important, thought-provoking book. Recommended." Tony Ficociello
    Library J 103:2323 N 15 '78 120w
Reviewed by Frank Kermode
    N Y Times Bk R p 1 Ja 14 '79 1250w

"[This book] takes a number of Lasch's recent essays, adds some new material, and reworks the whole into a continuous argument. . . . It is boldly conceived and gracefully, sometimes eloquently expressed. But in detail, the book is uneven; it suffers from a superficiality in historical explanation and a tendency to substitute assertion for argument. In part, the difficulties stem from Lasch's unwillingness fully to acknowledge his cultural conservatism. He clings to some of the honorable values in Victorian culture—moral discipline, parental authority, the work ethic—without making his allegiance explicit. As a result, while [the book] is an exciting and suggestive critique loses polemical focus; sometimes it degenerates into a repetitive tirade. In short, while [the book] is an exciting and suggestive book, it could have been a vastly more persuasive one." Jackson Lears
    Nation 228:91 Ja 27 '79 1200w
Reviewed by Robert Boyers
    New Repub 180:28 F 18 '79 2850w
Reviewed by Robert Coles
    New Yorker 55:98 Ag 27 '79 2800w

"[Lasch's] grasp of history, literature and psychology is sure: he can use Woody Allen to illustrate a point as well as he can use psychoanalyst Melanie Klein. . . . If there is anything wrong with Lasch's book, it is its almost total pessimism. . . . Lasch does not believe there is time for qualification. He suggests no way out of our dilemma, merely calling for a revival of the 'traditions of localism, self-help and community action.' But he has brilliantly performed the first job of a social critic by prompting us to look at our reflection—shorn of vanity." Valerie Lloyd
    Newsweek 93:75 Ja 22 '79 400w

Figure 4-3   From *Book Review Digest*

There are sources for some academic disciplines that provide summaries and evaluations of articles in periodicals. Consult the list of reference works in Chapter 10 to see if there is one related to your topic or ask a reference librarian; you might also ask an instructor who specializes in the field. In the area of American literature, for example, there is *American Literary Scholarship* (Durham: Duke UP, 1963 to date), an annual that consists of bibliographical essays describing and evaluating selected articles, books, and doctoral dissertations written about American literature in a given year.

After finding several reviews of a source, you may discover that the reviewers' evaluations do not entirely agree. Don't let this confuse or intimidate you. Instead, you may find that the disagreements and conflicting points of view can be turned into an opportunity for developing a research topic. Efforts to resolve a controversy or provide a sense of balance often lead to interesting syntheses and even new ideas.

TAKING NOTES

After you are satisfied that a source from your working bibliography is both relevant and reliable, you will need to read the source carefully and record accurate notes on the information related to the central point you want to make about the topic. At this stage you will be reading the material closely rather than skimming. In order to take accurate notes, your reading should reflect the exact meaning of the passages you quote or summarize. Avoid being reductive or simplistic. Good notes succinctly reflect the essential points of a source; they do not misrepresent them. Consider, for example, the problem that arises if a reader misses the irony in a humorous newspaper editorial that calls for a return to the Pony Express as an alternative to ever-increasing postal rates. One student, having missed the ironic humor of the essay, actually wrote a rebuttal to the editorial and pointed out that so many horses would be expensive to maintain and would represent a sanitation problem in city streets all across the land. The student was earnest but missed the point of the editorial, which was not a serious analysis of the financial problems of the postal system but simply an effort to poke some fun at the system's failure to operate efficiently. As you gather information, be alert to the subtleties, qualifications, and sometimes even humor that writers use to make their points.

Preparing Note Cards

Many researchers, both students and professionals, develop their own system of recording information as they become more experienced in putting together a research project. There is no prescribed method that everyone follows, but there are some basic principles that have been proven useful by most experienced researchers. Information must be organized carefully as it is gathered so that it can be retrieved from your notes efficiently when you organize and write the paper. The points listed below should help you to keep track of the notes you take on your reading.

1. Use note cards rather than sheets of notebook paper. Cards can be easily sorted into topical categories that will be useful when you organize the outline for the paper. Cards can be added or dropped and they are easy to handle either in an indexed file box or simply with rubber bands. Since you will probably be juggling a considerable amount of information as you organize the paper, you'll want that information to be mobile. Notes recorded on notebook paper do not travel well; cards do.

2. Use either three-by-five or four-by-six cards (or whatever your instructor requires). The bigger cards will allow for more information on a single card and will also accommodate large handwriting, but the smaller cards are less bulky and fit comfortably into most pockets, a feature many researchers find convenient as they move about the library taking notes.

3. Identify the source of information in the upper right-hand corner of the card. There are several ways to do this. Rather than writing all bibliographic information recorded on the bibliography cards, it is simpler to use some shortened form that will direct you to the correct bibliography card when it is needed for documenting your notes. Usually, the last name of the author will do (e.g., Lasch 46). You can also use a shortened form of the title. Christopher Lasch's *The Culture of Narcissism* might be listed as *Culture* 46, but the author's last name is preferable because your bibliography cards are already organized alphabetically by author and the source would be easier to find that way. If you are using more than one source by the same author, be sure to combine the author and shortened form of the title to distinguish between them (e.g., Lasch, *Culture* 46). Another way to indicate a source is to number your bibliography cards consecutively and then record the number for a particular source on the note card. This system works but it can be a problem if you lose your bibliography cards. Using the author's name is probably the more reliable method. And don't forget to include the page number(s) on which you found the information you record.

4. Write a short subject heading indicating what the note is about in the upper left-hand corner of the card (it makes no difference, by the way, which corner of the card is used for the subject heading or the source of the information; what is important is consistency so that you can sort through the cards efficiently). These headings will be useful when you get to the paper. Try to make them as specific as brevity will allow.

5. Write only one idea on a card. There may, of course, be several facts or points related to the idea, but you should have only one central

idea or subject per card, which will allow you the flexibility to organize information as the paper is developed.

6. Try to write on only one side of the card to avoid missing material. If your note does spill over onto the back, then draw an arrow in the lower right-hand corner to remind yourself that there is information on the back. If you use more than one card for a single idea, staple them together and/or number the cards. The first card of three, for example, would be numbered 1 of 3, the second 2 of 3, and so on.

7. Use ink and write clearly. The cards needn't be models of neatness and penmanship, but remember that you'll be handling them frequently and that penciled notes are likely to smudge. Several weeks may pass between your writing the note and your using it, so don't count on remembering what you've written.

In sum, three important elements will appear on each note card:

1. the source of the information, including the specific page number(s)
2. the subject heading identifying the nature of the information
3. the information itself (facts, ideas, opinions, quotations)

Figure 4-4 shows what a note card looks like. Notice that the information is prefaced with the phrase "According to Lasch." The student has distinguished between the author's facts and opinions. There may be facts to support this opinion, but at this stage of reading the student makes clear that the information recorded is Lasch's opinion. The bracketed

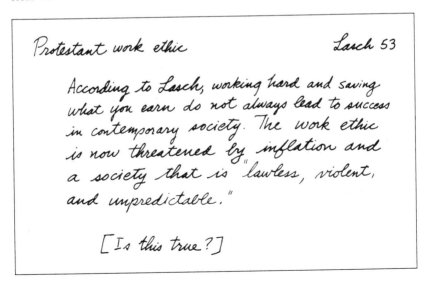

Figure 4-4 Sample Note Card

comment is a note by the student. You will find that the questions, notes, and comments you write on the cards while you are recording information will be useful as you compose the paper. Insights or questions that you have while you are reading may be forgotten later. Record them as you think of them.

Types of Note Cards

There are basically three types of note cards to record the information that will provide the supporting evidence for the thesis of your paper: (1) quotation, (2) summary, and (3) paraphrase. Each type is useful in particular situations; they can also be combined.

Quotation

A direct quotation is an exact, word-for-word reproduction of the original source. Indicate a direct quotation by beginning and ending the passage with quotation marks; without them you might mistakenly assume later on that the material is a paraphrase rather than a quotation. If you use quoted material that way, you could find yourself charged with plagiarism, a form of cheating (for a discussion of this important problem, see pages 92–97). If you leave out words to condense material or add words to clarify material, you must indicate that you have done so by using ellipses for deletions (see pages 83–86) and brackets for additions (see pages 86–87). Even if a word is spelled incorrectly or some other error appears in the quotation, you must record it as it appears and then write in brackets the word "sic," a Latin term meaning that the passage has been written exactly the way the original reads (see page 87).

Quotations should be used sparingly. A paper with too many quotations (the proportion usually cited as excessive is around 10 to 15 percent) is often perceived by instructors as padded. Moreover, because part of your task is to digest and evaluate information, a paper that consists mainly of chunks of other writers' words raises the suspicion that the student has little to say. Your cards will very likely include a number of quotations, but when you write your paper many of them should be summarized. As you take notes, try to put as much information as you can into your own words, which will save you time and effort later. Use direct quotations for passages with language so vivid and striking that tinkering with the passage would spoil the effect. Direct quotations are also useful when the passage focuses on a controversial topic and you want to invoke the authority (or outrageousness) of your source. Be certain to proofread your note card carefully while you still have the source in front of you. It is all too easy to leave out a word or skip a line when copying

Literary merit of novels   Fink 16
"Alger is a monument to bad taste. He comes to us
from the world of Victorian furniture and
architecture. Like them, he is terrible; however, he
is such a special instance of the terrible that
he exercises a fatal fascination. As long
as any reader has the slightest touch of
artistic masochism, an hour with an
Alger novel will bring to life a bit of
agonized fondness for him."

Figure 4-5 Quotation Note Card

material. Figure 4-5 shows a note card concerning the literary merit of
Horatio Alger's novels; the source is Rychard Fink's introduction to *Ragged Dick and Mark, the Match Boy* (New York: Collier, 1962). The author's assertion that "Alger is a monument to bad taste" would be difficult
to condense, and if it were reworded, much of its impact would be lost.
Clearly, it is a sentence worth quoting if the point is to make its way into
the paper.

Lengthy quoted passages that you think are important for both their
language and detailed information can be photocopied on machines in the
library, thus allowing you to gather information you can take notes on
later if it is not convenient to work in the library. It will also save a lot of
time. For such information write up a note card with a subject heading
along with the source of information and indicate something like: see
photocopy. Be sure to record the source on the photocopy too. Of course,
you will still have to make note cards for the photocopied passages, but
you may by then have a better idea of what information you'll need for
the paper and you will have saved the time spent on copying long passages
unnecessarily.

Summary

A summary note condenses an idea into *your own words*. It strips a passage
or chapter or even a book down to its essential kernel of thought. A
summary is useful when detailed descriptions and examples are not

needed or when the point of an argument rather than the evidence used to support it is what you are after. This kind of note can be written once you have a firm grasp of what you've read; its major purpose is to record information without concern for how the material is worded in the original source. Although the note must be accurate, it need not reflect the details or style of the original, and a good summary note can often make its way into your first draft. The more information you are able to condense and put into your own words as you take notes, the less rereading and rewriting you will have to do later when the material is not as immediate and fresh.

Literary merit of novels.   Fink 16

Alger's novels are so badly written that some readers find them strangely interesting.

Figure 4-6   Summary Note Card

Figure 4-6 shows a summary note that condenses the passage quoted in Figure 4-5. Notice that the card credits the point to Fink. Even though the words are yours, in your paper you must give Fink credit for the idea.

The summary makes basically the same point as the original but much more concisely. In addition, this note could easily become the topic sentence of a paragraph explaining why some readers find Alger's writing fascinating. The condensation and the student's own words represent work that won't have to be done later. A significant part of a paper can be written this way.

A summary does not have to be a complete sentence, but it is wise to write complete sentences if you think there is a chance the information can be used in the paper in that form. Figure 4-7 shows how the note card

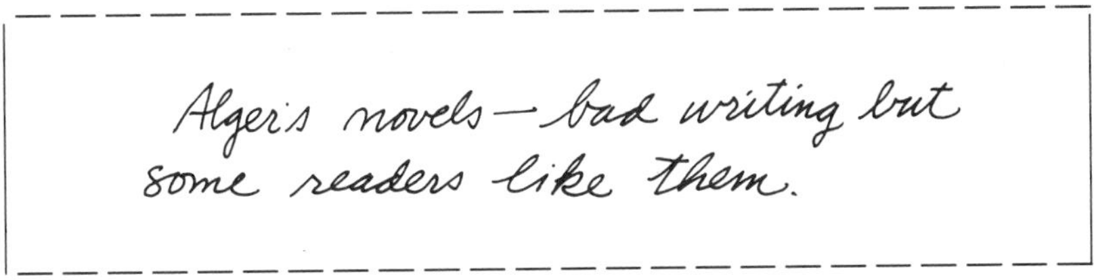

Alger's novels — bad writing but some readers like them.

Figure 4-7 Summary Note Card as an Incomplete Sentence

in Figure 4-6 could have been written. The point is preserved but if it is to be used in the paper, it will obviously have to be reconstructed in sentence form.

In contrast, a note that is cryptic and too sketchy may turn out to be useless two weeks after it is written and the passage is forgotten. Consider how difficult it would be to make sense of the note shown in Figure 4-8 on the literary merit of Alger's novels if you didn't recall the specific passage. Rather than generating a topic sentence for a paragraph, this sort of shorthand is more likely to produce something like "huh?"

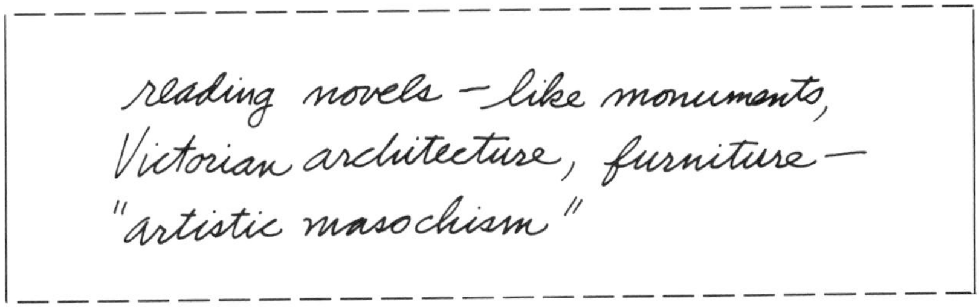

reading novels — like monuments, Victorian architecture, furniture — "artistic masochism"

Figure 4-8 Incoherent Summary Note Card

Paraphrase

A paraphrase, like a summary, is written in your own words, but instead of being significantly shorter than the original, a paraphrase follows more closely the sentence-by-sentence order, tone, and important vocabulary of a passage, and it is usually about the same length as the original. Paraphrases are useful because they demonstrate that you have understood the material in your source rather than simply quoting passage after passage. A research paper is not a string of quotations knotted together by parenthetical references; a good paper presents ideas and information that have been assimilated by the student.

Figure 4-9 shows a paraphrase of the quoted passage in Figure 4-5.

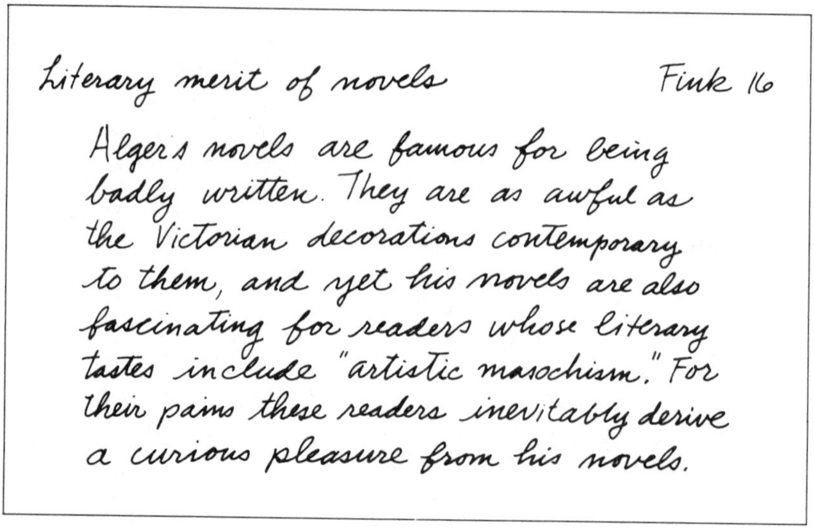

> Literary merit of novels   Fink 16
>
> Alger's novels are famous for being
> badly written. They are as awful as
> the Victorian decorations contemporary
> to them, and yet his novels are also
> fascinating for readers whose literary
> tastes include "artistic masochism." For
> their pains these readers inevitably derive
> a curious pleasure from his novels.

Figure 4-9   Paraphrase Note Card

This paraphrase represents something of a halfway point between a direct quotation and a brief summary of the passage (Figure 4-6). Unlike the summary, all the points are here in the paraphrase and so is much of the flavor of the passage (only a dedicated flagellant would attempt to reword "artistic masochism"). Paraphrasing is a sensible alternative to excessive quoting when you want to include most of the elements of a passage. Moreover, paraphrases are easily incorporated into the text of your paper when you compose the first draft, but remember that even though the words of the paraphrase are yours, you must give the author credit for the idea. If you don't you are plagiarizing.

A Few More Notes on Note Taking

1. Remember that quoting, summarizing, and paraphrasing can be combined on note cards. They are not mutually exclusive. Also, you shouldn't hesitate to include personal comments that make a point, raise questions, or refer you to other sources and ideas, and they needn't be recorded only on source cards. You can establish separate cards and cite yourself so that you won't think you neglected to record a source. The note cards are your tools; design them in whatever way helps you to get the job done.

2. Abbreviate names, titles, and other words that appear frequently on your note cards. So long as you are consistent, abbreviations such as A for Alger will be clear and save you time.

3. When the passage you are citing continues on to another page in the original, indicate in your notes with a slash where the page number changes, writing in the appropriate page numbers on each side of the slash (see Figure 4-10). If, however, you cite something that actually appears only on page 73, you won't know it if you have an inclusive reference to pages 73–74.

4. The number of note cards that you write for the paper will depend on the nature of the topic, what you know about it, and how well it was defined before you began. If you take many notes on material that ultimately doesn't get used, you're going to need more note cards than someone who knows exactly what the thesis of the paper will be from start to finish. Note taking can sometimes be exploratory as well as a search for specific information, but usually students end up with somewhere around 100 cards for a ten-page paper. Remember, however, that this is merely an average; many students will have more cards, and many will have fewer. More important than the number of cards is having enough material to write a solid, well-informed paper.

5. It is essential that you document the facts, ideas, and opinions from your sources. Any material that is quoted, summarized, or paraphrased must be attributed to its source (see Chapter 7 for a discussion of when and how to document your paper).

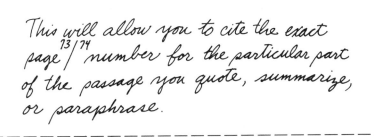

This will allow you to cite the exact
page 73/74 number for the particular part
of the passage you quote, summarize,
or paraphrase.

Figure 4-10 Page Reference Citations

As you take notes on information relevant to your topic, you should have ideas and questions that will serve as a guide to what information should be recorded. Just as you developed a preliminary thesis for the paper through exploratory reading, so too will you work up a preliminary outline of the paper as you gather information. The functions and techniques of outlining are discussed in the next chapter.

5 Using the Notes

As you become more comfortable finding your way in the library and more involved in recording information on your topic, you may be tempted to go on taking notes long after you have found enough material. That's natural enough; you have, after all, gotten to know the library and the topic. The problem, however, is that you may join the silent ranks of some other researchers who continued to take notes without ever organizing them into a finished paper. Most topics can probably be researched further, but remember that the time and space allotted for the project necessarily limit its scope. At some point it will be necessary to stop noting information and start writing. This is an obvious step, of course, but it is also something of a leap, because the many pieces of information that have been recorded on the note cards must now be organized around the central idea of the topic. This leap can be comfortably performed if you have prepared for it by keeping track of the information you've gathered. The process of outlining helps you to do that.

ORGANIZING THE INFORMATION

The Preliminary Outline

You begin organizing a paper as soon as you choose a topic and tentatively decide what your major point will be. The thesis, though it may be only tentative, will help you to determine what information will be included. Even before you start taking notes on the reading, a *preliminary outline* — a list of subtopics related to the thesis — can serve as a guide to the detailed reading and note taking that will be necessary.

Here is a tentative thesis for a paper about why so many Americans buy Japanese automobiles: "Americans buy Japanese cars because they are better designed, easier to repair, and less expensive to own than American cars, but this gain for individual buyers does not outweigh the negative impact such imports have by weakening the U.S. economy, an impact that affects the purchasing power of everyone, including buyers of imported cars." This thesis is useful because it indicates the two major areas that the paper will explore: (1) the quality of Japanese cars compared with that of American cars, and (2) the weakening effect imports have on the U.S. economy.

These two subtopics represent the beginnings of an outline for the paper. They can be readily subdivided into smaller units by jotting down ideas that are suggested by the thesis, your own reflections, and your reading. To begin a preliminary outline, list ideas as they come to you; they can be arranged in logical order later to conform to the conventions and rules of formal outlining, but for now they will help you to get started:

<u>Decline in the economy</u>   <u>U.S. versus Japanese cars</u>

unemployment   design

effect on related industries   repairs

tax losses   economy

welfare

weakened dollar

The above list offers some direction; as you read and take notes, further topics will surface and you can add them as you go along. Your working outline — at this early stage really a series of lists — will lead you to the information necessary to support your thesis.

Just as your working outline will provide a sense of direction for note taking, so too will your note taking flesh out the bare bones of your outline. This reflexive relationship means, in effect, that you are working on both at once. The subject headings on your note cards will often provide subdivisions for the topics in your preliminary outline. The section comparing the economy of Japanese and American cars could, for example, look like this after you take some notes:

<u>economy</u>

cost of parts

resale value

purchase price

gas mileage

These subdivisions will constitute the evidence required to support the comparison you make between the economic features of the Japanese and American cars. Also, because the information is on note cards, it will be a simple matter to collate all the data you've collected from various sources on resale values, for example, so that you have in one place the raw material necessary to write a solid paragraph or sequence of paragraphs. The preliminary outline will help you to see what information you need to support the thesis, and it will help you to organize the information you gather into an orderly and logical presentation.

Organizing the paper is a process of grouping related subtopics under main topics that logically follow one another. Here is one possible organizational scheme for the paper on Japanese imports. The outline is still in a preliminary form, but it has developed from a simple list of items to an ordering of them:

```
Japanese cars more competitive than American cars
   Economy
      Sticker price
      Gas mileage
      Repair costs
      Cost of parts
      Resale value
   Design
      Size
      Standard equipment
      Workmanship
      Reliability
      Durability
Japanese imports weaken U.S. economy
   Unemployment in Detroit
      Loss of tax revenue
      Welfare costs
      Budget cuts for state agencies
   Related industries nationwide
      Steel
      Tires
      Carpeting
      Accessories
   Diminished purchasing power for individuals
Possible solutions
   Restrict imports through quotas and taxes
   U.S. car makers should learn Japanese manufacturing
   techniques
```

Although hardly a completed formal outline (more on that shortly), this preliminary sketch serves as a useful guide for preparing one. Notice that "Repair costs," mentioned prominently in the thesis, has been incorporated here into the costs of owning the car. As the student reads more about the topic, the information gathered could affect the possible solutions offered at the end of the outline and perhaps the thesis as well. The student may discover that imposing import quotas on automobiles could seriously weaken U.S. exporting, if other nations imposed quotas on U.S. products. The point is that it is necessary to allow your research to shape your thinking and your conclusions, if they are to be supported by the evidence you find. This approach represents both an intelligent and honest use of your notes. Your preliminary outline can help you to discover relationships as well as organize them.

The sample preliminary outline moves logically from generalizations to particular bits of information that support the generalizations. This procedure is called a *deductive* approach and is one of two major ways to use supporting evidence. The thesis makes the generalization that Japanese cars are designed better than American cars, which is supported deductively in the outline by comparing the size, standard features, workmanship, reliability, and durability of imported cars with American cars. The strategy here is to make a statement and then support it with evidence. The other major way to use evidence is called an *inductive* approach. When you use evidence to lead up to a generalization, you are reasoning inductively. With this method you would first compare the elements of design in Japanese and American cars and then arrive at a generalization about them. No matter which method you use (and you may use both in a single paper), be sure you have enough evidence to support the generalizations that make up your thesis.

By indenting the headings in your preliminary outline, you make it clear which topics are subordinated to main topics; for example, the resale value of a car is obviously only part of the discussion of economic factors determining a car's competitiveness. At this stage indenting indicates this subordination well enough without your having to be concerned about whether or not the headings should be preceded by a Roman numeral or a capital letter. It is considerably more important to go through the *process* of outlining than it is to assign appropriate numbers and letters to your thought processes. Students who worry about these conventions prematurely usually end up writing the outline after the paper is written so that it doesn't get in the way of their thinking. Such an outline can certainly reflect what is in the paper, but it cannot serve to improve its organization. Indeed, what frequently happens is that the formal outline then betrays the paper's shaky structure.

The Final Outline

After you are satisfied that you have enough information to write the paper, sort your note cards into a final arrangement that reflects the subtopics of the preliminary outline. While sorting the cards, you will very likely add some topics and delete others as you did for the preliminary outline. This process will require you to revise the preliminary outline, and as you do so the final outline will begin to emerge. The *final outline* is highly conventional in its form, but it is also highly useful in its function. It will help you to organize information so that you can see the order in which your ideas should appear, and it will also indicate which ideas should be subordinated to others. You will then have a firm sense of when to begin new paragraphs and provide transitions between the sections of the paper so that it is clear and easy for a reader to follow. There is no single "correct" way to present the information you've gathered; there will, no doubt, be a number of ways to organize the material. The outline, however, will help you to discover the organizing principle that seems to work best for your treatment of the topic. In short, the outline equips you to present effectively what you have learned about your topic. For more specific information about how to organize different kinds of papers, such as comparison and contrast, process analysis, cause and effect, or definition, refresh your memory with a textbook that reviews these rhetorical patterns. You may draw a blank with these terms right now, but when you look them over, you'll probably realize that you've written papers like them before, even if you didn't refer to them as rhetorical patterns.

If your outline is to be handed in with the paper, it should conform to the conventions used for subdividing topics. Here is the formal structure of an outline:

```
    I.
   II.
       A.
       B.
           1.
           2.
               a.
               b.
  III.
```

There are three basic types of outlines: (1) *topic outlines* in which headings consist of a single word or phrase, (2) *sentence outlines,* and (3) *combinations* of both. The following is a topic outline for parts of the preliminary outline on Japanese imports. Note that the thesis has been revised and placed at the top of the page. No mention is made of an "introduction" or "conclusion," because the outline indicates what information is covered in the body of the paper.

Thesis: Americans buy Japanese cars because they are less expensive to own and better designed than Detroit's cars, but this gain for individual consumers does not outweigh the weakening effect imports have on the U.S. economy, an impact that affects the purchasing power of everyone, including buyers of imported cars.

I. Japanese cars are more competitive than U.S. cars
   A. Economy
      1. Sticker price
      2. Gas mileage
      3. Repair costs
      4. Resale value
   B. Design
      1. Size
      2. Standard equipment
      3. Workmanship
II. Japanese imports weaken U.S. economy
   A. Unemployment in Detroit
   B. Related industries nationwide
      1. Steel
      2. Accessories
         a. Air conditioners
         b. Radios
            (1) Speakers
            (2) Tape players
               (a) Cassettes
               (b) Cassette carrying cases
         c. Carpeting
      3. Tires
   C. Diminished purchasing power of individuals
III. Possible remedies

The essential organizing principle of outlines is that main topics appear in the left-hand margin while subtopics flow from them toward the right-hand margin. These indentations present a visual display of the relationship among the ideas in the paper. The numbers and letters are there to clarify the nature of those relationships. Roman numerals indicate main topics, capital letters the first subdivision, Arabic numerals the second, lower-case letters the third, Arabic numerals enclosed in parentheses the fourth, and lower-case letters enclosed in parentheses the fifth. In theory, these subdivisions could go on forever, but few outlines for a ten-page paper go beyond the third or fourth level, since these subdivisions ordinarily provide enough supporting information and details for the main topic. In the sample outline, the section under "Radios" is extensively subdivided because it is offered as a detailed example of the domino effect on manufacturing industries that supply auto makers with accessories.

With the exception of the numbers and letters enclosed in parentheses, each letter and number is followed by a period. The entries begin with a capital letter, but there is no period at the end of topic outlines as there is at the end of entries for sentence outlines.

Each level must be divided at least once. There is no I without II, no A without B, no 1 without 2, and so on. This rule reflects simple logic:

nothing can be *divided* into fewer than two elements. If you find yourself with a single subdivision, integrate it into the preceding heading or eliminate it. Consider the following portion of a sentence outline about outlining:

```
A.  Each level must be divided at least once.
    1.  Nothing can be divided into fewer than two
        elements.
B.  Entries for each level should be of equal im-
    portance.
```

Although 1 helps to explain A, 1 actually belongs as part of A:

```
A.  Each level must be divided at least once, because
    nothing can be divided into fewer than two ele-
    ments.
```

Topics at the same level should be parallel in importance so that they follow logically from the preceding topic. Part II.B. of the sample outline would be incorrectly placed if it were written:

```
B.  Related industries nationwide
    1.  Steel
    2.  Accessories
    3.  Diminished purchasing power of individuals
```

The entry for 3 does not explain the effect imports have on industries dependent on automobile production; instead, like B, it provides another example of how imports affect the economy. Hence, it should be entered under the parallel heading of a capital letter.

Topic headings should appear in the same grammatical structure so that they are easy to read. The following does not use parallel grammatical structures.

```
III.  Possible remedies
     A.  Restrict imports
     B.  To have Detroit learn Japanese techniques
```

In order to make A and B parallel in form, B should be revised to something like "Retool Detroit," which eliminates the infinitive phrase.

Sentence outlines present no problems in parallel phrasing because each entry is a complete sentence. Here is a portion of the topic outline on Japanese imports arranged as a sentence outline:

```
I. Many American buyers prefer Japanese cars to Detroit
   cars for a variety of reasons.
   A. Japanese cars are more economical.
      1. The purchase price is competitive.
      2. Gas mileage is significantly higher.
      3. They are cheaper to repair.
      4. They retain their value longer, and some
         even appreciate rather than depreciate in
         value.
   B. Japanese cars are better designed.
```

Sentence outlines offer more information and show relationships more clearly than topic outlines, especially for topics that are more abstract than factual. A sentence outline is a more detailed map of the paper and it is usually developed from a topic outline. Unless your paper is considerably longer than ten pages, a topic outline should suffice. If you are required to hand in the outline, be certain that you know which type your instructor expects. You may be able to combine the forms by using complete sentences for main topics (Roman numerals), which indicate relationships among the subtopics:

```
I. Many American buyers prefer Japanese cars to Detroit
   cars for a variety of reasons.
   A. Economy
      1. Sticker price
      2. Gas mileage
      3. Repair costs
      4. Resale value
```

Regardless of the type of outline you write, you should include in the final version any changes made while composing the final draft of the paper. That's not the same as writing the outline after you write the paper. Such changes are revisions that record the organizational adjustments you found necessary in the process of writing the paper, and as you write, it is likely that you will make discoveries that you previously hadn't seen in your notes or outline.

A sentence outline for the sample student paper appears on pages 200–205.

PRESENTING THE INFORMATION

Your outline indicates what information will be included in the paper and the order in which it will appear. The next step is to present the information effectively. As you write the first draft you will summarize, paraphrase, and quote the material from your note cards that supports the thesis. Your task now is to integrate this information into the paper so that it is readable, convincing, and adequately documented.

When to Quote

Working the information from your note cards into the paper requires a sense of tact; like almost any other kind of activity, the more experience you have the easier it becomes. Initially, however, some students may be tempted to quote excessively rather than relying on their own words, particularly if their note cards contain more quotations than summaries or paraphrases. Such students attempt to hide out among the quotations, emerging only occasionally to peep around a transitional sentence that introduces yet another quoted passage. Remember that you should have recorded quotations on your note cards only when (1) the language of the original was especially important or vivid and therefore worth preserving, and (2) when you wanted to invoke the authority of your source. The reason for quoting a source is to create an effect, not to avoid rephrasing the passage into your own words. A paper that merely assembles quoted passages from various sources is often disjointed and difficult to read; indeed, it usually reads more like a collection of note cards rather than like a well-integrated paper. Use quotations to enhance your writing, not as a substitute for it.

How to Quote

There are a variety of ways to integrate quotations into a paper, depending on the length and nature of the material. In each instance, however, you must indicate that the passage is a quotation, cite the source, and quote accurately.

Lengthy Quotations

Though they should be used sparingly, long quotations are at times useful, especially if you are discussing in detail the tone or style of a passage. In such cases it is important to give your reader a clear sense of what it is you are talking about. A quotation of four or more lines in the typescript should be set apart from the text of the paper. Your reader will find it easier to keep track of the passage this way. The quotation should smoothly be introduced by your own prose. Prepare your reader for the quotation by explaining whom you are quoting and why you are quoting. These transitions are important because they provide a context in which your reader can understand the passage. Here is a portion of a paper that discusses the portrayal of women by American writers.

According to Fiedler, American writers have had difficulty portraying sensuality (288); in fact, the sensuous
woman is often treated with fear or loathing. Consider
Giovanni's reaction when he first sees Beatrice Rappaccini:

> Soon there emerged from under a sculptured portal
> the figure of a young girl, arrayed with as much
> richness of taste as the most spendid of the
> flowers, beautiful as the day, and with a bloom
> so deep and vivid that one shade more would have
> been too much. She looked radiant with life,
> health, and energy; all of which attributes were
> bound down and compressed, as it were, and girdled
> tensely, in their luxuriance, by her virgin zone.
> Yet Giovanni's fancy must have grown morbid
> while he looked down into the garden; for the
> impression which the fair stranger made upon him
> was as if here were another flower, the human
> sister of those vegetable ones, as beautiful as
> they, more beautiful than the richest of them,
> but still to be touched only with a glove, nor
> to be approached without a mask. (Hawthorne 39)

It is the luxuriance of Beatrice's beauty, so much in
contrast to the Puritan standards of the day, that causes
this strange reaction and. . . .

The above method of presenting a lengthy quotation reflects the following
guidelines:

1. Introduce the quotation in the text of the paper.
2. Separate the double-spaced quotation from the text of the paper by triple spacing at the beginning and end of the passage.
3. Indent the quotation ten spaces from the left margin. The right margin for the quotation is the same as for the text.
4. If the quotation begins with a new paragraph, do not indent the first line unless you are quoting two or more paragraphs consecutively. When you do quote more than one paragraph, then indent the first line of each an additional three spaces.
5. Omit quotation marks at the beginning and end of the passage; the indentation and triple spacing indicate that the lines are quoted.
6. Place a parenthetical reference at the end of the passage to indicate its source. (See Chapter 8.)

Brief Quotations

Passages of fewer than four lines are integrated into the text of the paper.

```
Beatrice, however, turns out to be what Fiedler terms a

"Good Bad Girl" (295). When Giovanni discovers her secret,

she tells him: "Though my body be nourished with poison,

my spirit is God's creature, and craves love as its daily

food" (Hawthorne 55). However, since her body is

"nourished with poison," the antidote she accepts from

Giovanni causes her death.
```

This excerpt illustrates the guidelines for working brief quotations into the text:

1. Use quotation marks to indicate the quoted material.
2. Indicate the source of the quotation with a parenthetical reference. (See pages 144–154 for information on placing parenthetical references.)
3. When a quotation begins with the first word of a complete sentence and is formally introduced with a colon or comma, capitalize the first word of the quotation, unless the quoted material is used as part of the grammatical structure of your own sentence. Notice that the quotation above is a complete sentence and that it is preceded by a colon and begins with a capital letter. However, the last group of

quoted words begins with a lower-case letter, since it is not a sentence but only a fragment of the quotation that precedes it. (The quoted words "Good Bad Girl" reflect the capitalization of the original material.)

4. Help your reader to keep track of whom you are quoting. The critic's name is used in the text of the paper to introduce an assessment of Beatrice. Though it isn't always necessary to cite a name in the text — particularly when only factual information is presented — in this case the reference to Fiedler makes it easier for a reader to follow whose point of view is being offered.

A number of useful words can be used for introducing quotations into your text. Such words can help you to avoid repetitive constructions such as "Marcher says" or "Newton states," but they do more than provide variety; they provide exactness.

writes	thinks	agrees	contends
comments	believes	endorses	denies
notes	confirms	emphasizes	refutes
reports	affirms	argues	contradicts
discusses	declares	asserts	rejects
observes	accepts	claims	repudiates
suggests	acknowledges	insists	disputes
implies	grants	exposes	negates
judges	instructs	cautions	demands

A thesaurus will help you to find just the right word and make your writing more lively and precise. A source that "endorses" an idea is not the same as one that simply "states" one. Notice the way the following brief quotations are introduced:

In the spring of 1942, Douglas MacArthur mistakenly judged the U.S. Navy as "a fourth-class navy" (White 149).

"She is like a person walking a tight-rope," D. H. Lawrence wrote of H. D. "You wonder if she'll get across" (qtd. in Kazan 15).

Gore Vidal observes that "the written culture that was the core of every educational system since the fifth century

B.C. is now being replaced by sounds and images electron-
ically transmitted" (20).

According to Tuchman: "The gap between medieval Christianity's ruling principle and everyday life is the great
pitfall of the Middle Ages" (xix).

"Intellectual and spiritual disorientation," instructs
John Barth, "is the family disease of all my main
characters--a disease usually complicated by ontological
disorientation, since knowing where you're at is often
contingent upon knowing who you are" (36).

"Decoration," cautioned Frank Lloyd Wright, "can tell your
friends lots of things that you do not know and would not
like if you did" (4).

Quotations should be integrated into your prose as carefully as you construct your own sentences. Sometimes weaving a quotation into a sentence
requires a little ingenuity so that the complete sentence is grammatical.
As long as the meaning of a passage is not distorted or the results ungrammatical, quotations can be trimmed to fit into your sentences. Suppose
you wanted to quote this sentence from Thomas Paine: "I love the man
that can smile in trouble, that can gather strength from distress, and grow
brave by reflection." Consider these possibilities:

In an attempt to instill courage and confidence in his
countrymen, Paine expresses "love" for "the man that can
smile in trouble, that can gather strength from distress
and grow brave by reflection" (98).

In an attempt to instill courage and confidence in his
countrymen, Paine writes that "I love the . . ."(98).

not

```
In an attempt to instill courage and confidence in his

countrymen, Paine writes that he "love the . . ." (98).
```

This last example is clearly ungrammatical. It is corrected by altering the quotation and using brackets (see page 86). Check for ungrammatical constructions that can sometimes make their way into introductions to quoted material by reading the sentence aloud.

Omissions from Quotations

Although sources must be quoted accurately, they do not have to be quoted in their entirety. Words, phrases, and entire sentences can be omitted from quoted passages provided it is clear to your reader that the omissions have been made. The most common techniques for omitting parts of quotations follow:

1. It is often unnecessary to quote an entire sentence to make a point. When you omit a word or more in the middle of a quotation, you should use an *ellipsis mark* consisting of three spaced periods (. . .) to indicate the omission. For example:

```
"When you omit a word or more in the middle of a quotation,

you should use an ellipsis mark . . . to indicate the

omission."
```

2. When quoting only a phrase do not use an ellipsis at the beginning or end of the quotation:

```
Thomas Paine urged the "summer soldier and the sunshine

patriot" to take a stand.
```

not

```
Thomas Paine urged the ". . . summer soldier and the sun-

shine patriot . . ." to take a stand.
```

In the example immediately above, the ellipses are unnecessary because it is clear that the phrase is taken from a larger context that has been omitted from the quotation; hence, all those periods do little more than distract the reader.

3. When quoting the first part of a sentence but omitting the last part of it, use a period followed by an ellipsis:

```
Paine worried that "the summer soldier and the sunshine

patriot will, in this crisis, shrink from the service of

his country. . . ."
```

There is no space between the last word of the quotation and the period. If, however, something in parentheses had come after the final word of the quotation, then you would use three spaced periods at the end of the quote followed by the parenthetical material and then the sentence period:

```
country . . ." (98).
```

This final period is needed so that the parenthetical material is not set adrift outside the sentence.

4. To indicate the omission of an entire sentence or more, use four periods. Note that in such cases complete sentences must both precede and follow the four periods.

ORIGINAL QUOTATION
"These are the times that try men's souls. The summer soldier and the sunshine patriot will, in this crisis, shrink from the service of his country; but he that stands it *now* deserves the love and thanks of man and woman. Tyranny, like hell is not easily conquered; yet we have this consolation with us, that the harder the conflict, the more glorious the triumph. What we obtain too cheap, we esteem too lightly: it is dearness only that gives everything its value."

OMISSIONS INDICATED BY FOUR PERIODS

```
Paine fully acknowledged that the revolutionary

struggle would be difficult and costly: "These are the

times that try men's souls. The summer soldier and the

sunshine patriot will, in this crisis, shrink from the
```

service of his country. . . . What we obtain too cheap,

we esteem too lightly: it is dearness only that gives

everything its value"(98).

If you find yourself quoting more than is necessary just to have a complete sentence on both sides of the four periods, then it is better to integrate the parts of the quotation you need into your own prose.

5. To indicate a lengthy omission of more than one paragraph, type a single line of spaced periods across the width of the quotation:

Jack London is an American myth, a combination of

personal myths he created about himself and a national

myth he represented in his life and work.

. . . .

London not only showed the inherent virtues of the

American character--our energy and love of action and

the strenuous life, our generosity, courage, and concern

for social justice, he also portrayed our most pernicious

vices--our contentiousness and violence, our recklessness,

our materialism, and our love of change for its own sake.

(Rothberg 1-2)

In general, however, it is usually best to end the first part of the quotation and then begin again with your own prose leading into the second part of the quotation. An ellipsis should not be used as a substitute for transitions.

6. Be certain that when you use ellipses the meaning of the original is not changed. This sort of thing is most dramatically illustrated by advertisers who unscrupulously select only the words they want for a review of a film, book, or play:

ORIGINAL QUOTATION
    "This film is a significant failure coming from a producer who, in the past, enjoyed such success."

DISTORTED QUOTATION
```
"This film is a significant . . . success."
```

This use of an ellipsis is obviously dishonest, but even an inadvertent distortion can lead to a serious misrepresentation of a source.

Additions to Quotations

Any words that are added to a quotation should be enclosed in *brackets* so that a reader can distinguish your words from the original source. Brackets are used instead of parentheses because a reader would assume that the material in parentheses is the wording of the source rather than yours.

1. Use brackets when you clarify or explain a quotation:

```
"Unfortunately for London's express intention, the novel's

[White Fang's] most powerful sections are devoted to the

war of all against all, which London portrays with fidelity

and power" (Rothberg 11).
```

```
"She [Flora London] was constantly plunging into schemes

for making a fortune overnight" (Rothberg 2).
```

2. Use brackets to alter the grammatical structure of a quotation so that it can be integrated into your sentence:

```
In an attempt to instill courage and confidence in his

countrymen, Paine wrote that he "love[s] the man that can

smile in trouble, that can gather strength from distress,

and grow brave by reflection" (98).
```

```
"London . . . [adopted] the cloak that Hemingway would

later throw over his own literary shoulders" (Rothberg 1).
```

3. Use brackets to indicate that part of the quotation that has been underlined for emphasis:

> "When the colonists came to America, spelling was not a
> problem--if a man could write <u>at</u> <u>all</u> [emphasis added] he
> was lucky" (Flexner 212).

4. Use brackets with the Latin word "sic" (meaning "thus") to indicate that an error in the quotation is reproduced exactly as it appeared in the original. This informs the reader that you are aware of the error rather than responsible for it:

> Roethke compares the meadow mouse to "a miniscule [sic]
> puppy" (line 11).

Do not use "sic" for passages in which the spelling and capitalization do not conform to modern conventions. The following quotation written in the seventeenth century, requires no such notation:

> William Penn, the founder of Philadelphia, wanted his new
> city to be "a greene Country Towne, which will never be
> burnt, and allways be wholsome" (qtd. in Weigley 1).

Adding "sic" five times to this passage would be disruptive as well as unnecessary.

If your typewriter does not have brackets, leave space for them and draw them in with black ink.

Poetry Quotations

LENGTHY PASSAGES

Three or more lines of quoted poetry should be set apart from the text of the paper:

> The male speaker of Andrew Marvell's "To His Coy Mistress"
> would be a patient lover if there were "world-enough, and
> time" (line 1):

> But at my back I always hear
>
> Time's wingèd chariot hurrying near;
>
> And yonder all before us lie
>
> Deserts of vast eternity.
>
> Thy beauty shall no more be found,
>
> Nor in thy marble vault, shall sound
>
> My echoing song; then worms shall try
>
> That long, preserved virginity,
>
> And your quaint honor turn to dust,
>
> And into ashes all my lust:
>
> The grave's a fine and private place,
>
> But none, I think, do there embrace. (21-32)

This argument is effective owing to its vividness and grim truth.

Observe the following guidelines for quoting three or more lines of verse:

1. Introduce the quotation in the text of the paper.
2. Separate the quotation from the text by triple spacing at the beginning and end.
3. Double space the quotation unless the original lines call for different spacing. Reproduce the quoted passage so that the spacing and typographical features of the original are preserved.
4. If more than one stanza is quoted, triple space between them.
5. Indent ten spaces from the left margin, but if the quoted lines are very long, indent fewer spaces to avoid an unbalanced appearance.
6. If the quotation begins in the middle of a line, reproduce it that way; do not move the line over to the left margin.
7. Omit quotation marks at the beginning and end of the passage; the indentation and triple spacing indicate that the lines are quoted.
8. Provide a parenthetical reference citing the line numbers. For displayed quotations, place this citation after the final period. (The first time a parenthetical reference to a line or lines of verse appears in

text, spell out the word *line* or *lines*. All other times, simply provide the line number or numbers.)

9. To omit one or more lines of verse, type a line of spaced periods the width of the quoted lines:

```
But at my back I always hear

Time's wingèd chariot hurrying near;

. . . . . . . . . . . . . . . .

The grave's a fine and private place,

But none, I think, do there embrace. (21-32)
```

BRIEF PASSAGES

Poetry quotations of three lines or less are worked into the text of your paper:

```
The speaker in Marvell's poem has time on his side.  The

perspective he offers makes coyness seem tragic rather

than appealing.  We see "quaint honor turn to dust"

(line 29) when he concludes that "The grave's a fine and

private place, / But none, I think, do there embrace"

(31-32).
```

Follow these guidelines for brief poetry quotations:

1. Use quotation marks to indicate quoted material.
2. When quoting two or three lines of poetry in the text of the paper, use a slash (/) preceded and followed by a space to indicate where one line ends and another begins.
3. Provide a parenthetical reference citing the line number(s). For brief quotations worked into the text, place this citation after the quotation mark but before the final period. If the poet's name appears in the text, it is not necessary to include it in the parenthetical reference. Spell out the word *line* or *lines* the first time such a parenthetical reference occurs. Then, for all other times, simply provide the line number or numbers.

Punctuating Quotations

Punctuating quotations can sometimes be a bit confusing, because you have to make a choice between placing the punctuation either inside or outside the quotation marks. If you keep the following conventions in mind, however, you will have no problems:

1. *Commas* and *periods* are placed inside quotation marks, even if they do not appear in the original quotation:

   ORIGINAL QUOTATION
   "And your quaint honor turn to dust,"

   WORKED INTO PAPER
   "And your quaint honor," he warns, will "turn to dust."

Notice that the original quotation had no comma after "honor," but when it is worked into the paper, the comma is needed for grammatical purposes. Similarly, the comma at the end of the original line has been changed to a period, because it is needed to mark the end of a complete sentence.

You will see two exceptions to the rule of placing commas and periods inside quotation marks. When a quotation is followed by parenthetical reference, the punctuation comes after the parentheses:

"And your quaint honor," he warns, will "turn to

dust" (29).

The other exception you may encounter will be in your reading rather than in your paper, but you should be aware of it so that you are not bewildered. British usage places the period outside the quotation mark, and you will see that convention used in many books published in England. Use the American convention, unless you are prepared to defend your punctuation with a British accent.

2. *Colons* and *semicolons* are placed outside quotation marks:

It is clear what he means by "Deserts of vast eternity"

(24): death and decay.

The speaker grants that "The grave's a fine and private

place"; however, he also grimly notes that "none . . .

do there embrace" (31-32).

3. *Question marks* and *exclamation points* are placed inside quotation marks only if the quotation is a question or exclamation; otherwise, they are placed outside the quotation marks:

INSIDE
The student then asked, "What does this line mean?"

OUTSIDE
What does line 24 mean: "Deserts of vast eternity"?

INSIDE
"Jump!" he shouted.

OUTSIDE
He tried to write a paper about Marvell's attitude toward

women after reading only one poem, "To His Coy Mistress"!

4. *Single quotation marks* are used to enclose a quotation within a quotation:

Concerning Samuel Johnson's study of the metaphysical

poets, T. S. Eliot writes: "Johnson has hit, perhaps by

accident, on one of their peculiarities, when he observes

that 'their attempts were always analytical'" (1063).

The single quotation marks are used to set off the quoted material within the larger quotation. Notice that the period is placed after the parenthetical reference. If there had been no reference, the period would have been placed at the end of the sentence preceding the single quotation mark (. . . analytical.' ").

For quotations within lengthy quoted passages that are double spaced and indented use double quotation marks. Single quotation marks are used only inside double quotation marks.

ACKNOWLEDGING SOURCES OF INFORMATION

In writing a research paper, it is crucial to acknowledge the sources of the facts, ideas, opinions, and quotations that you've used. By documenting your sources, you demonstrate that you've drawn upon the work of experts and you inform your reader where that work can be found. Putting together a research paper is not, as one student put it, "the art of concealing your sources." This description may help to explain what deception, fraud, and misrepresentation mean, but it fails to define a research paper. Instead, it defines intentional *plagiarism:* the presentation of someone else's work as one's own.

Of course, the simplest and crassest form of plagiarism is handing in another student's paper or buying one from a term paper mill. If you've read this far, however, you're not likely to buy a paper or sell yourself. Morality is something we choose to abide by or not, so there's little point in sermonizing about it. The more common form of plagiarism appears in papers that inadequately document their sources. Whether this is done intentionally or not, it is a serious problem that can lead to serious consequences ranging from a failing grade for the assignment and course to academic probation or even expulsion. Remember that your instructor can evaluate only the results of your documentation, not your motive.

Quite apart from morality, plagiarism is totally unnecessary in a research paper, because you are *expected* to use sources of information that go beyond your own knowledge. After having spent so much time in the library, you shouldn't be shy about letting your reader know what you've found, but even if you're eager to acknowledge your findings, plagiarism can still be a problem for students who aren't entirely clear on when and how to document their sources. The following guidelines and examples should help you to acknowledge your sources accurately and with confidence. (For detailed information on how to write up your list of works cited and parenthetical references for the paper, see Chapters 7 and 8.)

When to Document

You will have no difficulty documenting the paper adequately if you keep in mind that you must acknowledge your use of a source whenever you (1) quote the exact wording from a work; (2) paraphrase or summarize someone else's ideas, opinions, or insights; (3) use any facts or information not regarded as common knowledge. These points can be illustrated by a description of Horatio Alger's novels from Russel B. Nye, *The Unembarrassed Muse: The Popular Arts in America* (New York: Dial, 1970) 67:

ORIGINAL PASSAGE

His books celebrated, in unmistakable terms, the values of individualism, self-reliance, and alertness to opportunity, and it was noticeable to his readers that success came to good boys, not bad ones. The old-fashioned virtues paid off in Alger's plots; it was not always exactly clear why, but they did, and the boy who was honest, punctual, respectable, and who honored his parents and his employer found success.

Here is a plagiarized version of this passage:

PLAGIARIZED

Alger's novels are populated by good boys who embody

the values of individualism, self-reliance, and alertness

that his books celebrated. The boys who were honest,

punctual, respectable, and who honored their parents and

employer were always rewarded for their old-fashioned

virtues.

The writer has changed a few words around, adding some while deleting others, but the passage is essentially the same as the original. Had a parenthetical reference been placed at the end of the passage acknowledging that the ideas had come from Nye, this version would still be plagiarized because the language of the passage is being passed off as the writer's own. Both the language and ideas of a source must be acknowledged. The next example is not so blatant as the version above, but it is a problem nonetheless:

PLAGIARIZED

Nye points out that all of Alger's heroes are self-

reliant individuals who stay alert to opportunity. These

boys are paid off for their old-fashioned virtues of

honesty, punctuality, and respectability (67).

This version makes clear that the ideas are Nye's — both by naming him in the text and the parenthetical reference at the end — but the language still relies too heavily on the original wording. Although some nouns and adjectives have been changed, the wording remains basically Nye's and so the passage is plagiarized. Even if quotation marks had been used for the exact wording ("opportunity," "paid off," and "old-fashioned virtues"), the paraphrase is too close to the original. Moreover, a string of quoted words would be awkward and distracting. The next version, however, represents an acceptable paraphrase:

ACCEPTABLE PARAPHRASE

Alger's boy heroes, according to Russel B. Nye, repre-

sented the individual's ability to help himself rise above

whatever circumstances limited him. The boy who was well-

behaved at home and at work could count on being well-

rewarded. As Nye puts it, "old-fashioned virtues paid off

in Alger's plots" (67).

In this paraphrase, the source is adequately acknowledged because the writer makes clear that the ideas are borrowed and that some of Nye's language has been used. The student used the quoted material because it served as an effective encapsulation of the original passage. The next version is an acceptable summary of the original passage:

ACCEPTABLE SUMMARY

Russel B. Nye points out that in an Alger novel virtue

is never simply its own reward; instead, good boys become

successful men (67).

Here the language is entirely the student's, except for the phrase "good boys," and although it is a concise summary rather than a paraphrase, the source of the idea must be acknowledged by a parenthetical reference.

It is not always necessary to name your source in the text of your paper. For example, when simply citing a piece of information, it is preferable to place the name of your source in your parenthetical reference:

Estimates of the total sales of Alger's novels since their

publication range from 15 million to 300 million, with the

greatest concentration of sales occurring from approxi-

mately 1900 to 1910 (Falk 151).

Identifying your source in the text, however, can be a useful signal to your reader that only the information framed by the identification and the parenthetical reference is from the source, not the entire paragraph. Suppose, for example, that the summary of the Nye passage above had been preceded by one of your own ideas:

```
In contrast to John Bunyan's Pilgrim's Progress, in which

there are spiritual rather than material rewards, Alger's

stories are filled with gold watches and full purses.

Russel B. Nye points out that in an Alger novel virtue is

never simply its own reward; instead, good boys become

successful men (67).
```

Without the reference to Nye in the text, a reader might think that the comparison between Alger and Bunyan also came from Nye rather than from you. Give credit where credit is due — including to yourself. Your reader will assume that material not documented in the paper represents either your own insights or common knowledge.

Common Knowledge

Information that is common knowledge requires no documentation. Common knowledge consists of facts and observations that are widely known and available in a number of sources. They are frequently acquired the way you catch a cold; they are in the air. It is not necessary to document historical facts such as "President Kennedy was assassinated in 1963." Even if you had to look up the years, the dates of World War II do not require a source, because this information is so basic. Similarly, the observation that the cost of imported oil has contributed to inflation or that fewer families today can afford to get by on one income compared with ten years ago does not need documentation. Information that can be regarded as generally known or basic to a particular field of study may be regarded as common knowledge.

Information that has been interpreted by a particular source must be documented, however. It is common knowledge, for example, that the United States declared war on Japan in December of 1941; no documentation is needed for that. If, however, you found a source arguing that war would have been declared during that month even if the Japanese had not bombed Pearl Harbor, it would have to be documented. It is common knowledge that the cost of imported oil has fueled inflation, but a citation would be required if you used a source saying that American oil producers conspired with foreign producers to keep the prices high.

Opinions and judgments that you reach independently or prior to your sources needn't be documented. If after reading a novel by Horatio Alger, for example, you concluded that it was badly written but easy to read, you would not have to document that perspective in a paper just because you found the same assessment in one of your sources. You would have to explain why you reached that conclusion by using illustrations from the novel, but you wouldn't have to cite a critic. Indeed, you'd probably find that point of view expressed in virtually all your sources. You would have to document that view of the novel only if you quoted a particularly significant or vivid source on the subject.

Occasionally it is difficult to determine when something should be documented or regarded as common knowledge. What is considered common knowledge for a paper written for an upper division journalism seminar that focuses exclusively on a comparison of print journalism with television news probably is not common knowledge for a paper on news coverage in a freshman English course. The seminar student will have access to more common knowledge than the freshman would be likely to have, just as a professional journalist would know more than the seminar student. Perhaps the wisest strategy to use when determining if you are dealing with common knowledge or specialized knowledge that must be documented is to ask yourself if your reader is likely to question what the information is based on. If you hear your reader saying "Where did you get this from?" then cite a source. Otherwise, the most sensible guideline to follow is to seek advice from your instructor when you are uncertain about what is considered common knowledge in the field you are researching. If that isn't feasible, then provide documentation when in doubt. As you do your research, notice how your own sources handle citations; also, the sample paper on pages 206–239 should help you to develop a sense of tact for documentation.

In order to use sources honestly and accurately, and, to avoid plagiarism, keep in mind the following guidelines:

1. Indicate that you have used the exact wording of a source by enclosing the material in quotation marks or displaying the quoted material by spacing and indenting. Place a parenthetical reference at the end of the quotation to document the source.

2. Any ideas, opinions, or insights taken from a source and used in your paper as a quotation, paraphrase, or summary must be acknowledged by a parenthetical reference.

3. Any facts or information not regarded as common knowledge must be acknowledged by a parenthetical reference.

4. Introduce borrowed language, ideas, and information in the text of your paper so that your reader can readily see what is yours and what is from your sources.

5. Never present someone else's language, ideas, or information in such a way that it might be mistaken for your own.

6 Writing the Drafts

Your paper is still unwritten, but don't despair. Given the planning and work you have already put into it, you shouldn't have too much difficulty. Consider, after all, what you have already done:

1. You've chosen a manageable topic.
2. You've found relevant materials in the library.
3. You've read and evaluated a variety of sources.
4. You've developed a thesis.
5. You've gathered and organized relevant and documented material on note cards.
6. You've composed an outline to use as a guide for your writing.

This chapter offers some practical advice about writing your paper. The topics covered are really reminders for you to consider as you compose. For fuller discussions, consult a recent composition handbook. If you haven't used one in a course or don't own one, ask your instructor to recommend an appropriate guide to writing.

As you compose the paper, remember that the very process of writing can be a way of learning about your topic as well as a vehicle for explaining your thesis. Think of your writing as more than simply the way in which your research project takes its finished form. As you write about your findings, you will have one more opportunity to explore ideas and discover relationships. Be alert for those discoveries. Few writers think through a topic so thoroughly that they know exactly what they're going to say when they sit down to write. (Those who do are also probably capable of knowing every move they'll make before they sit down to a chess game. For most of us, however, life — and writing — are not so predictable.) You'll probably discover much of what you want to say while you're actually in the process of writing. Strategies and ideas evolve as you write: your emphasis may change; your thesis may require qualification; and your organization may shift. This reflexive process is both natural and desirable. Writing is, after all, a way of thinking — one of the best.

SOME PRELIMINARY CONSIDERATIONS

Planning Ahead

Give yourself the time to write a good paper. You've spent a significant amount of time working up the topic, but unless your writing reflects your grasp of the material and the care with which you have put it together, your work in the library will be apparent only to you, not to your instructor. Even if you are required to hand in your outline and note cards with the paper, it is the finished paper that ultimately represents the time and effort that went into the project.

Only you know how much time you will need to write the first draft. If you spend several hours on the paper each day and it comes to about ten pages, you will probably need two or three days to write the first draft. After allowing it to sit for a day, you should then leave time for revisions and rewriting. Once it is typed, proofread it the following day so you will be more likely to catch errors. In short, you'll very likely need at least five or six days to do an adequate job of writing and editing the paper — assuming, of course, that you have other work to do as well. If you begin writing about a week before the paper is due, you shouldn't feel any panic. Remember that most of the work is already on your note cards.

Determining the Audience

Before you begin writing, you should consider the audience your paper is aimed at. This process is similar to the kind of decisions you make daily when you talk with a friend, or a child, or a parent, or an instructor. Imagine yourself explaining to each of these people why you are attending college. When you change your audience, you also alter what you say and how you say it. The same is true with writing: if you consider whom you are writing for, you are more likely to communicate effectively.

Suppose you were writing a paper on abortion. The course for which you wrote the paper would be a factor in determining its audience. The content and style of a paper written for a biology course would be different from one written for psychology, sociology, history, or philosophy. Your readers' expectations would cause you to adjust your emphasis, thesis, terminology, and supporting details. There would be no point, for example, in providing an overview of the moral issues associated with abortion if your paper were a qualitative analysis of outpatient abortion clinics.

More specifically, you should determine if you are expected to write for a general audience, such as your fellow students, or for a specialist in a particular field, such as your instructor. Writing done for a general audience assumes that the reader will be less familiar with the material than a specialist. Suppose you are writing a paper for an English course about Hemingway's view of war in *For Whom the Bell Tolls*. If the paper were to be read by students who have not been assigned the novel, you would have to provide a sense of what the book is about. Were the paper written only for your instructor, that kind of summary would be unnecessary. Or to take another example: a paper written for a psychology course wouldn't have to define widely used clinical terms, but a paper written on a psychology topic for an English composition course would present problems for most English teachers if it were freighted with terms such as "phenylketonuria" or "reciprocal inhibition psychotherapy." Highly specialized and technical language should be reserved for an audience that can understand it without being driven to reference books. Use language appropriate for your audience. Don't make the mistake frequently seen on signs at subway stations that read "Do Not Expectorate." That message is lost on its audience: the people who spit in subway stations. If you have any questions about who your audience is and what you can assume about that audience, ask your instructor for advice.

Adopting a Tone

Closely related to the question of audience is the tone you use in the paper. Tone is the attitude you adopt toward your subject (and, indirectly, toward your reader and toward yourself). It is established by the nature of your subject, your purpose, and your audience. Tone is a matter of degree; it may range from a highly formal presentation of the material to an informal one. It may be serious or casual, sober or humorous, factual or ironic, detached or involved. For research papers the tone is usually serious but that does not mean that it must be dour. Wit and humor, when appropriate, can go a long way toward engaging your readers as well as informing them. Some topics lend themselves more readily to an informal, light approach than others. Probably any attempts to be witty or humorous about a topic such as abortion would be a mistake. A paper about changing attitudes toward sex roles, however, could easily have some light moments, since the subject, though serious, has its humorous side as people attempt to cope with those changes. Surely a light and informal approach to comic book heroes could be appropriate, but a similar approach to international terrorism could easily backfire. Very likely the tone of your sources will affect the tone of your paper, because you will sense how others have deemed it appropriate to handle the subject. Notice, for example, the use of tone in the sample research paper (pages 206–231).

Tone, like fashion, has a good bit to do with personal taste. In general, academic writing, particularly in the humanities, has loosened up in recent years. It has become less formal and rigid, and there is a greater range of styles apparent in journals and books. These styles range from conservative to more open approaches to language. You may run across informal prose in your sources or highly abstract specialized language. You'll probably choose a middle ground that is compatible with your own writing habits and the inescapable fact that your instructor will be grading the paper. Before you use contractions or colloquial expressions (e.g., "uptight" for "anxious"), it is a good idea to check with your instructor.

Usually, students are advised to write in the third person and to avoid pronouns such as "you" and "I." A research paper is different from a letter home to a friend. Your task is to report your findings so that they support a thesis, which is different from writing a chatty, intimate letter. It may be, however, that you will refer to yourself at some point in the paper because you want to distinguish your own point of view from your sources. If you do refer to yourself, don't resort to awkward, passive constructions such as "in the opinion of this writer, doubt should be cast on. . . ." Simply write "I doubt." Don't abandon what is natural, sensible, and effective just because you're writing a research paper. That doesn't mean that you should groove on the research paper in laid back, mellow prose (prose that, as you can see, is as silly as it is embarrassing), but it does mean that you can write a relatively formal paper and still write graceful, readable prose.

Using the Outline and Note Cards

Before you begin writing, use your outline to organize sections of the paper and arrange the note cards so that they are in the same order. Cards that no longer seem relevant to your thesis should be set aside; you may also find yourself regrouping some cards because you now see a better way to organize them. Use the information from the organized cards to provide the detailed information necessary to construct the paragraphs indicated by your outline. You'll probably feel that you're making good progress if you write up one or two sections of your outline at a sitting. Many writers find this satisfying; they have a sense of having accomplished something, and they know where to begin when they resume their work (precisely the way this book was written). Also, by writing up one section at a time, it is easier to relate each part of the paper to the thesis and to determine how each part leads into the next section of the outline. On the other hand, if you have the stamina and an entire day, you might find that you can write a complete first draft in one sitting. Do what comes naturally. Regardless of which way you write the paper, your outline will map the route you take through all those note cards.

THE FIRST DRAFT

The first draft is the preliminary form that your writing will take. It will be rough, not finished, and tentative, not final. Follow your outline, but feel free to write as the words come to you without worrying about the mechanics of writing or grammatical correctness. Those concerns will only slow down your thinking and your writing. Walt Whitman made the point as well as anyone: "Let everything be as free as possible," he urged. "There is always danger in constipation." Freedom is important at this stage because you can discover relationships as you write even while you're explaining them. If you get caught up in agonizing over whether or not to use "who" or "whom" in a sentence, you might easily lose your train of thought and the momentum you had. Give yourself a chance to write something before you worry about how you've written it. Save that for your revisions.

Similarly, for your first draft, do not worry about the exact form of your parenthetical references. At this stage it is enough to place in parentheses the source's name and the page number (plus any other information you will need to identify this source):

```
There was a steady increase of tourism the following year;

nearly 4,000 Japanese traveled to China in 1966 (Cook 45).
```

Keep your note cards in the order you have used them. Then, after you have used your note cards to prepare your list of works cited, you can check your parenthetical references against this list to make sure that they contain enough information and are in standard form.

You can prepare for the revisions in your first draft by leaving generous margins and skipping every other line if you write in longhand (triple space if you type). The more space you leave, the more room you will have to add words or entire sentences. Some students find that writing only one paragraph to a page allows them the flexibility of shifting whole paragraphs around if that turns out to be desirable. It also leaves room to write transitions that, at first, didn't seem to be needed. Using this method will make the draft easier to read, and it will eliminate unnecessary copying.

The paper has three basic parts: the introduction, the body, and the conclusion. (The documentation — list of works cited and parenthetical references — are discussed in Chapters 7 and 8.) An overview of these three parts should provide you with a better sense of how to make the most of the information in your outline.

The Introduction

Although the introduction informs your reader of what it is you are going to discuss, you may find, as many writers do, that the introduction is easier to write after the body of the paper is completed. Beginnings — especially reluctant ones — are always difficult, and some writers prefer to plunge right into the body of the paper. Your introduction is more for your reader than for you. Equipped with your thesis and outline, you already know what you are going to do. If you have any problems writing the introduction, put it off until you've written the body of the paper rather than getting stalled at the very start.

An introduction has two essential purposes: to engage your reader and to explain clearly what the paper is about. The idea is to both interest and inform the reader. Examine the opening paragraphs of the articles and books you've used for your notes and you will see a variety of ways to introduce topics. The approach you use for your own introduction will depend on the nature of your topic, your audience, and the prevailing tone of the paper. Consider the following strategies for introducing topics:

1. Begin with an arresting fact that is central to the topic. Here is the opening sentence for a paper about Herman Melville's reputation:

   Early readers looked to Moby-Dick for an adventure story

   along the lines of Typee and White-Jacket but found instead

   a long tale about whaling that they considered "spoiled by

   murky metaphysical speculations" (Chase 880). So dis-

   appointed were they that this novel sealed Melville's

   decline into obscurity and . . .

2. Begin with a quotation that is especially fitting and incisive. The following quotation introduces a paper about the early years of American involvement in Vietnam:

   "Anybody who commits the land power of the United States

   on the continent of Asia ought to have his head examined,"

   cautioned Douglas MacArthur (qtd. in White 149). How dif-

   ferent might have been the history of American involvement

   in Vietnam if we had heeded his admonition.

3. Begin with a forceful assertion that challenges a belief or an assumption. Here is a passage introducing a paper on the decline of quality in America.

America is no longer a producer of quality goods. In fact,

our famous "Yankee know how" seems to be dead. Nowhere is

this more evident than in the automotive industry. In

1977, 9,300,000 new cars, many of them foreign cars, were

sold. However, in that same year, 10,400,000 American cars

of various model years were recalled (Swyrydenko 30).

4. Begin with a paradox that your paper resolves. The following statement introduces a paper on the issue of gun control:

If freedom in America is to survive, Americans are going

to have to give up some freedom.

5. Begin with a reference to a current event. Observe the parallel drawn in this paper about eighteenth-century sentimental stories written for young women:

The sentimental romances that were popular toward the end

of the eighteenth century in England are not very different

from the romances found beside check-out counters at super-

markets today.

These strategies are meant to be suggestive, not exhaustive. Your own sources will yield other devices. Some writers find that a personal anecdote explaining why they became interested in the topic is useful. Others survey the major work done on the topic and then choose a particular point of view to develop. It is also helpful to introduce some topics with important background information so that you provide a context for your reader. Whatever strategy you use, the time is well spent because in the space of a paragraph or two your reader will either look forward to the rest of the paper or begrudge you the time. Since first impressions are so important you should also be conscious of what often leads to bad impressions:

1. Avoid special pleading. If something genuinely interests you, make it interesting. Don't write:

   ```
   Hair styles have always interested me.
   ```

2. Avoid apologizing for your topic. Don't write:

   ```
   Although there was little material in the library about

   nineteenth-century men's fashions, there was a lot about

   women's hair styles.
   ```

3. Avoid repeating the title in the introduction unless it is part of a quoted line or phrase that your introduction explains.
4. Avoid dictionary definitions of terms. Don't write:

   ```
   According to Webster, boredom is. . . .
   ```

   This sort of thing is as predictable as it is deadly.
5. Avoid asking questions unless they are provocative. Don't write:

   ```
   What is Keynesian economics?
   ```

   and then immediately proceed to answer it.

The Body

Your thesis and outline are your guides here, but don't allow them to tyrannize your thought processes. If, as you write, you discover better ways to organize the paper, use them. The outline will indicate the points that need to be developed and your note cards will supply the detailed information for that development (see pages 70–91 for discussions of how to organize and present the information). At this stage you will unify your notes for each subdivided topic of your outline and work your quotations, paraphrases, and summaries into a coherent whole.

Unity, Coherence, and the Use of Transitions

As you work through the outline be sure that all the material included in the paper is related to your thesis. You jeopardize the *unity* of the paper if you allow extraneous information to creep in. No doubt you worked hard for that information on the note cards and you may be tempted to work it all in one way or the other, but if you do, the irrelevant material will distract and confuse your reader. A paper on the reception of *Moby-Dick* would lack unity if you tucked in a paragraph about recent campaigns to save whales. On a smaller scale unity is also necessary in paragraphs. Each element of a paragraph should be related to its central idea.

Your unified topic will have *coherence* if your reader can follow its progression from one idea to the next. The paper must be constructed so that a reader can understand how the topics relate to one another. You have to provide the connective tissue that holds the paper together. It can be unified (all the topics related to the thesis) but still incoherent if the topics, instead of being tied together, lurch in every direction. Don't treat your reader like a pinball machine. Use transitions to help make your discussion easy to follow.

Transitions connect the parts of the paper and show logical relationships. There are a number of words and phrases suitable for this purpose. Remember that you are much closer to the material you're presenting than your reader. The more thoughtful you are with transitional devices the more likely your reader will be able to follow your discussion and appreciate your work. The following sampling of transitional words and phrases can be used to signal relationships within paragraphs and between paragraphs:

TO SIGNAL CONTRAST
but, nevertheless, on the contrary, on the other hand, still, though, yet, despite, although, whereas, however

TO SIGNAL RESULTS
then, as a result, therefore, hence, consequently, otherwise, because, thus, so

TO SIGNAL AN ADDITIONAL RELATIONSHIP
first, second, furthermore, in addition, besides, equally, another, also, last, finally

There are many other useful transitions to indicate examples ("for instance," "an illustration," "such as," "specifically"), time ("next," "then," "until," "finally," "afterward," "earlier," "later," "subsequently"), or a conclusion ("finally," "in short," "in brief," "in other words").

These transitional devices are enormously helpful to your reader because they indicate the relationships that you have established among the ideas and information you are presenting. It certainly isn't necessary or desirable to begin every paragraph with a transition; that would be monotonous. Nor should you identify the parts of the paper (introduction, body, conclusion) with headings naming them. Remember that an important word or phrase that appeared at the end of a paragraph can be repeated toward the beginning of the next as a transitional device too.

The Conclusion

The conclusion is as important as the introduction. Leave your reader with a firm sense that the information you have provided in the body of the paper has made the point you introduced in the opening paragraphs. Your conclusion should satisfy the reader that you have said all that is reasonably necessary to establish the credibility of your thesis. The last thing you want to do is to leave the impression that you've run out of things to say. Instead, you should make clear the significance of the work you've done and explain how it sheds light on the topic you've chosen. Here is the concluding paragraph from an article by Katherine G. Simoneaux entitled "Color Imagery in Crane's *Maggie: A Girl of the Streets*" (*CLA Journal* 18 [Sept. 1974]: 91–100) which does just that:

> Color then is not only a vital part of Crane's work but an aspect of it which is of primary importance, indispensable to an understanding of his art. To convey emotional or sense impressions, Crane depends on color-words which, though perhaps not always realistically accurate, cause the reader to appreciate and remember characters and events. Thus Crane associates black primarily with Maggie; red with her mother and her brother; red, blue, black, and white with Pete; and yellow with the environment. Black in *Maggie* is related to death; red to anger and violence; and yellow to the harshness of the grim environment and the discontent of its inhabitants. Crane's philosophy found little use for delicate colors such as green, pink, or blue except when these colors are used for irony or for contrast with the harsh world that the strong, plain colors portray. The frequent use of color creates a poetic texture in Crane's prose and contributes to the power of his impressionistic writing.

This detailed conclusion makes absolutely clear what the paper has discussed and why it was worth discussing.

Conclusions, like introductions, are unique to the paper they are written for; there is no magic formula for creating a conclusion, but here are some general guidelines to consider as you write one:

1. Make sure the conclusion *ends* the paper; don't trail off or stop your discussion abruptly with the last subdivision of your outline. Provide a retrospective view that summarizes your major points and explains their significance.

2. Don't simply repeat your thesis; instead, elaborate on it or perhaps suggest further directions for research.

3. Use the conclusion to tie the paper together. One way to do this is to develop or allude to some point mentioned in the introduction.

4. Don't claim more than you have actually done. Notice that the color symbolism discussed in the quoted paragraph restricts its relevance to *Maggie*, not to all of Crane's works.

5. Don't undercut your own work:

```
This evidence may not convince you, but:
```

```
I am convinced.
```

6. Don't take up a new topic or idea that requires more development; avoid afterthoughts.

7. Don't write concluding paragraphs that begin:

```
In conclusion
```

or its equivalents. This kind of signaling is unnecessary and about as useful as starting an introduction by intoning:

```
In the beginning
```

The Title

Choose a final title only after you have completed at least a draft of the paper. Until you've finished the paper you won't know for certain what it is that you've actually done. You may already have a working title, but now you should refine it. Your title should, like the introduction, both interest and inform the reader about the nature of the paper. Consider these suggestions:

1. Be specific rather than vague; avoid titles that consist only of unqualified nouns:

Vague	*Specific*
Prison Reform	Prison Reform Efforts of the 1830s
Uncle Tom's Cabin	Racial Stereotypes in Uncle Tom's Cabin
Terrorism	Strategies for Ending International Terrorism

2. Be sure that your title accurately describes what you actually write about. If you titled a paper "Marvell's View of Women" but discussed only one poem, "To His Coy Mistress," then the title should be restricted to something like:

```
Marvell's View of Women in "To His Coy Mistress"
```

3. Do not underline or use quotation marks for *your own* title, unless part of your title includes the title of another work:

```
Recent Psychological Interpretations of Hamlet

Hawthorne's Use of History in "Young Goodman Brown"
```

4. A witty or eye-catching title, when appropriate for the topic, can help to create interest in the rest of the paper. Barbara Lawrence entitles her analysis of obscene language: "Four-Letter Words Can Hurt You."

REVISING THE DRAFTS

After you have completed a draft, set it aside for a day so that you can distance yourself from what you have written. You can then revise it more effectively. Through the process of revision an adequate paper that supports its thesis can become a first-rate paper that is a pleasure to read. The really good writers are the ones who revise, and when they finish, they revise again. Revision involves considerably more than correcting punctuation and spelling errors.

For your first round of revising, read the paper through to see if the organization holds up. Check to see if there are any gaps. Should any transitional paragraphs be added? Check, too, to see if there are irrelevancies. Should any paragraphs be deleted? Any organizational shifts you make at this point should also be reflected in your final outline if you are expected to hand one in. Also, any changes in your thinking that may cause you to adjust your thesis should be recorded in the thesis. If you wrote each paragraph on a separate sheet of paper, you will find this process of moving material around easy to do, because you won't have to disrupt whole sections to make changes. Now is the time to add any necessary information to paragraphs that need further development and supporting evidence and to delete sentences that are irrelevant or repetitive.

Approach your paper with an eye toward your audience. Try to adopt your reader's point of view so that you can anticipate problems. Check to see that you have provided transitions between paragraphs and between sentences within paragraphs. Does each topic or idea follow logically from the next? When you feel confident about the paper's organization — when it appears to be unified and coherent — you can then focus on more detailed matters. If the revisions are heavy, it might be wise to rewrite or type the draft so that you can more easily see smaller problems that have to be dealt with.

You will read your paper through many times during the process of revision. As you do, check for the items included in the following checklist. It will be a useful reminder of the elements that go into making an effective paper. Try to be as thorough as possible because what you don't catch in your revisions will, no doubt, be caught by your instructor. If you need more detailed information about a specific element in the checklist consult a composition handbook.

Revision Checklist

General Questions

1. Is your thesis — the point of the paper — clear?
2. Have you included enough information to support the thesis?
3. Is there any extraneous information that should be deleted?
4. Does the body of your paper develop logically and appear well organized? Is it unified and coherent?
5. Is your material proportioned effectively so that important elements are emphasized?
6. Have you documented all the borrowed words, facts, and ideas you have used?
7. Is your introduction interesting and does it give the reader a clear sense of what the paper is about?
8. Have you quoted excessively when a paraphrase or summary would be better?
9. Is your tone appropriate for the subject matter and the audience?
10. Are your points made clearly and concisely? Do you use concrete examples to illustrate your points?
11. Have you maintained a consistent point of view that does not shift from *you* to *one* to *he* or *she?*
12. Does your conclusion end the paper effectively?
13. Does your title engage the reader and suggest the nature of the topic?

Paragraphs

1. Does each paragraph develop logically and have a central point to make? Is the point related to the thesis?
2. Are your paragraphs adequately developed? Are there any paragraphs only one or two sentences in length?
3. Are any of your paragraphs too long? Can they be divided?
4. Are there smooth transitions between your paragraphs?
5. Are you satisfied that each sentence in the paragraph relates to its central point?

Sentences

1. Are your sentences varied in length?
2. Are they clear and complete? Are there any run-on sentences, comma splices, or fragments?
3. Are modifiers near what they modify?
4. Are your sentences varied in form? Are there simple, complex, and compound sentences? Have you used coordination, subordination, and parallelism for variety and emphasis?
5. Have you used transitions where they are needed?
6. Have you correctly punctuated each sentence?
7. Are any of your sentences wordy or vague? Can any of them be written more concisely?

Words

1. Have you used a dictionary for the spelling or definition of any words unfamiliar to you?
2. Have you used any words inappropriately (e.g., "imply" for "infer")?
3. Is your choice of words clear, accurate, and precise?
4. Have you used the appropriate word in context? Is it too formal or informal?
5. Have you avoided jargon or overly technical words?

This checklist should help you to write the best paper you can out of the materials that you've researched.

PREPARING THE FINAL DRAFT

After the paper has been thoroughly revised, the list of works cited compiled, and the parenthetical references written (see Chapters 7 and 8), you are ready to prepare the final draft that you will hand in to your instructor. Many instructors give specific directions for manuscript form. If your instructor establishes a particular format for you to use, then follow it. The purpose of any format is to create a legible, clean paper that is easy to read. Use the following standard guidelines if your instructor expresses no particular preferences regarding the format of the paper. You should also examine the sample paper in Chapter 9.

Typing

Research papers must be typed. Don't expect your instructor to read handwritten copy. Type on only one side of white bond paper (8½″ × 11″); do not use flimsy paper. Be sure that the ribbon (preferably black) is fairly fresh and the letters not clogged with ink. All of this is simple courtesy: your instructor will be reading many papers, and it is only common sense to realize that no one is going to be grateful for a paper that strains one's eyes or one's patience. In addition, follow these typing conventions: To type a dash use two hyphens with no space between, before, or after them. If your typewriter has no number 1 use the lower case l, not the capital I.

Title Page

A separate title page should include the title of the paper, your name, the course number and section, your instructor's name, and the date. Center the title about a third of the way down the page. Do not use quotation marks and do not underline your own title; omit a period at the end. Capitalize the first word, the last word, and any word after a colon; also capitalize all other words except articles, conjunctions, and prepositions. An inch below the title center the word "By," and two spaces below that center your name. An inch below your name center and double space the course number, your instructor's name, and the date. Do not number the title page.

Your instructor may prefer your following the 1984 MLA guidelines, which recommend not using a separate title page. You can present the identifying information on the first page of the text. Place your name, your instructor's name, the course number and section, and the date on separate double-spaced lines in the upper left-hand corner of the page, observing the same left-hand margin as the text. Double space below the date and center your title on the page; then quadruple space between your title and the first line of the text.

Outline

If an outline is required, place it immediately after the title page and before the text of the paper. Follow the format for outlining on pages 73–77. Use small Roman numerals (i, ii, iii) to number the pages of the outline; they are located on the page in the same place as Arabic numbers (see next item below).

Page Numbering

The title page and the outline are not given Arabic numerals (1, 2, 3, etc.). The first page to be numbered is the first page of the text. Place the page number in the upper right-hand corner about a half inch from the top of the page and in line with the right margin. Do not use parentheses, periods, or other marks with page numbers. Number the pages consecutively, including any notes and the list of works cited. Type your last name before the page number for all pages after the first page.

Margins and Spacing

Use one-inch margins at the top, bottom, and sides of each page. The first page of the "Notes" and "Works Cited" sections are handled differently: center the word "Notes" (or "Works Cited") one inch from the top of the page and then quadruple space between it and the text. Double space the text, notes, and list of works cited (see pages 157–159 for spacing of notes when placed at the foot of the page). See pages 78–80 for handling long quotations in the text. Indent the first line of each paragraph five spaces.

Tables and Illustrations

Depending on the nature of your topic, you may find tables and illustrations useful. You can convey a good bit of information this way without having to resort to lists in your prose. These materials should be placed as closely as possible to the section of the paper that refers to them. Tables consist of information listed in columns. They are assigned Arabic numerals, identified as "Tables," captioned, and double spaced (see Figure 6-1). Unless you have compiled the table yourself, place the source of the information at the bottom. A reader will assume that a table without a source is the result of your own investigations.

In addition to tables, illustrative materials such as graphs, charts, maps, drawings, and photographs may be useful. Each of these is labeled as a "Figure," often abbreviated "Fig.," given an Arabic numeral, and identified by a title, along with the source of the material (the absence of a source will indicate that you have provided the material). (See Figure 6-2.)

Table 2

ANNUAL AVERAGE RATES OF CLEARING

(thousands of acres)

| | 1850s | | 1900s | |
	Forest	Nonforested Area	Forest	Nonforested Area
Northeast	570	---	30	---
South	1,590	20	950	20
Midwest	1,330	150	370	120
West	480	750	890	5,010
United States	3,970	920	2,240	5,150

Source: Martin Primack, "Land Clearing Under Nineteenth-
Century Techniques: Some Preliminary Calcula-
tions," Journal of Economic History 22 (December
1962): 492.

Figure 6-1 Sample Table

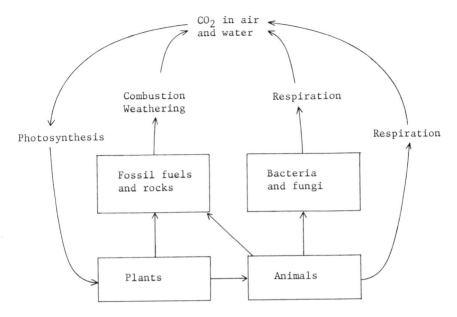

Figure 12   Some major pathways in the carbon cycle

Source: Charles K. Levy, <u>Elements of Biology</u>, 2nd. ed.

(Reading: Addison, 1978) 483.

Figure 6-2   Sample Figure

Proofreading

Check the final draft of your paper very carefully for errors in spelling, punctuation, grammar, syllabication, capitalization, and typing. If a word should be deleted, draw a single, horizontal line through it: don't make a mess by scratching it out. To add a letter or a word use a caret (^) at that place in the line and write in the addition over the caret in the space above the line:

Many colleges are now ~~now~~ moving toward more stringent

requirements for graduation. Is‸good or bad?

When three or four errors appear on a page or you need to add a number of words, it is better to retype the page. Otherwise your paper will look shabby. The use of correction tape or correction fluid will minimize the number of pages you have to retype.

Reading your paper aloud is an effective way to proofread. It will slow you down enough to look at the paper carefully; it's also a useful technique to catch awkward sentences: if a passage doesn't sound right, it very likely isn't right. If you have a devoted friend, you might persuade him or her to read aloud from the draft you typed while you follow closely with the final typed draft. Have the person read the punctuation and capitalizations as well as the text, which will be especially helpful in catching errors in the notes and list of works cited. Obviously, you'll need a good friend for such an arduous task, but you can always return the favor. This method is the most reliable way to proofread a paper.

Handing in the Paper

Use a paper clip (rather than a stapler) to hold the paper together when you hand it in so that your instructor can take it apart to read it. Don't waste money on elaborate covers or plastic folders since your instructor will have to remove the paper from the folder to read and comment on it anyway. Save your money for a pizza and a beer; you've earned it.

Works Cited 7

PURPOSE

The list of works cited provides the sources from which you have borrowed quotations, ideas, and facts included in your paper. Its purpose is to provide your reader with a convenient listing of the sources that inform the paper, and since it is arranged alphabetically by author, it allows a reader to scan quickly for the range of your sources. Although the list of works cited comes at the end, many readers examine it before beginning to read a paper in order to get a sense of where the writer has been in the library and what is to come. Just because your list of works cited appears last, do not think you can give it little attention or consideration. If your list of works cited consists of only a few sources or if it is haphazardly or carelessly put together, the first page of your paper may address itself to an antagonistic reader rather than a sympathetic one.

Different academic disciplines employ different styles for giving information. Although the content remains pretty much the same, you will find variations, for example, among the social sciences, the sciences, and the humanities. Many disciplines have their own style manuals; for a brief discussion and listing of some of them, see pages 177–185. The style generally followed in this book is suggested by the Modern Language Association (an organization comprised chiefly of college English and foreign-language teachers) in the *MLA Handbook for Writers of Research Papers*. This style is widely accepted in the humanities and in many other fields as well. Unless your instructor tells you to use another manual of style or instructs you on specific matters that are to be handled differently from the format shown in this chapter and in Chapter 8, you can feel confident using the format recommended here. Of course, it is the information rather than the style that finally matters, but once you choose a style, follow it scrupulously and consistently.

The 1984 *MLA Handbook* recommends documenting sources with parenthetical references in the text. Prepare your list of works cited before you prepare your parenthetical references, since the information in the list will affect the information in these references. Fortunately, the final list of works cited is easy to prepare because it is based on the file cards of your working bibliography (see pages 49–53). You already have the necessary information, so all you have left to do is arrange it in a conventional format. Once your bibliography cards are organized alphabetically by author, you can turn that information into your final list of works cited.

Your final list of works cited must include all the sources from which you quoted, paraphrased, or summarized. However, it should not contain any sources that you merely glanced at or didn't use. Any source listed in the list of works cited must be documented by a parenthetical reference in the text.

FORMAT

Placement

Place the list of works cited at the end of the paper after any endnotes, and follow these directions for typing it:

1. The first page of the list of works cited begins one inch below the top of the page (see Figure 7-1). Subsequent pages are typed, like the text, one inch from the top of the page.

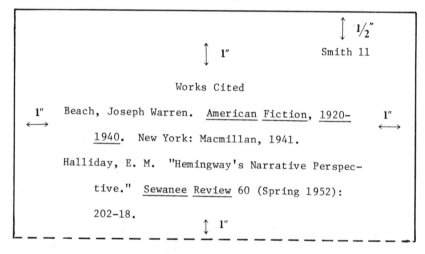

Figure 7-1   Sample Works Cited Style

2. Center the heading "Works Cited." Double space between the heading and the first entry.
3. Use one-inch margins on each side. Type the first line of each entry flush with the left-hand margin. If the entry runs for more than one line, indent the additional lines five spaces.
4. Double space within and between entries.
5. Within each entry, skip two spaces after each period.
6. Place a page number one-half inch from the top in the upper right-hand corner of each page, including the first page, of the list of works cited. This number (preceded by your name) should continue the numbering of the text. For example, if the last page of the text is 12, the first page of the list of works cited should be 13. (If you include endnotes, the list of works cited would follow the endnotes.)

Alphabetizing

Entries are arranged in alphabetical order by author. For that reason the author's name is reversed. If there is more than one author, reverse only the name of the first author and follow it with a comma: Kennedy, Patricia, and Edward J. Leary. For anonymous works, use the first word of the title, disregarding definite or indefinite articles ("A Wolf in Sheik's Clothing" is alphabetized under *W*). For two or more works by the same author, give the name of the author in the first entry, but for subsequent entries substitute three hyphens followed by a period for the name. If the author served as a compiler, editor, or translator on one of the books, place a comma after the three hyphens, follow the comma with the appropriate abbreviation (comp., ed., trans.), and follow the abbreviation with a period. Skip two spaces after the period and follow the period by the title. Alphabetize entries by the same author by the title.

```
Rosenthal, M. L.  The Modern Poets: A Critical Introduc-

    tion.  1960.  London: Oxford UP, 1969.

---, ed.  The New Modern Poetry: An Anthology of American

    and British Poetry Since World War II.  1967.  New

    York: Oxford UP, 1970.

---.  The New Poets: American and British Poetry Since

    World War II.  1967.  London: Oxford UP, 1970.

---.  A Primer of Ezra Pound.  1960.  New York: Universal

    Library-Grosset, 1966.
```

When a title begins with a number, alphabetize the way you would if it were spelled out: "10 Days in Rome" is entered as if the first word were "Ten."

Sample Entries for Books

The examples in this section and the following sections on periodicals and other sources should equip you to write entries for your list of works cited. There are numerous variations on the information to be included depending on the nature of the source (for example, the author may be anonymous). However, if you do not find the exact form that fits a particular source you are using, then improvise by using the logic you derive from reviewing the following sample entries.

Each book entry has at least three parts separated by periods:

1. the author's name in reverse order (last, first, middle)
2. the title of the book
3. the publication information

Always consult the title page of the book itself for this information.

A Book with One Author

> Boller, Paul F., Jr. <u>Presidential Anecdotes.</u> New York:
>
> Oxford UP, 1981.
>
> Flesch, Rudolph. <u>Lite English: Popular Words That Are OK</u>
>
> <u>to Use--No Matter What William Safire, John Simon,</u>
>
> <u>Edwin Newman, and the Other Purists Say!</u> New York:
>
> Crown, 1983.

NAME

The name of the author is in reverse order (last, first, middle) and is followed by a period. Use the author's full name as it appears on the title page. If the author uses initials for his or her first or middle name and you wish to provide the author's full name, you may include this information in brackets: (T[homas] S[tearns] Eliot).

TITLE

The title of the work is underlined in your paper to indicate italics. It is followed by a period unless the title ends with a question mark or an exclamation point. Do not underline this period, but do underline a question mark or exclamation point that is part of the title. Use the complete title from the title page. If there is a subtitle, be sure to include it. The subtitle is indicated by the colon. Do not reproduce the typography of the title page. Here, for example, is how one title appears on its title page:

A SECOND

FLOWERING

works and days of the

lost generation

In a list of works cited, however, the title is written like this: *A Second Flowering: Works and Days of the Lost Generation.*

PLACE OF PUBLICATION

The place of publication is the city in which the book was published. This information should be taken from the title page or the copyright page on the reverse side of the title page. If more than one city is listed, use only the first city given. Do not list the state in which the book was published. Place a colon after the city of publication.

PUBLISHER

Use a shortened form of the publisher's name: hence Prentice-Hall, Inc. becomes Prentice; Little, Brown and Company becomes Little; Alfred A Knopf, Inc. becomes Knopf; Oxford University Press becomes Oxford UP; State University of New York Press becomes State U of New York P. (See pages 141–143 for a listing of abbreviated forms of publishers' names.) Separate the publisher from the date of publication with a comma.

DATE OF PUBLICATION

Unless a date appears on the title page, use the most recent copyright date, the last year listed after © on the reverse side of the title page. However, if the book has gone through several printings by the same publisher, use the original publication date. (See pages 127–128 for books that have been reprinted.) Place a period at the end of the date of publication.

PAGE NUMBERS

In general, you do not include page numbers for books in your list of works cited. However, if you are citing a shorter piece within a book (e.g., an essay, an article, a chapter, a poem), you do need to cite the page numbers for the entire piece. (See page 124 for a work in a collection of writings by the same author.)

A Book with Two Authors

> Harding, Walter, and Michael Meyer. The New Thoreau Hand-
>
> book. New York: New York UP, 1980.

Notice that only the first author's name is reversed.

A Book with Three Authors

> Purves, Alan, Sauli Takala, and Avon Crismore. How to
>
> Write Well in College. San Diego: Harcourt, 1984.

A Book with More than Three Authors

> Spiller, Robert E., et al. Literary History of the United
>
> States. New York: Macmillan, 1946.

ET AL.
This abbreviation means "and others." Instead of listing all the authors, use "et al." or "and others." Observe that a comma comes between the author's name and "et al."

A Book with a Corporate Author

> The Diagram Group. Woman's Body: An Owner's Manual. New
>
> York: Paddington, 1977.

AUTHOR
List the group or the corporation as the author and alphabetize accordingly.

A Book with an Anonymous Author

> Margaret: A Tale of the Real and Ideal, Blight and Bloom.
>
> Boston: Jordon, 1845.

or, if the author is known but not indicated:

> [Judd, Sylvester]. Margaret: A Tale of the Real and Ideal,
>
> Blight and Bloom. Boston: Jordon, 1845.

AUTHOR
Do not use "Anon." or "Anonymous" in place of the author's name. If the author's name is known but not indicated on the title page, enclose it in brackets.

PUBLISHER

For books published before 1900, you may omit the name of the publisher (. . . *Blight and Bloom.* Boston, 1845).

A Book with a Pseudonymous Author

```
Optic, Oliver [William T. Adams].  Haste and Waste; or, The

    Young Pilot of Lake Champlain.  Boston: Lothrop, 1894.
```

AUTHOR

Notice that the author's actual name follows in normal order and is enclosed in brackets.

A Work in More than One Volume

To cite the entire set of a multivolume work, place the volume numbers before the publication information. Use Arabic numerals for volume numbers. Follow this format:

```
Sewall, Richard B.  The Life of Emily Dickinson.  2 vols.

    New York: Farrar, 1974.
```

To cite just part of the set, however, place the number of the volume(s) that you used after the publication information:

```
Sewall, Richard B.  The Life of Emily Dickinson.  2 vols.

    New York: Farrar, 1974.  Vol. 2.
```

To cite a single volume of a multivolume work that has individual titles, use this format:

```
Copleston, Frederic, S. J.  Medieval Philosophy.  Vol. 2 of

    A History of Philosophy.  10 vols.  Garden City:

    Doubleday, 1962.
```

To cite a multivolume work that has been published over a period of years, use the following format:

> Costain, Thomas B. A History of the Plantagenets. 4 vols.
>
> Garden City: Doubleday, 1949–1962.
>
> Trent, William Peterfield, et al. The Cambridge History of
>
> American Literature. 3 vols. New York: Macmillan,
>
> 1917–1921.

A Work in a Collection of Writings by the Same Author

> Saroyan, William. "Ancient History." The Human Comedy.
>
> By Saroyan. New York: Harcourt, 1943. 51–61.

Observe that page numbers are included at the end of the entry, since the citation is to a single work in the collection. However, no abbreviation for pages (pp.) is used.

A Work in a Collection of Writings by Different Authors

Notice that, as in the previous example, page numbers are given for a single work in a collection.

AN ESSAY
> Melville, Herman. "Hawthorne and His Mosses." The Theory
>
> of the American Novel. Ed. George Perkins. New York:
>
> Holt, 1970. 71–82.

Inform your reader of the original publication information when it is available. You can usually find this information in a list of works cited or in a copyright acknowledgment. Note its presentation in the following example:

> Bewley, Marius. "Scott Fitzgerald's Criticism of America."
>
> Sewanee Review 62 (Spring 1954): 223–46. Rpt. in The
>
> Great Gatsby: A Study. Ed. Frederick J. Hoffman.
>
> New York: Scribner's, 1962. 263–85.

This format is particularly useful for researchers using collections of essays and casebooks. The abbreviation "rpt." means that Bewley's article is reprinted in Hoffman's collection of essays. Notice too that the title of the novel, *The Great Gatsby,* included in Hoffman's book title is *not* underlined. Do not underline the titles of novels or plays when they appear in a book's title. If, however, the title of a short story, poem, or essay appears in a book title, include the quotation marks and underline the entire title.

A SHORT STORY

    Poe, Edgar Allan.   "A Tale of the Ragged Mountains."

        Future Perfect: American Science Fiction of the

        Nineteenth Century.   Ed. H. Bruce Franklin.   New

        York: Oxford UP, 1968.   104-113.

A NOVEL

    Stevenson, Robert Louis.   The Strange Case of Dr. Jekyll

        and Mr. Hyde.   Minor Classics of Nineteenth-Century

        Fiction.   Ed. William E. Buckler.   2 vols.   Boston:

        Houghton, 1967.   2: 61-109.

Notice that the volume number followed by a colon precedes the page numbers (2: 61–109). This tells the reader that the novel appears in Vol. 2 of *Minor Classics of Nineteenth-Century Fiction* on pages 61–109.

A POEM

    Creeley, Robert.   "The Door."   The New American Poetry.

        Ed. David M. Allen.   New York: Grove, 1960.   83-86.

A PLAY

    Wilde, Oscar.   The Importance of Being Earnest.   The Norton

        Anthology of English Literature.   Ed. M. H. Abrams et

        al.   4th ed.   2 vols.   New York: Norton, 1979.

        2: 1675-1731.

A Cross-Reference to a Work in a Collection

When citing two or more works in the same collection, you can avoid needless repetition by cross-referencing each work to the collection. To do this, give all the necessary bibliographic information about the collection and then refer the reader to the collection by providing the editor's name and page numbers after the work's author and title.

> Auden, W. H. "Writing." Gibbons 240-53.
>
> Gibbons, Reginald, ed. The Poet's Work: 29 Masters of
>
> 20th Century Poetry on the Origins and Practice of
>
> Their Art. Boston: Houghton, 1979.
>
> MacDiarmid, Hugh. "Poetry and Science." Gibbons 121-135.
>
> Shapiro, Karl. "What Is Not Poetry?" Gibbons 92-109.

If two books by Gibbons were included in your list of works cited, a short form of the title would be needed to avoid confusion:

> Auden, W. H. "Writing." Gibbons, Poet's Work 240-53.

Classic Works and the Bible

> Milton, John. Paradise Lost. John Milton: Complete Poems
>
> and Major Prose. Ed. Merritt Y. Hughes. New York:
>
> Odyssey, 1957. 211-530.
>
> Shakespeare, William. The Tempest. Shakespeare: The
>
> Complete Signet Classic Shakespeare. Gen ed. Sylvan
>
> Barnet. New York: Harcourt, 1972. 1537-1568.
>
> The Bible.

No other documentation is necessary for the Bible unless you use some version other than the King James version.

The Bible. Revised Standard Version.

Notice that the Bible, like other sacred books, such as the Koran, is not underlined.

Encyclopedias and Other Reference Works

"Poe, Edgar Allan." The New Encyclopaedia Britannica.

1984 ed.

"Faulkner, William." Current Biography. 1951 ed.

Russell, Don. "Cody, William Frederick." Encyclopedia

Americana. 1973 ed.

For well-known encyclopedias, yearbooks, annuals, and other such reference works that are alphabetically arranged, it is not necessary to include volume and page numbers or publication information except for the edition. If the article is signed, provide the name of the author as you would for any book entry; otherwise just use the title of the entry, title of the work, and the year of the edition. For reference works that are not well known, supply all the facts of publication.

A Work in a Series

Scholnick, Robert J. Edmund Clarence Stedman. Twayne's

United States Author Series 286. Boston: Twayne,

1977.

Do not underline or enclose in quotation marks the title of the series. When the series is not numbered, place a period after the series name and follow this immediately with the publication information.

Reprints

Gohdes, Clarence L. F. The Periodicals of American

Transcendentalism. 1931. New York: AMS, 1970.

Williams, Stanley T. The Spanish Background of American

Literature. 2 vols. 1955. n.p.: Archon, 1968.

The date of original publication is supplied so that your reader does not mistakenly assume the book is a recent work. The abbreviation n.p. before the colon indicates that no place of publication is listed on the title page. The appreviation n.p. after the colon indicates that no publisher is listed. The abbreviation n.d. after the comma indicates that no date is listed. If you can determine any of the missing information yourself, include it in brackets: . . . 1955 [Hamden]: Archon, 1968.

If the book was originally published in a foreign country, indicate the place of publication after the title and before the original date.

Dickens, Charles. <u>Hard Times</u>. London, 1854. New York:

AMS, 1970.

An Edition of a Book

Spiller, Robert E., et al. <u>Literary History of the United</u>

<u>States</u>. 3rd ed. New York: Macmillan, 1963.

This is a later revised edition of the work cited on page 122.

An Editor of an Anthology or Collection

Carr, Terry, ed. <u>Classic Science Fiction: The First</u>

<u>Golden Age</u>. New York: Harper, 1978.

An Editor of a Book by Another

Donaldson, Scott, ed. <u>On the Road</u>. By Jack Kerouac.

Viking Critical Library. New York: Penguin, 1979.

The preceding entry cites the work of the editor. To cite the author's work, use this format:

Kerouac, Jack. <u>On the Road</u>. Ed. Scott Donaldson.

Viking Critical Library. New York: Penguin, 1979.

An Introduction, Preface, Foreword, or Afterword to a Book

> Gingrich, Arnold.   Introduction.   The Pat Hobby Stories.
>
> By F. Scott Fitzgerald.   New York: Scribner's, 1962.
>
> ix–xxiii.
>
> Rothberg, Abraham.   Introduction.   The Call of the Wild
>
> and White Fang.   By Jack London.   New York: Bantam
>
> Pathfinder-Bantam, 1963.   1–17.

These entries cite the introductions by Gingrich and Rothberg respectively. Note that the word Introduction is not underlined or enclosed in quotation marks. This form also applies to a preface, foreword, or afterword, provided it is not written by the author or the editor of the work. To cite the work of the author, use this format:

> Fitzgerald, F. Scott.   The Pat Hobby Stories.   Intro.
>
> Arnold Gingrich.   New York: Scribner's, 1962.
>
> London, Jack.   The Call of the Wild and White Fang.
>
> Intro. Abraham Rothberg.   New York: Bantam Path-
>
> finder-Bantam, 1963.

To cite an introduction, preface, foreword, or afterword written by the author or the editor of the work, use the following format:

> Cheney, Anne.   Introduction.   Millay in Greenwich Village.
>
> By Cheney.   University: U of Alabama P, 1975.   1–6.

A Translated Book

> Frechtman, Bernard, trans.   The Screens.   By Jean Genêt.
>
> New York: Grove, 1962.

The entry above cites Frechtman's translation; to cite Genêt's work, use this format:

Genêt, Jean.   The Screens.   Trans. Bernard Frechtman.

New York: Grove, 1962.

A Publisher's Imprint

Pritchett, V. S.   Midnight Oil.   1971.   New York: Vintage–

Random, 1973.

Wharton, Edith.   Afterword.   The House of Mirth.

Louis Auchincloss.   New York: Signet–NAL, 1964.

Place the name of the imprint followed by a hyphen before the publisher's name.

A Pamphlet

Hubbard, S. Dana.   Facts About Marriage Every Young Man &

Woman Should Know.   New York: Claremount, 1922.

Wherever possible, pamphlets are cited in the same way as books.

A Government Publication

United States.   Dept. of Housing and Urban Development.

Wise Home Buying.   Washington: GPO, 1978.

This entry uses the name of the government and the government agency in place of the author. The abbreviation GPO means "Government Printing Office."

Cong. Rec.   5 Apr. 1957: 14471–75.

For the *Congressional Record,* you need include only the date and the page numbers.

United States.   Cong.   Senate.   Communism in Labor Unions.

83rd Cong., 2nd sess.   S. Rept. 526.   Washington: GPO,

1954.

The preceding entry is read as follows: Name of government; the agency of the government (had it been the House of Representatives, it would have read "House"; had it been issued by both the Senate and the House, it would have read "Joint"); the title of the document; the number and the session of Congress; the number of the report; and then the usual publication information (place, publisher, date).

A Legal Reference

Legal citations are, as you might expect, even more complex and irregular than those for other government documents. If you find yourself writing a paper with many legal references in it, use as a guide *A Uniform System of Citation.* 13th ed. Cambridge: Harvard Law Review, 1981.

Sample Entries for Periodicals

The following examples illustrate the format used for the kinds of materials you will likely encounter in periodicals. A periodical consists of any regularly published journal, magazine, or newspaper. An entry for a periodical presents information in the following order:

1. the name of the author in reverse order (last, first, middle)
2. the complete title of the article in quotation marks
3. the name of the periodical underlined to indicate italics
4. the volume and/or date of publication
5. the inclusive page numbers of the article

An Anonymous Entry

"A Wolf in Sheik's Clothing." <u>Time</u> 13 Apr. 1981: 54.

"Notes and Comment." <u>New Yorker</u> 7 May 1984: 41-42.

When the author isn't named (which happens in many newspaper and magazine pieces), begin with the title. Omit the initial article from the title of the publication (*New Yorker,* not *The New Yorker*). Notice that the date of publication is followed by a colon and the page number(s). Since the first article appears entirely on one page, only one page number is given.

A Signed Article

Rainer, Dachine.   "Who Are the Anarchists?" <u>Liberation</u> 8

(April 1963): 26-27.

When an article ends with a question mark or exclamation point, it is not followed by a period. For multiple authors of an article, follow the same guidelines as for multiple authors of a book (see pages 121–122).

A Journal with Continuous Pagination Beyond a Single Issue

Hauck, Richard.   "The Dickens Controversy in the Spirit of

the Times."   PMLA 85 (1970): 278-83.

Cite journals that number issues consecutively (i.e., if issue 1 ends on page 165, then issue 2 begins on page 166) only by volume number and year. The month or season is unnecessary because there will be only one set of pages 278–83 in volume 85 of the 1970 issue of *PMLA*. If you are uncertain whether a journal numbers issues consecutively or separately, then supply the month or season. However, a much better idea is to avoid this uncertainty by checking for this information while you are in the library.

A Journal with Separate Pagination for Each Issue

Scharnhorst, Gary F.   "The Alger Problem: The Hoax About

Horatio Revealed."   Ball State University Forum 15

(Spring 1974): 61-65.

Here the season (another journal could have a month) is included with the year because each issue of the journal is numbered separately: each of its four issues per year begins with page 1; therefore, pages 61–65 would appear four times. Save your readers the trouble of looking through all of the issues. Be specific.

If you use a journal with separate numbering for each issue that does not designate a season or month, then include the issue number after the volume number, like this: *Journal Title* 52.4 (1980): 5–17. The 52.4 tells the reader that the article appears in volume 52, issue 4 of the journal. Notice that the issue number follows the volume number after the period (but with no space between it and the period) and precedes the year in parentheses. The issue number is an important bit of information in this instance because your reader would otherwise have to look in each of the four issues for pages 5–17.

A Monthly Magazine

> Goodman, Hirsch, and Zeev Schiff. "The Attack on the
>
> Liberty." Atlantic Sept. 1984: 78-84.

Do not use a volume or issue number for monthly magazines.

A Weekly Magazine

> Otto, Herbert A. "Communes: The Alternative Life Style."
>
> Saturday Review 24 Apr. 1971: 16-21.

Use the complete date (24 Apr. 1971) instead of a volume and issue number.

A Newspaper

> Broad, William J. "Tesla, A Bizarre Genius, Regains Aura
>
> of Greatness." New York Times 28 Aug. 1984, late ed.:
>
> C1+.

Omit the introductory article from the title of the newspaper (*New York Times,* not *The New York Times*). Use the complete date (28 Aug. 1984) instead of a volume and issue number. If an edition is given on the masthead, include this after the date, followed by a colon.

If the newspaper is divided into sections and each section is paginated separately, indicate this. The Monday through Friday *New York Times,* for example, is divided into sections A, B, C, and D and the section letter is included with each page number; therefore, the first page of the third section is C1. If the article does not appear on consecutive pages, indicate the first page and follow this page number with a plus sign (C1 +).

If the section letter or number is not included with the page number, use this form: *Periodical* 28 June 1982, sec. B: 1 + .

If the pages are paginated separately, no section number is needed. The page numbers follow the colon after the edition.

> Cox, Meg. "Parents' Approach to Child Rearing Is Becoming
>
> More Goal-Oriented." Wall Street Journal 29 Aug.
>
> 1984, eastern ed.: 25+.

An Editorial

Oppel, Richard. "The Story That Wasn't True." Editorial.

Charlotte Observer [N.C.] 19 Apr. 1981, sec. B: 2.

An unsigned article would simply begin with the title of the article. Do not underline or put in quotation marks the word Editorial. Notice the information in brackets. If the city is not included in the masthead of the paper or if the city is not as well known as New York or Boston, include the city and/or state in brackets after the name of the paper.

A Letter to the Editor

Johnson, George. Letter. New Republic 18 Apr. 1981: 40.

Do not underline or put in quotation marks the word *Letter*.

A Review

Pinckney, Darryl. "Every Which Way." Rev. of Tar Baby, by

Toni Morrison. New York Review of Books 30 Apr. 1981:

24-25.

Smith, Gaddis. "What the Diplomats Really Thought." Rev.

of War Diaries: Politics and War in the Mediterranean

--January 1943-May 1945, by Harold Macmillan. New

York Times Book Review 16 Sept. 1984: 7.

The reviewer's name is followed by the review's title. This, in turn, is followed by the words "Rev. of" and then the name of the work being reviewed, the author of the work (notice the comma after the name of the work being reviewed), and the publication information. Use the following format for an untitled review:

Fiociello, Tony. Rev. of The Culture of Narcissism:

American Life in an Age of Diminishing Expectations,

by Christopher Lasch. <u>Library Journal</u> 15 Nov. 1978:

2323.

For a review that is unsigned and untitled, begin this way:

Rev. of <u>Maggie: A Girl of the Streets</u>, by Stephen Crane.

<u>New York Tribune</u> 31 May 1896: 26.

A Published Interview

Kesey, Ken. "An Impolite Interview with Ken Kesey." <u>One</u>

<u>Flew Over the Cuckoo's Nest: Text and Criticism</u>. Ed.

John Clark Pratt. New York: Viking, 1973: 348–58.

Place the name of the person interviewed in the author position of the entry.

A Quotation in the Article's Title

Boyers, Robert. "Attitudes Toward Sex in American 'High

Culture.'" <u>Annals of the American Academy of</u>

<u>Political and Social Science</u> 376 (March 1968): 36–52.

Sample Entries for Other Sources

Examples of entries for sources other than books and periodicals are listed in this section. There is a variety of sources available to researchers that cannot be classified as books or periodicals. Although there is no single format that covers them all, the organizing principle governing the information provided in the entries remains the same. For each item, provide when possible:

1. the author(s)
2. the title
3. the publication information (or the nature of the material if not published)
4. the page reference (or other pertinent location references)

An Unpublished Manuscript or Typescript

> Minutes of the Psi Gamma and Alpha Kappa Library Societies.
>
> Ms. Dawes Memorial Library of Marietta College,
>
> Marietta.

Supply the following information when available: author, title or descriptive label, form — whether manuscript (Ms) or typescript (Ts), any identifying numbers if in a library, and location of material, including city.

A Lecture

> Gross, Robert. "Emily Dickinson and Amherst." American
>
> Literature Symposium. Middlebury College, Middlebury,
>
> 24 Apr. 1981.
>
> Johnson, Lyman. History 109 class lecture. City College,
>
> New York, 19 Jan. 1979.

Supply the speaker's name, the title of the talk (or the circumstances), the sponsoring agency if applicable, the location of the lecture, and the date.

A Film

> Deliverance. Dir. John Boorman. With Jon Voight and Burt
>
> Reynolds. Warner Bros., 1972.

Begin the entry with the title of the film. Underline the title. Follow this with the name of the director, if known, the distributor, and the date. You may include additional information such as the actors and the length of the film — whatever is relevant to your discussion. However, if you wish to emphasize the work of a particular person (director, screenwriter, producer, etc.), begin your entry with this information.

> Boorman, John, dir. Deliverance. With Jon Voight and Burt
>
> Reynolds. Warner Bros., 1972.

Cite videotapes, filmstrips, and slide programs by using the same information provided for films, and indicate the type of medium following the
title.

> Financial Planning. Slide program. Dir. James Fawn.
>
> Mandell Institute, 1983.

A Theatrical Performance

> The Night Thoreau Spent in Jail. By Jerome Lawrence and
>
> Robert E. Lee. Dir. Roy Bowen. Ohio State U,
>
> Columbus, Ohio. 21 Apr. 1970.
>
> Fools. By Neil Simon. Dir. Mike Nichols. Eugene O'Neill
>
> Theater, New York. 15 Apr. 1981.

The guidelines for theatrical performances are similar to those for films,
but you should also include the playwright, theater, city, and date of
performance. As with films, if you wish to emphasize the work of a
particular person, begin your entry with the name of this person.

> Bowen, Roy, dir. The Night Thoreau Spent in Jail. By
>
> Jerome Lawrence and Robert E. Lee. Ohio State U,
>
> Columbus, Ohio. 23 Apr. 1970.
>
> Simon, Neil. Fools. Dir. Mike Nichols. Eugene O'Neill
>
> Theater, New York. 15 Apr. 1981.

A Musical Composition

> Tchaikovsky, Peter Ilich. Piano concerto no. 1 in B,
>
> op. 23.
>
> Stravinsky, Igor. Petrouchka.

Do not underline or put in quotation marks a musical composition you
cite by only its form, key, and number. Do underline a musical composition you cite by name.

A Work of Art

> Munch, Edvard. The Scream. Museum of Modern Art, New
>
> York.

Use the name of the artist, the title of the work underlined, the name of the museum or other location housing the work, and the city. To identify the source of a photographic reproduction in a published work, use this form:

> Bellows, George. Dempsey and Firpo. Whitney Museum of
>
> American Art, New York. Illus. in George Bellows:
>
> Painter of America. By Charles H. Morgan. New York:
>
> Reynal, 1965.

A Radio or Television Program

> "How Much Loyalty Is Owed to the Boss?" Firing Line. PBS.
>
> WUNG, Atlanta. 19 Apr. 1981.

Include the title of the episode (when appropriate) in quotation marks, the program (underlined), the network, the local station and the city, and the date. If the program is part of a series, include the series title, but do not underline it or put it in italics. Use the name of the director, writer, narrator, or producer if the name(s) relates to your discussion. If you wish to emphasize the work of a person rather than the program itself, include this person's name in the author's position of the entry.

A Recording

> Taylor, James. Mud Slide Slim and the Blue Horizon.
>
> Warner Bros., BS2561, 1971.

The entry consists of the performer or composer (or other person you wish to emphasize; for example, the conductor), the title of the record or tape, the artist(s), if appropriate, the manufacturer, the catalog number, and the year of issue (if unknown, use "n.d."). Here is an entry for a particular song on an album:

```
Seeger, Pete.  "Talking Union."  Pete Seeger's Greatest

    Hits.  Columbia, CS9416, n.d.
```

For entries for spoken word recordings, list first the person you want to emphasize. The following entry focuses on the speaker rather than the writer:

```
Welles, Orson.  Walt Whitman's Song of Myself from Leaves

    of Grass.  CMS, 636, 1972.
```

For entries for jacket notes, list the author first:

```
Cunliffe, Marcus.  Jacket notes.  Walt Whitman's Song of

    Myself from Leaves of Grass.  CMS, 636, 1972.
```

An Unpublished Personal Letter

```
Gatlin, Leon.  Letter to the author.  12 Mar. 1980.
```

Do not underline unpublished material. For an unpublished letter housed in a collection (rather than one sent to you personally as in the previous case), use this form:

```
Parker, Theodore.  Letter to Oliver Wendell Holmes.

    13 Sept. 1858.  Theodore Parker Papers.  Library of

    Congress, Washington, D.C.
```

A Personally Conducted Interview

```
Josephson, Harold.  Personal interview.  18 Oct. 1978.

Graves, Ralph.  Telephone interview.  12 Jan. 1981.
```

Do not underline or place in quotation marks the type of interview.

An Unpublished Doctoral Dissertation

> Brian, Michael. "Cynicism and the Problem of Political
>
> Consciousness." Diss. U of California, Berkeley,
>
> 1976.

Notice that the title is in quotation marks. Dissertation is abbreviated "Diss." with two spaces between it and the name of the university that granted the degree. If you refer only to the abstract of a dissertation in *Dissertation Abstracts International,* use this form:

> Brian, Michael. "Cynicism and the Problem of Political
>
> Consciousness." DAI 37 (1977): 6030A. U of Cali-
>
> fornia, Berkeley.

Prior to volume 30 (1969) *Dissertation Abstracts International (DAI)* was known as *Dissertation Abstracts (DA).* In volumes 27 to 36 *DA* and *DAI* are paginated in two series: *A* for humanities and social sciences, and *B* for the sciences. Hence the reference in the note above is to page 6030 in the *A* series. With volume 37, a third series was added: *C* for European dissertations.

Computer Software

> Word Weaver III. Computer software. Synergistic Software,
>
> 1983. Apple III.

The preceding entry includes the title of the program, a description of the program, the distributor, and the date of publication. Since this program was created for a specific program, this information appears at the end of the entry. If you know the name of the creator of the program, place this information in the author position. If you wish, you may include at the end of the entry the amount of memory and the form of the program.

ABBREVIATED FORMS OF PUBLISHERS' NAMES

Publishers' names are abbreviated in the list of works cited, because the full names are readily available in such publications as *Books in Print.*

Unless detailed publication information is central to your paper (particularly if it is a bibliographical study), abbreviate publishers' names.

Guidelines:

1. Omit initial articles. Omit the abbreviations Co., Corp., Inc., Ltd., and the words Books, House, Press, Publishers. Thus The Viking Press, Inc. becomes Viking.
2. If the publisher's name consists of the name of a person, use only the last name of this person. Thus George Braziller, Inc. becomes Braziller.
3. If the publisher's name consists of the names of several people, use only the last name of the first person listed. Thus Harcourt Brace Jovanovich, Inc. becomes Harcourt.
4. Use abbreviations for Academy (Acad.), Association (Assn.), and Society (Soc.). Thus National Geographic Society becomes National Geographic Soc.
5. If the publisher's name is usually abbreviated and the abbreviation is commonly understood, use this abbreviation. Thus The National Council of Teachers of English becomes NCTE.
6. If the publisher is a university press, use the abbreviation U for University and P for Press. Thus University of New Mexico Press becomes U of New Mexico P.

Samples:

Abrams	Harry N. Abrams, Inc.
Allyn	Allyn and Bacon, Inc.
Andrews	Andrews and McMeel, Inc.
Appleton	Appleton-Century-Crofts
Avenel	Avenel Books
Ballantine	Ballantine Books, Inc.
Bantam	Bantam Books, Inc.
Basic	Basic Books
Beacon	Beacon Press, Inc.
Black Sparrow	Black Sparrow Press
Bobbs	The Bobbs-Merrill Co., Inc.
Bowker	R. R. Bowker Co.
Braziller	George Braziller, Inc.
Cambridge UP	Cambridge University Press
Clarendon	Clarendon Press

Columbia UP	Columbia University Press
Cornell UP	Cornell University Press
Crown	Crown Publishers, Inc.
Dell	Dell Publishing Co., Inc.
Dial	Dial Press, Inc.
Dodd	Dodd, Mead, and Co.
Dorset	Dorset Press
Doubleday	Doubleday and Co., Inc.
Dover	Dover Publications, Inc.
Dutton	E. P. Dutton
Farrar	Farrar, Straus, and Giroux, Inc.
Feminist	The Feminist Press
Free	The Free Press
GPO	Government Printing Office
Grove	Grove Press, Inc.
Harcourt	Harcourt Brace Jovanovich, Inc.
Harper	Harper & Row Publishers, Inc.
Harvard Law Rev. Assn.	Harvard Law Review Association
Harvard UP	Harvard University Press
Heath	D. C. Heath and Company
Holt	Holt, Rinehart and Winston, Inc.
Houghton	Houghton Mifflin Company
Indiana UP	Indiana University Press
Information Please	Information Please Publishing, Inc.
Johns Hopkins UP	The Johns Hopkins University Press
KIP	Knowledge Industry Publications, Inc.
Knopf	Alfred A. Knopf, Inc.
Larousse	Librairie Larousse
Lippincott	J. B. Lippincott Co.
Little	Little, Brown and Company
Macmillan	Macmillan Publishing Co., Inc.
McGraw	McGraw-Hill, Inc.
MIT P	The Massachuetts Institute of Technology Press
MLA	The Modern Language Association of America
Morrow	William Morrow and Company, Inc.
NAL	The New American Library, Inc.
National Geographic Soc.	National Geographic Society
NCTE	The National Council of Teachers of English
NEA	The National Education Association

New Directions	New Directions Publishing Corporation
North Point	North Point Press
Norton	W. W. Norton and Co., Inc.
Nostalgia	Nostalgia Press
Ontario Review	The Ontario Review Press
Overlook	The Overlook Press
Oxford UP	Oxford University Press
Penguin	Penguin Books, Inc.
Persea	Persea Books, Inc.
Pocket	Pocket Books
Pomegranate	Pomegranate Press
Potter	Clarkson N. Potter, Inc.
Prentice	Prentice-Hall, Inc.
Princeton UP	Princeton University Press
Putnam's	G. P. Putnam's Sons
Rand	Rand McNally and Co.
Random	Random House, Inc.
St. Martin's	St. Martin's Press, Inc.
Scott	Scott, Foresman, and Co.
Scribner's	Charles Scribner's Sons
Sierra	Sierra Club Books
Simon	Simon and Schuster, Inc.
State U of New York P	State University of New York Press
Straight Arrow	Straight Arrow Publishers, Inc.
Swallow	The Swallow Press
UMI	University Microfilms International
U of Chicago P	University of Chicago Press
U of Illinois P	University of Illinois Press
U of Nebraska P	University of Nebraska Press
U of New Mexico P	The University of New Mexico Press
UP of Florida	The University Presses of Florida
Viking	The Viking Press, Inc.
Warner	Warner Books, Inc.
Wesleyan UP	Wesleyan University Press
Yale UP	Yale University Press

8 References

PURPOSE AND STYLE

A carefully prepared and complete list of works cited does not provide sufficient documentation of the sources of information you used for your paper. This list must be accompanied by additional documentation indicating the exact location of specific information. The 1984 MLA guidelines recommend providing this documentation in parenthetical references in the text. (For a discussion of when to provide documentation for your sources, see pages 92–97.)

A parenthetical reference serves two purposes. It directs your readers to a particular work in your list of works cited, and it indicates the exact location in this work of the information used. Usually, for a one-volume work the reference can accomplish these two purposes simply by including the last name of the author of the work and the page number(s) on which the information can be found. For example:

```
The young Jack London had his first taste of success when

he steered a schooner through a savage storm during a voyage

to the Bonin Islands (Sinclair 16-17).
```

This reference first tells the reader the author of the book — Sinclair. With this information, the reader can consult the list of works cited to find the entry for the work:

```
Sinclair, Andrew.  Jack: A Biography of Jack London.  New

York: Harper, 1977.
```

The reference next tells the reader the exact location of the information. It can be found on pages 16–17 of the work.

If the author's name is included in the text, the reference need include only the page number(s).

```
According to Sinclair, the young Jack London had his first

taste of success when he steered a schooner through a

savage storm during a voyage to the Bonin Islands (16-17).
```

Of course, the information presented in parenthetical references varies depending on the nature of the source. This chapter discusses most of these variations and offers a consistent way of presenting the information. It also discusses briefly the various styles employed by different academic disciplines for giving information.

Where to Place Parenthetical References

Place your parenthetical reference where it will least disrupt the sentence. In general, this means placing it at the end of a sentence before the closing punctuation mark.

```
It was not London's beliefs, but his charisma, his personal

appeal, that made him useful to the Socialists (Sinclair

130).
```

Notice that the reference comes before the period. Within the reference there is no punctuation mark between the author's name and the page number.

```
London's interest in the ideal of the perfect male body is

expressed in his novel The Game--a novel "which began a new

minor genre--the American boxing story" (Sinclair 113).
```

Notice that the reference occurs after the closing quotation mark but before the period.

However, at times the material referred to or quoted occurs at the end of a clause or other syntactical unit while the remainder of the sentence contains other information. When this is the case, place the reference within the sentence at the end of the appropriate syntactical unit.

```
Sinclair claims that when Jack taught himself how to ride

a horse, he "treated it like a boat, luffing and steering

it roughly in the right direction" (109), and that image

of Jack is also presented in the title of Irving Stone's

biography of London, Sailor on Horseback.
```

At times the reference is to an entire quoted passage. When this is the case, place the parenthetical reference at the end of the passage after the final punctuation mark.

Sinclair vividly describes the routine business of seal hunting, an experience which gave London his first insight into determinism.

> This wholesale murder, this daily slaughter-house was the young sailor's first sight of nature red in tooth and claw. The men were more bestial than the beasts they killed. It was a crude commercial struggle to survive, dictated by the market in furs. Jack began to see that the struggle to live among humans was part of the struggle to live among animals. The men got the wages, the captain took the profits, the women wore the furs, the sharks devoured the meat, the herds of seals suffered. He began to understand the connection between nature, man, and the market before reading Darwin or Marx. (17)

Sample Parenthetical References

The following examples illustrate most of the variations you will have in your parenthetical references. They correspond with the entries listed in Chapter 7 and with the preceding sample entry. If you find a work that doesn't fit one of these patterns, write your parenthetical reference following the principles of guidelines that follow.

An Entire Work (see page 144)

If you are referring to the entire work, you do not need to include a parenthetical reference. By simply including the author's name in the text, you provide the reader with enough information to find the work on your list of works cited (unless there are several books listed by this author).

```
Sinclair helps us understand how London, at that time the
most successful writer in the world, could come to such a
tragic end.
```

If you choose not to use the author's name in text, you need to include the name (or names if there are multiple authors) in a parenthetical reference.

```
The biography offers an insightful look at a man who lived
at both poles, balancing notoriety with respectability,
adventure with comfort and security (Sinclair).
```

An Article or a Book Published in a Single Volume (see page 129)

```
During the period when Fitzgerald wrote the Pat Hobby
stories, interest in his work was at an all-time low
(Gingrich ix-x).
```

Use only the author's last name. (By author we also mean any person who fills the author position in the entry for the list of works cited — editor, translator, compiler.) Do not use abbreviations indicating role such as ed., tr., and comp. Do not place a comma between the author's name and the page number(s). Do not use an abbreviation for page (p.) or pages (pp.). If the author's name appears in the text, include only the page number(s) in the reference.

```
Throughout his professional life, Fitzgerald was in need of
money, and, according to Gingrich, "wrote for his living,
as opposed to living for his work, more than any other
author of our time" (xxii-xxiii).
```

A Work by One Author (see page 120)

```
Did you know that the word lousy is no longer considered
slang by three major desk dictionaries (Flesch 117)?
```

Flesch claims that Americans now consider _machismo_ "a
quaint aberration" (118).

A Work by Two Authors *(see page 133)*

The assumption by Israeli intelligence that the explosion
and smoking coming from El Arish was caused by shelling
from sea was one factor leading to the Israeli's fatal
attack on the American ship _Liberty_ in 1967 (Goodman and
Schiff 82).

According to Goodman and Schiff, during the Arab-Israeli
war of 1967, the Israeli navy treated any unidentified ship
that moved at a speed faster than twenty knots through a
battle area as an enemy ship (82).

A Work by Three Authors *(see page 122)*

Even a process paper has an interpretive level which can
be achieved through a cause and effect structure (Purves,
Takala, and Crismore 84).

Purves, Takala, and Crismore divide the comparison-contrast
composition into two structures: the all-about-A, all-about-
B structure and the pendulum structure (84).

A Work by More than Three Authors *(see page 124)*

American poetry did flourish in the second half of the
twentieth century, but although it became less rigid and
more experimental, it remained regional and provincial
(Trent et al. 3: 32).

Note that there is no comma separating the author's name from the abbreviation et al. (The 3 preceding the colon indicates the volume number.)

> It is interesting to note that in 1921 Trent et al. ranked
>
> Emily Dickinson as a minor Eastern poet with about the
>
> same standing as her contemporaries Thomas Bailey Aldrich,
>
> Bayard Taylor, R. H. Stoddard, E. C. Stedman, R. C. Gilder,
>
> and Richard Hovey and further claimed that in the future
>
> her rank in American literature would be "inconspicuous but
>
> secure" (3: 32-34).

A Work by a Corporate Author or a Government Document (see page 122)

> The compulsive eater is someone who not only eats a lot,
>
> but also is addicted to food and uses it as a drug (The
>
> Diagram Group 346).

Use the name of the group or government body as the author. Since many names of corporate authors or government bodies are long, you may find it preferable to include the name in the text:

> According to The Diagram Group, not all diseases trans-
>
> mitted by sexual activity are officially classified as
>
> VD (370).

Two or More Works by the Same Author (see page 119)

> It is in his "greenhouse" poems that Roethke harnesses his
>
> emotional tumult and makes his first major artistic advance
>
> (Rosenthal, The New Poets 117).

Include the title preceded by a comma after the author's last name and before the page number(s). If the title is long, use a shortened form. However, if you prefer to include the author's name in the text, use only the title page number(s) in the reference:

Rosenthal claims that when reading a poet's reviews and

comments on another's poetry, we must keep in mind that

the criticism is as much grounded in the poet's own poetry

as in his or her own analysis of the other's work (The New

Poets 139).

If you prefer to include the author's name and the title in the text, use only the page number(s) in the reference.

In The New Poets, Rosenthal defines one force at work in

Thom Gunn's poem "My Sad Captains" as "preoccupation with

existential emptiness" (256).

A Work Listed by Title (see page 131)

Frank Sinatra once wrote to Mabel Mercer, "Everyone who has

ever raised his voice in song has learned from you" ("Notes

and Comment" 41).

You may find it preferable to shorten the title. However, be careful to shorten it in a way that still allows your reader to find the corresponding entry easily in the list of works cited.

Among the people influenced by Mabel Mercer were such

diverse artists as Leontyne Price, Billie Holiday, Bobby

Short, Eileen Farrell, and Frank Sinatra ("Notes" 41).

You may wish to include the title in the text.

According to "Notes and Comment," there were actually two

distinct sides of Mabel Mercer's personality: one was the

regal singer who wore beautiful gowns draped with brilliant,

colorful shawls; the other the country bumpkin who lived in

a small farmhouse, dressed in old clothes, and weeded her

garden (42).

A Multivolume Work (see page 127)

During his first stay in Spain, Irving decided that his

goal as a writer would be to portray the life of the common

people of this country (Williams 2: 25).

Williams claims that it was unfortunate that Irving accepted

the invitation to serve as secretary of the American lega-

tion in London, since this appointment ended "an experience

particularly suited to Irving's talents" (2: 27).

The numeral preceding the colon indicates the volume number. If, however, you wish to refer to the entire volume, use this form:

This volume rectifies the inattention paid to the influence

of Spain and Spanish literature on specific American

writers (Williams, vol. 2).

Notice that an abbreviation for volume is used and that a comma separates
this abbreviation from the author's name. If you include the author's
name in the text, use this form:

Williams is a useful source for information about the

Spanish influence on specific American writers (vol. 2).

If, however, you have listed only one volume of a multivolume work in
your list of works cited, do not include a volume number in your parenthetical reference.

An Indirect Source

We seldom think of Eisenhower as a "behind-the-scenes"

person, but his skillful work for others should not be

overlooked. He once boasted to Arthur Larson, "You know

that General MacArthur got quite a reputation as a silver-

tongued speaker when he was in the Philippines. Who do

you think wrote those speeches? I did" (qtd. in Boller

296).

If an original source is unavailable to you, but you want to use something from it that is quoted in another work you've read, then you can cite an indirect source by placing "qtd. in" before the author of the indirect source. Always try, however, to find the original source first. (You may find it preferable to use a note giving the original source.

Literary Works

CLASSIC PROSE WORKS (see page 130)
After Rosedale catches Lily in a lie, she wonders: "Why

must a girl pay so dearly for her least escape from routine.

Why could one never do a natural thing without having to

screen it behind a structure of artifice" (Wharton 18;

bk. 1, ch. 2).

After the semicolon, give any other identifying information possible, since the material referred to or quoted may appear on a different page in another edition. Use the following abbreviations: bk. (book), pt. (part), sec. (section), and ch. (chapter). If you use the author's name in text, use the following form:

When Wharton writes that Lily was beginning to lose her

"girlish smoothness . . . after eleven years of late hours

and indefatigable dancing," we suspect that some change is

in store for her (6; bk. 1, ch. 1).

CLASSIC VERSE PLAYS AND POEMS (see page 126)

Shakespeare has Miranda tell Prospero, upon her seeing

Ferdinand: "I might call him / A thing divine; for nothing

natural / I ever saw so noble" (Tempest I.ii.420-422).

Use an abbreviated form of the title. Separate the divisions by periods. The entry above refers to the play *The Tempest*, Act I, Scene ii, lines 420–22. Notice that page numbers have been omitted entirely. If you include the title in the text, use this form:

In The Tempest, when Prospero pretends to believe Ferdinand

a spy, Miranda defends Ferdinand by saying: "There's

nothing ill can dwell in such a temple" (I.ii.460).

More than One Work in a Single Parenthetical Reference (see pages 129 and 144)

London claimed that he was unaware of the thematic sig-

nificance of The Call of the Wild when he was writing it

(Rothberg 7; Sinclair 95), but its dog-eat-dog theme cannot

be missed by any careful reader.

Separate each citation with a semicolon. If your parenthetical reference is particularly long, consider placing it in a note (see page 156).

One-Page Articles, Works Arranged Alphabetically, and Nonprint Sources (see pages 125 and 134)

Although Poe's behavior was attributed to drug addiction,

medical evidence indicates that he had a brain lesion

("Poe").

According to Smith, ingrained class prejudice made it

difficult for Harold Macmillan to respond warmly to

ordinary Americans.

Omit any page numbers. If you cite the author's name in text, omit any parenthetical reference. If the article in a work arranged alphabetically is long, you may include page numbers:

> Some of the poems in <u>Tamerland and Other Poems</u> hint at
>
> Poe's love for his first sweetheart, Sarah Elmira Royster
>
> ("Poe" 597).

Writing Notes with Parenthetical Documentation

You may find it necessary to supplement your parenthetical references with content notes and bibliographic notes. There are two ways of placing notes in the paper. Footnotes are typed at the bottom of the page to which they refer. Endnotes are collected in a separate section of pages at the end of the paper. Footnotes are undoubtedly more convenient for the reader because they make it unnecessary to look at the end of the paper for the information. However, since footnotes can be cumbersome, endnotes are generally preferred. Therefore, unless your instructor specifically calls for footnotes, use endnotes.

Indicate the material being referred to with a superscript numeral at the end of the information or quotation. Indicate the note with a superscript numeral at its beginning. For example:

Text

> It is with joy and wonder that Miranda exclaims upon seeing
>
> Alonso, Sebastian, and Gonzalo: "O brave new world / That
>
> has such people in't!"[1] (<u>Tempest</u> V.i.183).

Note

> [1]When Miranda uses the word <u>brave</u> here, she means fine
>
> (Barnet 1544).

(For specific information on typing notes, see pages 157–159.)

Content Notes

You can use content notes to explain or qualify points in the text and to provide full publishing information for the original source of quoted material when you have used an indirect source. Resist the urge to include in a content note an interesting bit of information that is not really related to your topic but which you want to share with your reader anyway. Here are samples of several kinds of content notes:

Explanation

[1]There are nearly as many different spellings of

Pottawatomie as there are sources for this paper; I have

silently regularized the variants in the passages I quote.

This information allows the writer to avoid an excessive use of "sic" in the paper; the information belongs in an explanatory note so that it does not disrupt the text of the paper. Note 2 explains the meaning of a term:

[2]Bowdlerize derives from the name of an English

physician, Thomas Bowdler, who, in 1818, removed what he

regarded as offensive passages from an edition of Shake-

speare's writings.

Qualification

[3]Although it is true that individual incomes have

increased, buying power has remained relatively constant

for this group; hence, more data might suggest further

problems to consider here.

Indirect Source

[4]Peter Lyon, Eisenhower: Portrait of a Hero (Boston:

Little, 1974) 641, qtd. in Boller 296.

The source used was Boller; the original source is Lyon.

Bibliographical Notes

Reference

[5]For a thorough comparison of these two writers, see

Stephen Donadio, Nietzsche, Henry James, and the Artistic

Will (New York: Oxford UP, 1978).

You can use bibliographical notes to refer your reader to additional information about a topic or contrasting points of view and to cite more than one source.

More than One Source

[6]Both Sinclair 95 in his excellent biography and

Rothberg 7 in his introduction to The Call of the Wild

make mention of this.

[7]For the background information on John Brown's life,

I am indebted to Richard O. Boyer, The Legend of John

Brown: A Biography and a History (New York: Macmillan,

1971) 85-112; Stephen B. Oates, To Purge This Land with

Blood: A Biography of John Brown (New York: Harper, 1970)

158-65; and C. Vann Woodward, "John Brown's Private War,"

America in Crisis, ed. Daniel Aaron (New York: Knopf,

1952) 109-30.

Note that each source is separated by a semicolon with the final source preceded by "and."

There is a variety of useful combinations for these kinds of notes, limited only to the circumstances you run into. Here, for example, is a note combining a qualification and reference.

[8]This description seems plausible, but for a more

detailed analysis, see Julia Epstein, "Voltaire's Ventrilo-

```
quism: Voices in the First Lettre Philosophique," Studies

on Voltaire and the Eighteenth Century 182 (1979): 219-35.
```

ANOTHER METHOD OF DOCUMENTATION IN THE HUMANITIES

Some instructors prefer the earlier style of MLA documentation, which uses notes instead of parenthetical references. First check with your instructor to see if this style is preferred, and if it is, whether a list of works cited or bibliography is also required. If your instructor does prefer this style, follow the guidelines below.

How to Write Notes

Use endnotes, called "Notes," instead of footnotes, unless your instructor specifies otherwise.

Endnotes

Figure 8-1 shows how to set up notes at the end of the paper. Follow these directions for typing the notes:

1. The first page of the "Notes" begins one inch below the top of the page. Subsequent pages are typed, like the text, one inch from the top of the page.
2. Leave two spaces between the heading and the first line of the note.
3. Indent the first line of the note five spaces. Type the note number a half space above the line. Leave one space between the number and the note. Do not indent subsequent lines.
4. Double space within and between notes.
5. Number all note pages as you would text.

Footnotes

The entire footnote should appear at the bottom of the page to which it refers (see Figure 8-2). Plan ahead when you type, and follow these directions:

1. Leave four spaces between the last line of the text and the first note.

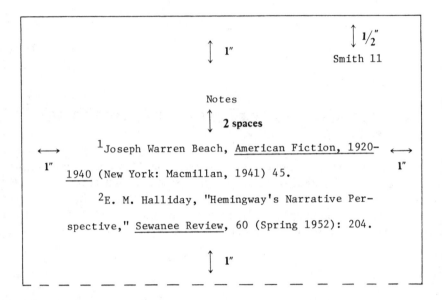

Figure 8-1   Sample Endnote Style

2. Indent the first line of the note five spaces. Type the note number a half space above the line. Leave one space between the number and the note.
3. Single space within each note; double space between each note.

Numbering

Number the notes consecutively through the paper. If you use footnotes, don't number them only for each page. In the text, place the note number *at the end* of the information or quotation cited. The numbers are typed right after a word or punctuation with no extra space coming between them:

WRONG
Although Atkinson[7] liked the film's "quick pace and excel-

lent camera work," he found the acting melodramatic.

WRONG
Although Atkinson liked the film's "quick pace and excellent

camera work,"[7] he found the acting melodramatic.

instruction played the major role in the education

of children during this period.[12] Therefore books

↑ **4 spaces**

1″
⟵⟶   [11]James Steel Smith, <u>A Critical Approach to</u>   1″
<u>Children's Literature</u> (New York: McGraw, 1967) 28.   ⟵⟶

[12]Zena Sutherland and Mary Hill Arbuthnot,
<u>Children and Books</u> (Glenview: Scott, 1977) 78.

↑ 1″

Figure 8-2   Sample Footnote Style

RIGHT
    Although Atkinson liked the film's "quick pace and excellent

camera work," he found the acting melodramatic.[7]

Notice, however, that the note is placed closest to what it documents in this next example:

RIGHT
    Although Atkinson praised the film's "quick pace and excel-

lent camera work,"[7] Jordan found it "slow and badly

edited."[8]

An alternative way of handling the preceding example is to use only one note at the end of the sentence and to cite both Atkinson and Jordan in a single note.

Notes Compared with Entries in the List of Works Cited

Notes are similar to entries in the list of works cited in the basic information they contain, but there are three chief differences in form: (1) indentation, (2) order of the author's name, and (3) punctuation. Compare the following two entries:

Works Cited Entry

> Keiser, Albert. College Names: Their Origin and Signifi-
>
> cance. New York: Bookman, 1952.

Note Entry

> [1]Albert Keiser, College Names: Their Origin and Sig-
>
> nificance (New York: Bookman, 1952) 42.

1. Indentation. Visually, the difference is immediately apparent. The works cited entry indents all lines five spaces except the first line, whereas only the first line of the note entry is indented five spaces.
2. Author. In the works cited entry, the author's name appears in reverse order so that it can be alphabetized, whereas in the note entry the author's name appears in normal order.
3. Punctuation. In the works cited entry, there are three main categories of information (author, title, and publishing information), each ending with a period. However, since the note entry is to be read as if it were a sentence, the period comes only at the end. A comma comes between the author's name and the title while publishing information is placed in parentheses.

Sample Notes for Books

The examples in this section and the following sections on periodicals and other sources should equip you to write notes for the sources you encounter. If you don't find the exact form that fits a particular source you're using, then improvise by employing the logic you will find in the sample notes that follow. These notes correspond to the sample works cited entries listed in Chapter 7. Keep in mind when you type your notes that they will be double spaced.

A Book with One Author (see page 120)

> [1]Paul F. Boller, Jr., Presidential Anecdotes (New
>
> York: Oxford UP, 1981) 296.
>
> [2]Rudolph Flesch, Lite English: Popular Words That
>
> Are OK to Use--No Matter What William Safire, John Simon,

<u>Edwin Newman, and the Other Purists Say!</u> (New York: Crown,

1983) 117.

Notice that no comma comes between the publishing information and the page number and that no abbreviation for page is used.

A Book with Two Authors (see page 121)

³Walter Harding and Michael Meyer, <u>The New Thoreau</u>

<u>Handbook</u> (New York: New York UP, 1980) 40.

A Book with Three Authors (see page 122)

⁴Alan Purves, Sauli Takala, and Avon Crismore, <u>How to</u>

<u>Write Well in College</u> (San Diego: Harcourt, 1984) 84.

A Book with More than Three Authors (see page 122)

⁵Robert E. Spiller et al., <u>Literary History of the</u>

<u>United States</u> (New York: Macmillan, 1946) 482.

Notice that there is no comma between the author's name and "et al."

A Book with a Corporate Author (see page 122)

⁶The Diagram Book, <u>Woman's Body: An Owner's Manual</u>

(New York: Paddington, 1977) 346.

A Book with an Anonymous Author (see page 122)

⁷<u>Margaret: A Tale of the Real and Ideal, Blight and</u>

<u>Bloom</u> (Boston: Jordan, 1845) 30-31.

Note that neither "Anonymous" nor "Anon." is substituted for the name. If you determine the author's name for a book published anonymously, place it within brackets followed by a comma: [Sylvester Judd], *Margaret* . . .

A Book with a Pseudonymous Author (see page 123)

[8]Oliver Optic [William T. Adams], Haste and Waste;
or, The Young Pilot of Lake Champlain (Boston: Lothrop,
1894) 25.

Notice that the author's actual name appears in brackets after the pseud-onym.

A Work in More than One Volume (see page 123)

To cite the entire set of a multivolume work, use this form:

[9]Richard B. Sewall, The Life of Emily Dickinson,
2 vols. (New York: Farrar, 1974).

To cite just one volume of a set, however, place the volume number before the page reference.

[10]Richard B. Sewall, The Life of Emily Dickinson,
2 vols. (New York: Farrar, 1974) 2: 123.

If Sewall's two-volume work had been published in different years, the volume number in the above example would have preceded the publishing information: . . . *Dickinson, 2* (New York . . .). For a single volume of a multivolume work that has individual titles, use this format:

[11]Frederick Copleston, S. J., Medieval Philosophy,
Vol. 2 of A History of Philosophy, 10 vols. (Garden City:
Doubleday, 1962) 48.

A Work in a Collection of Writings by the Same Author (see page 124)

[12]William Saroyan, "Ancient History," The Human
Comedy by Saroyan (New York: Harcourt, 1943) 51.

A Work in a Collection of Writings by Different Authors

AN ESSAY (see page 124)

[13]Herman Melville, "Hawthorne and His Mosses," The

Theory of the American Novel, ed. George Perkins (New York:

Holt, 1970) 72.

If possible, indicate original publishing information by using this format:

[14]Marius Bewley, "Scott Fitzgerald's Criticism of

America," Sewanee Review 62 (Spring 1954) 223-46; rpt. in

The Great Gatsby: A Study, ed. Frederick J. Hoffman (New

York: Scribner's, 1962) 263-64.

A SHORT STORY (see page 125)

[15]Edgar Allan Poe, "A Tale of the Ragged Mountains,"

Future Perfect: American Science Fiction of the Nineteenth

Century, ed. H. Bruce Franklin (New York: Oxford UP, 1968)

105-06.

A NOVEL (see page 125)

[16]Robert Louis Stevenson, The Strange Case of Dr.

Jekyll and Mr. Hyde, Minor Classics of Nineteenth-Century

Fiction, ed. William E. Buckler, 2 vols. (Boston: Houghton,

1967) 2: 78-79.

A POEM (see page 125)

[17]Robert Creeley, "The Door," The New American Poetry,

ed. David M. Allen (New York: Grove, 1960) 83.

A PLAY (see page 125)

[18]Oscar Wilde, The Importance of Being Earnest, The

Norton Anthology of English Literature, ed. M. H. Abrams

et al., 4th ed., 2 vols. (New York: Norton, 1979), 2:
1685-86.

Classic Works and the Bible *(see page 126)*

[19]John Milton, Paradise Lost, John Milton: Complete

Poems and Major Prose, ed. Merritt Y. Hughes (New York:

Odyssey, 1957) 305 (V.110-28).

[20]William Shakespeare, The Tempest, The Complete

Signet Classic Shakespeare, gen. ed. Sylvan Barnet (New

York: Harcourt, 1972) 1549 (I.ii.420-421).

For classic works, besides providing the page reference you should also provide information that will enable a reader to locate a passage regardless of which edition of the work is used. In note 19 (V.110–28) refers to Book V, lines 110–28; in note 20 (I.ii.420–421) refers to Act I, scene ii, lines 420–421. Use large Roman numerals for large sections of a work (books, acts), small Roman numerals for subsections (cantos, scenes), and Arabic numerals for lines.

The Bible is cited only by book, chapter, and verse. Like other sacred books such as the Koran, it is not underlined. No other documentation is necessary unless you use some version other than the King James version:

[21]Matthew 7:24-29.

[22]Luke 17:12 (Revised Standard Version).

Encyclopedias and Other Reference Works *(see page 127)*

[23]"Edgar Allan Poe," The New Encyclopaedia Britannica,

1984 ed.

If your reference is to only one page of an article longer than one page, you may supply the page number. For reference works that are not well known, supply all the facts of publication.

A Work in a Series *(see page 127)*

[24]Robert J. Scholnick, Edmund Clarence Stedman,

Twayne's United States Author Series 286 (Boston: Twayne,

1977) 61.

Reprints *(see page 127)*

[25]Clarence L. F. Gohdes, The Periodicals of American

Transcendentalism (1931; New York: AMS, 1970) 187.

[26]Williams, Stanley T., The Spanish Background of

American Literature, 2 vols., 1955 (n.p.: Archon, 1968)

2: 27.

An Edition of a Book *(see page 128)*

[27]Robert E. Spiller et al., Literary History of the

United States, 3rd ed. (New York: Macmillan, 1963) 95.

This is a later revised edition of the work cited in note 5.

An Editor of an Anthology or Collection *(see page 128)*

[28]Terry Carr, ed., Classic Science Fiction: The First

Golden Age (New York: Harper, 1978) 345.

An Editor of a Book by Another *(see page 128)*

[29]Scott Donaldson, ed., On the Road, by Jack Kerouac,

Viking Critical Library (New York: Penguin, 1979) x-xiii.

To cite the author's work, use this form:

[30]Jack Kerouac, On the Road, ed. Scott Donaldson,

Viking Critical Library (New York: Penguin, 1979) 99.

Place the editor's name first when discussing the editor's work, but place the author's name first when citing the work of the author. Be certain that you distinguish between a writer who actually edits a work and one who provides only an introduction to a work. Editors are identified as such on the title page.

An Introduction, Preface, Foreword, or Afterword to a Book (see page 129)

[31]Arnold Gingrich, introduction, The Pat Hobby

Stories, by F. Scott Fitzgerald (New York: Scribner's,

1962) x.

To refer to the work of the author rather than to the introduction, use this form:

[32]F. Scott Fitzgerald, The Pat Hobby Stories, intro.,

Arnold Gingrich (New York: Scribner's, 1962) 37-39.

A Translated Book (see page 129)

[33]Bernard Frechtman, trans., The Screens, by Jean

Genêt (New York: Grove, 1962) 20.

In the preceding example, some aspect of Frechtman's translation is cited; hence his name comes first. A citation for Genêt's work, however, looks like this:

[34]Jean Genêt, The Screens, trans. Bernard Frechtman

(New York: Grove, 1962) 29.

A Publisher's Imprint (see page 130)

[35]V. S. Pritchett, Midnight Oil (New York: Vintage–

Random, 1973) 144.

A Pamphlet (see page 130)

[36]Dana S. Hubbard, Facts About Marriage Every Young

Man & Woman Should Know (New York: Claremount, 1922) 12.

A Government Publication (see page 130)

[37]United States, Dept. of Housing and Urban Develop-

ment, Wise Home Buying (Washington: GPO, 1978) 26.

[38]Cong. Rec., 5 Apr. 1957: 14471-75.

[39]United States, Cong., Senate, Communism in Labor

Unions, 83rd Cong., 2nd sess., S. Rept. 526 (Washington:

GPO, 1954) 48.

A Legal Reference

Since citations for law are complex and irregular, use as a guide *A Uniform System of Citation*, 13th ed. (Cambridge: Harvard Law Review, 1981).

Sample Notes for Periodicals

An Anonymous Entry (see page 131)

[40]"A Wolf in Sheik's Clothing," Time 13 Apr. 1981: 54.

A Signed Article (see page 131)

[41]Dachine Rainer, "Who Are the Anarchists?"

Liberation 8 (April 1963): 26-27.

For multiple authors of an article, follow the same guidelines used for multiple authors of books (see pages 120–122).

A Journal with Continuous Pagination Beyond a Single Issue (see page 132)

[42]Richard Hauck, "The Dickens Controversy in the

Spirit of the Times," PMLA 855 (1970): 280.

A Journal with Separate Pagination for Each Issue (see page 132)

[43]Gary F. Scharnhorst, "The Alger Problem: The Hoax About Horatio Revealed," Ball State University Forum 15 (Spring 1974): 61.

A Monthly Magazine (see page 133)

[44]Hirsh Goodman and Zeev Schiff, "The Attack on the Liberty," Atlantic Sept. 1984: 79.

A Weekly Magazine (see page 133)

[45]Herbert A. Otto, "Communes: The Alternative Life Style," Saturday Review 24 Apr. 1971: 17.

A Newspaper (see page 133)

[46]William J. Broad, "Tesla, a Bizarre Genius, Regains Aura of Greatness," New York Times 28 Aug. 1984, late ed.: C3.

[47]Meg Cox, "Parents' Approach to Child Rearing Is Becoming More Goal-Oriented," Wall Street Journal 29 Aug. 1984, eastern ed.: 25.

If an article does not appear on consecutive pages, the entry in the list of works cited provides the number of the first page followed by a plus sign (C1+, 25+). However, the note provides the specific page of the reference (C3, 25).

An Editorial (see page 134)

[48]Richard Oppel, "The Story That Wasn't True," editorial, Charlotte Observer [N.C.] 19 Apr. 1981, sec. B: 2.

A Letter to the Editor (see page 134)

[49]George Johnson, letter, New Republic 18 Apr. 1981:

40.

A Review (see page 134)

[50]Darryl Pinckney, "Every Which Way," rev. of Tar

Baby, by Toni Morrison, New York Review of Books 30 Apr.

1981: 24.

Use the following form for an untitled review:

[51]Tony Fiociello, rev. of The Culture of Narcissism:

American Life in an Age of Diminishing Expectations, by

Christopher Lasch, Library Journal 15 Nov. 1978: 2323.

Use the following form for a review that is untitled and unsigned:

[52]Rev. of Maggie: A Girl of the Streets, by Stephen

Crane, New York Tribune 31 May 1896: 26.

A Published Interview (see page 135)

[53]Ken Kesey, "An Impolite Interview with Ken Kesey,"

One Flew Over the Cuckoo's Nest: Text and Criticism, ed.

John Clark Pratt (New York: Viking, 1973) 349.

A Quotation in the Article's Title (see page 135)

[54]Robert Boyers, "Attitudes Toward Sex in American

'High Culture,'" Annals of the American Academy of Political

and Social Science 376 (March 1968) 37-39.

Sample Notes for Other Sources

An Unpublished Manuscript or Typescript (see page 136)

[55]Minutes of the Psi Gamma and Alpha Kappa Library
Societies, ms., Dawes Memorial Library of Marietta College,
Marietta.

A Lecture (see page 136)

[56]Robert Gross, "Emily Dickinson and Amherst,"
American Literature Symposium, Middlebury College, Middlebury, 24 Apr. 1981.

[57]Lyman Johnson, History 109 class lecture, City
College, New York, 19 Jan. 1979.

A Film (see page 136)

[58]Deliverance, dir. John Boorman, with Jon Voight and
Burt Reynolds, Warner Bros., 1972.

If you wish to cite a person's role rather than the film itself, use this form:

[59]John Boorman, dir., Deliverance, with Jon Voight and
Burt Reynolds, Warner Bros., 1972.

A videotape, filmstrip, or slide program is cited the same way as a film, except that the type of medium is indicated following the title.

[60]Financial Planning, slide program, dir. James Fawn,
Mandell Institute, 1983.

A Theatrical Performance (see page 137)

[61]The Night Thoreau Spent in Jail, by Jerome Lawrence
and Robert E. Lee, dir. Roy Bowen, Ohio State U., Columbus,
Ohio, 21 Apr. 1970.

To cite the work of a person rather than the performance itself, use this form:

[62]Roy Bowen, dir., The Night Thoreau Spent in Jail,

by Jerome Lawrence and Robert E. Lee, Ohio State U.,

Columbus, Ohio, 21 Apr. 1970.

[63]Neil Simon, Fools, dir. Mike Nichols, Eugene O'Neill

Theater, New York, 15 Apr. 1981.

A Musical Composition (see page 137)

[64]Peter Ilich Tchaikovsky, Piano concerto no. 1 in B,

op. 23.

[65]Igor Stravinsky, Petrouchka.

A Work of Art (see page 138)

[66]Edvard Munch, The Scream, Museum of Modern Art,

New York.

Use this form for a photographic reproduction in a published work:

[67]George Bellows, Dempsey and Firpo, Whitney Museum

of American Art, New York, illus. in George Bellows:

Painter of America, by Charles H. Morgan (New York:

Reynal, 1965) 310.

A Radio or Television Program (see page 138)

[68]"How Much Loyalty Is Owed to the Boss?" Firing

Line, PBS, WUNG, Atlanta, 19 Apr. 1981.

A Recording (see page 138)

[69]James Taylor, Mud Slide Slim and the Blue Horizon,

Warner Bros. BS2561.

To cite a particular song, use this form:

[70]Pete Seeger, "Talking Union," Pete Seeger's Greatest
Hits, Columbia, CS9416, n.d.

For citations to spoken word recordings, list the speaker first:

[71]Orson Welles, Walt Whitman's Song of Myself from
Leaves of Grass, CMS, 636, 1972.

In citations for jacket notes, list the author first:

[72]Marcus Cunliffe, jacket notes, Walt Whitman's Song
of Myself from Leaves of Grass, CMS, 636, 1972.

An Unpublished Personal Letter (see page 139)

[73]Leon Gatlin, letter to author, 12 Mar. 1980.

Use this form for an unpublished letter housed in a collection:

[74]Theodore Parker, letter to Oliver Wendell Holmes,
13 Sept. 1858, Theodore Parker Papers, Library of
Congress, Washington, D.C.

A Personally Conducted Interview (see page 139)

[75]Harold Josephson, personal interview, 18 Oct. 1978.

[76]Ralph Graves, telephone interview, 12 Jan. 1981.

An Unpublished Doctoral Dissertation (see page 140)

[77]Michael Brian, "Cynicism and the Problem of Political Consciousness," diss. (U of California, Berkeley, 1976)
48.

To refer to the abstract of a dissertation in Dissertation Abstracts International, use this form:

78Michael Brian, "Cynicism and the Problem of Politi-

cal Consciousness," DAI 37 (1977): 6030A (U of California,

Berkeley).

Computer Software (see page 140)

79Word Weaver III, computer software, Synergistic

Software, 1983, Apple III.

Subsequent References

The sample notes just listed are used to acknowledge a source the first time it is referred to or quoted in the paper. Although the form of the note varies when the material cited comes from a book, periodical, or some other source, the purpose of the note remains the same: to provide information that fully identifies the source.

Once you have fully identified a source in a note, you needn't repeat all the information in subsequent references. Use a shortened form. Here is a first full reference to a book followed by a subsequent reference:

80Milton R. Stern, The Golden Moment: The Novels of

F. Scott Fitzgerald (Urbana:. U of Illinois P, 1970) 194.

81Stern 268-71.

Note 81 saves you and the reader some time and effort. The author's last name and page number constitute a clear and concise reference. If you use more than one work by the same author or cite two authors with the same last name, add a shortened form of the title to the name to avoid any confusion. Suppose that you had also cited another book by Stern:

82Milton R. Stern, The Fine Hammered Steel of Herman

Melville (Urbana: U of Illinois P, 1957) 95.

Subsequent references to both books pose no problem provided that it is clear which work of Stern's is cited.

83Stern, Fitzgerald 34.

84Stern, Melville 104.

When you shorten the title, choose a key word or two that readily identifies the work. For example, *Moment* and *Steel* identify the above works, but each would probably force the reader back to the first full reference of each book. *Golden Moment* and *Fine Hammered Steel* would be better, but the shortened form in notes 83 and 84 is best because it clearly indicates the subject of each book. Use the same method for subsequent references to periodicals and other kinds of sources. You may cite sources that don't entirely lend themselves to this method; an anonymous work, for example, would require you to begin the subsequent reference with a shortened form for the title:

> [85]"A Wolf in Sheik's Clothing," Time 13 Apr. 1981: 54.
>
> [86]"Wolf" 54.

In unusual cases your method may have to be slightly adjusted, but your purpose and note logic remain the same: use a subsequent reference that is concise and clear.

Latin Abbreviations

The use of Latin abbreviations in subsequent references is now generally considered unnecessary. The abbreviations "op. cit." for *opere citato* ("in the work cited"), "loc. cit." for *loco citato* ("in the place cited"), and "ibid." for *ibidem* ("in the same place") were once common in scholarly writing. For that reason you should know what they mean, because you may encounter them in your reading. Most contemporary writers avoid them, however, because the abbreviations confuse many readers rather than help them. Some writers continue to use "ibid." although its use is no longer recommended. However, in case you encounter it in your reading, its usage is illustrated in the following sequence of notes.

> [87]Casey Miller and Kate Swift, The Handbook of Non-sexist Writings for Writers, Editors and Speakers (New York: Lippincott and Crowell, 1980) 43.
>
> [88]Ibid. 39.
>
> [89]Ibid.
>
> [90]Peter Elbow, Writing with Power: Techniques for

Mastering the Writing Process (New York: Oxford UP, 1981) 145.

[91]Miller and Swift 98.

[92]Elbow 148.

[93]Ibid. 12.

Note 87 is the first full reference to the Miller and Swift book. Because "ibid." is always used to refer to the work in the immediately preceding note, note 88 indicates that the material cited will be found in Miller and Swift on page 39. When "ibid." appears without a page reference, it refers to the same work and the same page number. Hence, note 89 also refers to page 39 of Miller and Swift. In note 91 "ibid." cannot be used to refer to Miller and Swift because note 90 cites a different book; the same is true for note 92: Elbow's name must be used because the preceding note refers to a different book. Since "ibid." requires the use of an author's name when another work is cited between "ibid." and its referent, there is little sense in using "ibid." at all. The author's name and page number can be consistently used instead, as described in the discussion of subsequent references above.

Internal Documentation

Sometimes it is necessary to cite a single work many times throughout a paper, especially if you are writing an analysis about a work such as a novel or play. Rather than include many distracting notes that repeatedly direct your reader to the author's name and page number cited, you can provide internal documentation by placing the page number in parentheses in the text of the paper. Here, for example, is the first full reference to a short story referred to later in the text of the paper:

[94]David Porush, "The Misogynist," Rope Dances (New

York: Fiction Collective, 1979) 49-67. Subsequent

references to this work appear in the text.

And here is how the source is subsequently documented in the text of the paper:

The narrator of the story finds himself in a "hyper-

imaginative state": "I groaned. I tried to remember the

number of my psychoanalyst, but realized I didn't have a

psychoanalyst, that only characters in my stories do" (58).

Notice that the period comes after the parentheses. Had the passage been a long one and therefore set off from the text of the paper, however, the period would come inside the quotation and before the parenthetical information, with no punctuation following the closing parenthesis.

If you were to cite frequently more than one story by Porush, then you could use a shortened version of each title within the parentheses to indicate which story is cited. Or if you were to compare this story to a work by someone else, then you could supply each author's name along with the page number within the parentheses. The strategy is a simple one: try to avoid sending your reader to the bottom of the page or to the back of the paper for information that can be unobtrusively documented within the text of the paper.

Another form of internal documentation employs a full citation to a source enclosed in parentheses within the text of the paper. This form can be used if your paper cites only a few sources or if the paper is a bibliographical essay. There are several ways of supplying this kind of documentation in the text of the paper, but the same principle applies to all of them — provide the same information for the first full reference to a source that you would for a footnote or endnote:

John P. McWilliams, Jr. (Political Justice in a Republic:

James Fenimore Cooper's America [Berkeley: U of Calif. P,

1972] 204) points out that. . . .

In "Black Writers of the South" (Mississippi Quarterly 31

[1978]: 170), Julian Mason provides. . . .

John B. Watson--Behaviorism (New York: Norton, 1925) 84

--acknowledges that. . . .

Ann J. Jawin (A Woman's Guide to Career Preparation:

Scholarships, Grants and Loans [New York: Doubleday, 1979]

340-42) lists. . . .

DOCUMENTATION IN THE SCIENCES

Scientific fields such as biology, chemistry, engineering, geology, mathematics, physics, and psychology have their own style manuals for documenting papers. If you write a paper about one of these fields for a humanities course, you will use the system of documentation described in this book, but if you write a paper for a course offered in a specific scientific discipline, you probably will be expected to use a format that conforms to the style manual endorsed by that discipline. Here is a listing of some of the manuals available. Check with your instructor to determine if you should use such a manual; some departments recommend their own style sheets.

Biology: Council of Biology Editors, Style Manual Committee. *CBE Style Manual.* Bethesda: Council of Biology Editors, 1983.

Chemistry: American Chemical Society. *Handbook for Authors.* Washington: American Chemical Soc., 1978.

Engineering: Engineers Joint Council, Committee of Engineering Society Editors. *Recommended Practice for Style of References in Engineering Publications.* New York: Engineers Joint Council, 1966.

Geology: U.S. Geological Survey. *Suggestions to Authors of Reports of the United States Geological Survey.* 6th ed. Washington: Dept. of the Interior, 1978.

Linguistics: Linguistic Society of America. *LSA Bulletin* 71 (December 1976) 43–45.

Mathematics: American Mathematical Society. *A Manual for Authors of Mathematical Papers.* 7th ed. Providence: American Mathematical Soc., 1980.

Physics: American Institute of Physics. *Style Manual.* Rev. ed. New York: American Inst. of Physics, 1978.

Psychology: American Psychological Association. *Publication Manual of the American Psychological Association.* 3rd ed. Washington: American Psychological Assn., 1983.

As the *MLA Handbook* points out, the principal difference in documentation between the humanities and the sciences is in the form of the parenthetical references. For the sciences, these references take three basic forms: (1) author-date, (2) author-title, or (3) number.

1. Author-date:

   Analysis of the effects of low light intensity on this species of grass (Burne, 1978, 23–24) demonstrates that. . . .

2. Author-title:

   Analysis of the effects of low light intensity on this species of grass (Burne, "Shade Tolerance," 23–24) demonstrates that. . . .

3. Number:

   Analysis of the effects of low light intensity on this species of grass (*17*, 23–24) demonstrates that. . . .

For the preceding examples, the complete bibliographical information for the parenthetical citations would be found at the end of the paper. In the last example, *17* refers to a numbered list of references in the bibliography (usually labeled "References" or "Works Cited") at the end of the paper. Hence, number 17 would refer to Burne's work.

Again, this brief description of parenthetical documentation for the sciences indicates only the basic note logic of the system; for specifics consult with your instructor or an appropriate style manual.

DOCUMENTATION IN THE SOCIAL SCIENCES

The following method of citation is drawn from the *Publication Manual of the American Psychological Association*. Because undergraduate research papers in psychology are quite common, the stylistic conventions for psychology papers represent a useful opportunity to offer at least one detailed example of documentation in the social sciences.

Author-Date Method

The American Psychological Association (APA) uses the author-date method for citations in the text of the paper:

```
In contrast to an earlier study of how children use

language (Piaget, 1962), Allen (1970) argues. . . .
```

In the preceding example, because Allen's name is mentioned in the text, his name is not included in the parenthetical citation. Subsequent references in the text to Piaget or Allen need not include the year, provided that no other studies by them are included in the paper.

Observe the following additional guidelines for author-date citations:

A Work by a Single Author

Cite the author's name and the year of publication.

    A recent article on learning with home computers (Hively,

    1984) . . .

    Hively (1984) provides guidance for parents purchasing

    computers . . .

Notice the comma between the author's name and the date in the parenthetical reference. If both the author's name and the date appear in the text, no parenthetical reference is needed.

    In 1984, Hively rated various computer programs . . .

A Work by Two Authors

Use both names each time the work is cited in the text.

    . . . as has been indicated (Miller & McKean, 1964).

    As Miller and McKean (1964) have indicated. . . .

Notice that an ampersand (&) is used in place of "and" when it appears inside a parenthetical reference.

A Work with More than Two Authors (but Fewer than Six)

Cite all of the authors in the first entry.

    Lieberman, Cooper, Shankweiler, and Studdert-Kennedy (1967)

    show . . . .

But use only the first surname plus "et al" for subsequent entries.

    . . . informed by these theories (Lieberman et al., 1967).

(Of course, if two different entries have the same shortened form, include the surnames of all the authors in subsequent entries to avoid confusion.)

A Work by Six or More Authors

Use the surname of the first author followed by "et al." in the first and all subsequent entries.

```
Christiansen et al. (1982) studied learning patterns of

animals in . . . .

This careful study (Christiansen et al., 1982) explains

how animals . . . .
```

(If the shortened form of two or more works is the same, use the surname of the first authors and as many other surnames as needed to avoid confusion.)

Corporate Author

Spell out short names and names that cannot be abbreviated in an easily identifiable way each time they appear in text.

```
The Fitness Group (1979) recommends . . . .

. . . according to this report (The Fitness Group, 1979).
```

Spell out names that can be abbreviated in an easily identifiable way the first time they appear in text. Include the abbreviation after the name.

```
. . . the effects of exercise on mental health (American

Medical Association [AMA], 1981).
```

Use the abbreviation in subsequent references.

```
In a study by the AMA (1981), the effects . . . .
```

A Work with No Author

Use a shortened form of the title so that it can be easily located in the reference list.

FULL REFERENCE LIST TITLE
```
"Psychological effects of deafness"
```

SHORTENED FORM
```
. . . as has been argued ("Psychological Effects," 1971).
```

A Work Signed by "Anonymous"

Use the word "Anonymous" in the author's position of the entry.

```
. . . a harrowing experience (Anonymous, 1982).
```

Authors with the Same Surname

Use the authors' initials to distinguish between them, even if the publication dates differ.

```
. . . resulting from this experiment (A. K. Austin, 1928),

while a later experiment (T. Austin, 1931) . . . .
```

Two or More Works Within the Same Parentheses

Place the works in the order in which they appear in the reference list.
    For two or more works by the same author published in different years, use this form:

```
Several case histories (Thompson, 1979, 1980). . . .
```

Notice that the book published first is placed first.
    For two or more works by the same author published in the same year, use this form:

```
These two studies (Piaget, 1962a, 1962b) indicate. . . .
```

Notice that lower-case letters identify the works. These letters also appear in the reference list.
    For two or more works by different authors, use this form:

```
. . . has been proven (Kingsley, 1984; Matthews 1983).
```

Notice that the works are placed in alphabetical order and are separated by a semicolon.

A Part of a Work

Provide the page, chapter, figure, table, or equation number.

```
In light of this experiment (Capshaw, 1980, chap. 4). . . .

Other evidence supports this finding (Weinberg, 1978,

p. 17).
```

Personal Communications

Provide complete information in text, since personal communications are not listed in the reference list.

```
. . . the morale of the staff (E. G. Parkinsen, personal

communication, August 24, 1984).

According to one staff member, E. G. Parkinsen (personal

communication, April 18, 1983), the morale. . . .
```

A Legal Reference

Use as your guide *A Uniform System of Citation,* 13th ed. (Cambridge: Harvard Law Review, 1981).

Reference Lists

Place reference lists at the end of the paper and include only those works actually cited in the text. Each work cited in the paper must appear in the reference list. Arrange the list alphabetically by the author's last name (or by the first important word of the title if no author is given).

Book Entry

A reference to a book contains the following basic information:

1. name[s] of author[s] in inverted order with only the initials of first or middle names
2. date of publication in parentheses and followed by a period
3. title of the book underlined to indicate italics with only the initial letter of the first word capitalized followed by a period

4. publication information:
   a. place of publication followed by a colon
   b. name of publisher followed by a period

Notice that in the sample reference list entries the first line is flush with the left-hand margin and that any subsequent lines for the entry are three indented spaces:

SAMPLE BOOK ENTRIES

Alper, L., & Holberg, M. (1984). Parents, kids, and

   computers: Learning adventures beyond the classroom.

   Berkeley: SYBEX.

Butterfield, H. (1965). The origins of modern science

   (rev. ed.). New York: Free Press.

Miller, G. A., & McNeill, D. (1969). Psycholinguistics.

   In G. Lindzey & E. Aronson (Eds.), The handbook of

   social psychology (2nd ed.), Vol. 3 (pp. 666-794).

   Reading, MA: Addison-Wesley.

Piaget, J. (1954). The construction of reality in the

   child. New York: Basic Books.

Sagan, C. (1977). The dragons of Eden: Speculations on

   the evolution of human intelligence. New York:

   Random House.

Turkle, S. (1984). The second self: Computers and the

   human spirit. New York: Simon and Schuster.

Article Entry

A reference to an article contains the following basic information:

1. name[s] of author[s] in inverted order with only the initials of first or middle names
2. date of publication in parentheses and followed by a period
3. title of the article *not* enclosed in quotation marks, followed by a period

4. publication information:
   a. name of the journal underlined to indicate italics with each important word capitalized, followed by a comma
   b. volume number underlined, followed by a comma
   c. page references, followed by a period

SAMPLE PERIODICAL ENTRIES

Braby, R., & Kincard, J. P. (1981). Computer aided authoring and editing. Journal of Educational Technology Systems. 10(2), 109–123.

Gallini, J. K. (1983, April). What computer-assisted instruction can offer toward the encouragement of creative thinking. Educational Technology, pp. 7–11.

Gardner, H. (1980, April). Composing symphonies and dinner parties. Psychology Today, pp. 18–25.

Johnson, C. (1983, March). Problem solving: Your key to creative thinking. Media & Methods, pp. 12–14.

Klein, R. D. (1982). An inquiry into the factors related to creativity. The Elementary School Journal, 82, 256–265.

Teachers' interest in computers. (1982, May). Instructor, pp. 76–77.

Here is a brief sample reference list; examine the order in which the entries appear:

Brown, R. (1970). *Social psychology.* New York: Free Press.
Brown, R., & Bellugi, U. (1964). Three processes in the child's acquisition of syntax. *Harvard Educational Review. 34*, 133–151.
Cofer, C. (1960). Experimental studies in the role of verbal processes in concept formation and problem solving. *Annals of the New York Academy of Science, 91*, 94–107.

Cofer, C. N. (Ed.). (1961). *Verbal learning and verbal behavior*. New York: McGraw-Hill.

Cofer, C. N., & Musgrove, B. S. (Eds.). (1963). *Verbal behavior and learning: problems and processes*. New York: McGraw-Hill, 1963.

Miller, G. A., & McKean, K. O. (1964). A chronometric study of some relations between sentences. *Quarterly Journal of Experimental Psychology*, *16*, 297–308.

Miller, G. A., & McNeill, D. (1969). Psycholinguistics. In G. Lindzey & E. Aronson (Eds.), *The handbook of social psychology* (2nd ed.), Vol. 3. (pp. 666–794). Reading, MA: Addison-Wesley.

Piaget, J. (1954). *The construction of reality in the child*. New York: Basic Books.

Piaget, J. (1962a). *Comments on Vygotsky's critical remarks concerning "The Language and Thought of the Child" and "Judgement and Reasoning in the Child."* Cambridge, MA: M.I.T. Press.

Piaget, J. (1962b). *Play, dreams and imitation in childhood*. New York: Norton.

The above sample reference list illustrates the following points:

1. All names are listed in inverted order.
2. When citing more than one work by the same first author observe these guidelines:
   a. Type out the author's name in each instance.
   b. Place single-author entries before multiple-author entries (see Brown entry above).
   c. Alphabetize by the surname of the second author when the first author is the same for two entries (see Miller entry above).
   d. Arrange multiple works by one author chronologically (see the Piaget entries above).
   e. Arrange multiple works by the same author published in the same year alphabetically by the first important word of the title (excluding "the" or "a") and place a lower-case letter in parentheses after the final period of the entry (see 1962 Piaget entries above).

For additional kinds of reference list entry forms, consult the *Publication Manual of the American Psychological Association*.

The following is a portion of a student's research paper. Study this portion carefully to note how sources are cited in the parenthetical references.

1 Place the title of the article at the top of each page, flush with the right-hand margin. The title of this paper by Angela Moore clearly relates to the thesis statement. Place the page number two lines below the title, aligned with the title at the right-hand margin.

2 Center the word Abstract two lines below the page number. Begin the paper two lines below this title.

3 Moore begins her paper with a series of facts showing how computers are becoming widely used.

4 Moore cites her source for the information from this survey. Since the article is unsigned, she uses a shortened form of the title. Notice that a comma comes between the shortened title and the year.

5 Moore's next source of information is an article by Schneiderman. Since she cites the author's name in the text, she includes only the year of the article in her reference.

6 Moore next uses a quotation by Andrew R. Molnar, whom she identifies. This quotation appears in an unsigned article. Since she uses the title of the article in the text, she includes only the year in her reference.

7 Moore found the next fact in two sources. Therefore, she cites both these sources in her parenthetical reference. Notice that a semicolon separates the sources.

8 Moore ends the paragraph with her thesis statement, which connects computers to creativity.

Computers and Creativity

2

Abstract

In 1981, Instructor, a magazine directed toward ele-

mentary school teachers, surveyed its readers to discover

their reactions to computers and how they felt computers

were affecting their lives. Of the more than 4,000

respondents, 86% had a high interest in computers and 39%

were already using them in school ("Teachers' Interest,"

1982). Schneiderman (1983) found that a typical high

school now has five computers, and this number is steadily

growing. In fact, in the article "Trying to Predict the

Future" (1984) Andrew R. Molnar, Program Manager in the

Division of Science Education Development and Research at

the National Science Foundation, states: "It used to be

that you couldn't have a school unless you had books and

a library; now you can't have a school of excellence with-

out having a computer or a computer-based system." Com-

puters are in the schools and their place is secure. Right

now, they are being used mainly to teach computer literacy

and for drill and practice (Schneiderman, 1983; Peterson,

1984). However, these uses overlook the unique capabili-

ties of computers that make them unparalleled tools for

enhancing a child's creativity.

9 | Moore provides transition between paragraphs by repeating the word creativity from the thesis statement at the start of the second paragraph.

10 | Moore cites the source for the quoted words. The citation appears immediately after the quoted words, since the rest of the sentence contains Moore's own thoughts. Since the author is not cited in the text, Moore uses both the author's name and the year in the citation.

11 | Moore summarizes information from a book written by two authors. The last name of both authors appears in the reference, joined by an ampersand.

12 | Moore reinforces the information from Alper & Holmberg with information from another source.

13 | Since Moore uses a special term here, she cites its source.

| 9 |

Creativity has been described as the ability to do

such divergent tasks as "composing symphonies and dinner

| 10 |

parties" (Gardner, 1980), choreographing dances and foot-

ball plays. What factors are inherent in creativity?

What makes some people gifted artists and others drones?

Johnson (1983) defines problem solving as a key to cre-

ativity. Certainly providing a problem for students to

solve in an open-ended fashion leads to greater student

involvement and the possibility of creative solutions.

Computers, if used with open-ended programs, can develop

| 11 |

skills in problem solving and logical thinking (Alper &

Holmberg, 1984). They can provide students with a struc-

ture that allows them to select, discover, and test alter-

| 12 |

nate strategies (Gallini, 1984). Computer simulations

allow children to enter worlds that might otherwise be

closed to them, worlds in which they can test and control

real-life variables (Alper & Holmberg, 1984). These simu-

lations create an environment in which children are free

to make mistakes, to change their minds, to explore possi-

| 13 |

bilities. They put children in a "freewheeling" frame of

mind, another factor considered necessary for creativity

(Davis, 1973).

14 Moore uses the author's name in the text here to emphasize the source. Notice that the citation appears at the end of the quotation, not after the author's name.

14   Turkle considers the computer "an evocative object, an
object that fascinates, disturbs equanimity, and precipi-
tates thought" (1984). This evocative quality accounts for
the computer's holding power. For computers to be effective, children must want to spend time with them. Anyone
who has observed a child in a computer game arcade has wit-
nessed the computer's holding power. This holding power,
if used properly, creates the conditions necessary for
other valuable things to happen (Turkle, 1984). Because
children are fascinated by computers, they will work at
them actively. They will formulate questions and test
solutions. They become "real inquirers rather than lesson
learners" (Gallini, 1983).

15   Place the title of the paper at the top of the page. Place the page number two lines below the title. Align at the right-hand margin.

16   Center the word References four lines below the page number.

17   Begin the entries two lines below the heading. Start at the left-hand margin. Indent subsequent lines three spaces. This is an entry for a book by two authors.

18   This is an entry for a book by one author.

19   This is an entry for an article in a monthly magazine. The article is by one author.

20   This is an entry for an unsigned article in a monthly magazine.

15

Computers and Creativity

12

16

References

17

Alper, L., & Holmberg, M. (1984). Parents, kids, and

computers: Learning adventures beyond the classroom.

Berkeley: SYBEX.

18

Davis, G. (1973). Psychology of Problem Solving. New

York: Basic Books.

19

Gallini, J. K. (1983, April). What computer-assisted

instruction can offer toward the encouragement of

creative thinking. Educational Technology, pp. 7-11.

Gardner, H. (1980, April). Composing symphonies and

dinner parties. Psychology Today, pp. 18-25.

Johnson, C. (1983, March). Problem solving: Your key to

creative thinking. Media & Methods, pp. 12-14.

Peterson, D. (1984, mid-October). Nine issues: Will

education be different (better) in the year 2000?

Popular Computing, pp. 10-18.

Schneiderman, M. (1984, mid-March). Making the case

for innovation. Popular Computing, pp. 88-95.

Turkle, S. (1984). The second self: Computers and the

human spirit. New York: Simon and Schuster.

20

"Teachers' interest in computers." (1982, May).

Instructor, pp. 76-77.

Trying to predict the future. (1984, mid-October).

Popular Computing, pp. 30-44.

ABBREVIATIONS FOR REFERENCE WORDS

The following abbreviations are commonly used in scholarly writing. You are likely to use some of them in your paper and you will most certainly run across them in your reading. The list does not include abbreviations for dates (Jan., Sept., 20th century) or countries and states; both frequently make their way into notes and bibliographies. Latin abbreviations needn't be underlined in your paper, although you may find them italicized in your reading. Most contemporary writers try to use English equivalents when Latin terms are cumbersome or confusing (see the discussion of Latin abbreviations on pages 174–175). Recent usage indicates that the space between capital letters and the periods used after them are often eliminated. Hence you are likely to encounter AD for A.D. or NY for N.Y. Notice the spacing and use of periods in the items listed below:

acad.	academy
A.D.	*anno Domini:* "in the year of our Lord"; precedes numerals (A.D. 204)
anon.	anonymous
app.	appendix
art., arts.	article(s)
assn.	association
assoc.	associate, associated
b.	born
B.C.	before Christ; follows numerals (51 B.C.)
bibliog.	bibliography, bibliographer, bibliographical
biog.	biography, biographer, biographical
bk., bks.	book(s)
bull.	bulletin
©	copyright (© 1981)
c., ca.	*circa:* "about"; used to indicate approximate dates (c. 1855)
cf.	*confer:* "compare"; used to compare one source with another; does not mean "see"
ch., chs. (or chap., chaps.)	chapter(s)
col., cols.	column(s)
comp., comps.	compiled by, compiler(s)
Cong.	Congress
Cong. Rec.	*Congressional Record*

d.	died
DAB	*Dictionary of American Biography*
dir., dirs.	directed by, director(s)
diss.	dissertation
DNB	*Dictionary of National Biography*
ed., eds.	edited by, editor(s), edition(s)
e.g.	*exempli gratia:* "for example"; preceded and followed by a comma
enl.	enlarged (as in "rev. and enl. ed.")
esp.	especially (as in "129–35, esp. 130")
et al.	*et alii:* "and others"
et seq.	*et sequens, sequentia:* "and the following." A reference to "25 et seq." means 25 and the following page(s). See also "f., ff." below.
etc.	*et cetera:* "and so forth." Do not use in the text of the paper.
ex., exs.	example(s)
f., ff.	and the following. It is better to use exact references: 55–56 instead of 55ff.; 57–62 instead of 57ff. But use ff. for a magazine or newspaper article with scattered page numbers.
fig., figs.	figure(s)
govt.	government
GPO	Government Printing Office (U.S.)
hist.	history, historian, historical
ibid.	*ibidem:* "in the same place," the immediately preceding title. Avoid using; see pages 174–175.
i.e.	*id est:* "that is." Do not use in text.
illus.	illustrated (by), illustrator, illustration(s)
inst.	institution
introd.	introduction; introduced by; (author of) introduction
jour.	journal
l., ll.	line(s)
L.C.	Library of Congress (U.S.)
loc. cit.	*loco citato:* "in the place cited." Used to cite the same passage referred to in a recent note. Avoid using; see pages 174–175.

mag.	magazine
ms, mss	manuscript(s). Capitalize and follow with a period when referring to a specific manuscript.
n., nn.	note(s). Write as "45n4."
nar., narrs.	narrated by, narrator(s)
N.B.	*nota bene:* "take notice, mark well"
n.d.	no date of publication
NED.	*New English Dictionary*
no., nos.	number(s)
n.p.	no place of publication, no publisher
n. pag.	no pagination
OED	*Oxford English Dictionary*
op.	opus, a work
op. cit.	*opere citato:* "in the work cited." Avoid using; see pages 174–175.
orch.	orchestra, orchestrated by
p., pp.	page(s)
par., pars.	paragraph(s)
passim	"throughout the work, here and there" (as in "21, 24, et passim")
philol.	philological
philos.	philosophical
pl., pls.	plate(s)
pref.	preface
proc.	proceedings
prod., prods.	produced by, producer(s)
pseud.	pseudonym
pt., pts.	part(s)
pub. (or publ.), pubs.	published by, publication(s)
q.v.	*quod vide:* "which see"; used as a cross-reference
rev.	revised (by), revision; review, reviewed (by). Spell out if confusing in context.
rpt.	reprinted (by), reprint
sc.	scene
sec., secs. (or sect., sects.)	section(s)
ser.	series
sic	"thus, so." Used between brackets to indicate an error in a quoted passage; see page 87.
soc.	society

st., sts.	stanza(s)
St., Sts.	Saint(s)
supp., supps.	supplement(s)
TLS	typed letter signed
trans. (or tr.)	translated by, translator, translation
ts	typescript. Cf. "ms."
U	University
UP	University Press
v.	*vide:* "see"
v., vs.	versus: "against." Cf. "v., vv."
v., vv. (or vs., vss.)	verse(s)
vol., vols.	volume(s).

9 Sample Research Paper

The sample research paper that follows includes an outline, the complete text of a paper, notes, and a list of works cited. The sample paper illustrates the parenthetical documentation system used in the *MLA Handbook for Writers of Research Papers* (1984). The facing pages discuss various elements of the paper and the strategies used in putting it together. Although the sample paper illustrates much of the advice offered in this book, no paper can incorporate all the possible choices you will have to make as you write your own. To answer any questions that are not covered in the sample paper, use the index of this book to locate information presented in the preceding chapters.

A reading of the sample paper and accompanying comments will provide you with a useful overview of the concerns you should keep in mind as you type the final draft. You might also want to check with your instructor to see if he or she keeps on file sample student papers that you can consult.

Alger's Novels: Remembered but Not Read

By

Timothy Matthews

English 101-102

Professor Ryan

March 17, 1984

The Final Outline

1 If your final outline must be handed in with the paper, place it between the title page and the text of the paper. Use lower-case Roman numerals to number the pages of the outline (though you don't have to number them at all), but do not number the first page; begin with page ii.

2 The title precedes the thesis statement. The thesis statement needn't be worded exactly the same way in the paper; compare this thesis statement with the last three sentences of the first paragraph in the sample paper. Notice that the thesis provides a rationale for what is included in the outline and the order in which it appears. Once Matthews establishes that Alger's novels are all similar in content in section I, he focuses on a representative novel in sections II and III to illustrate his points. Sections IV and V then contrast earlier reactions with contemporary reactions to Alger's novels.

3 This particular outline is in sentence form. Depending on what is required, your outline could be a sentence or topic outline or a combination of both.

1

2 Alger's Novels: Remembered but Not Read

Thesis: Although Alger's novels are all basically alike and
badly written, they were popular at the turn of the
century when his stories seemed more believable to
Americans than they do today.

3 I.   Alger wrote more than 100 novels that tell the same
basic story.

    A.   The central character is a poor boy who climbs up
the ladder of success because he is ambitious,
hardworking, and virtuous.

    B.   The villains lack all the virtues of the hero and
are eventually punished for their misdeeds.

II.   The plot and characters of <u>Digging for Gold</u> represent
a typical Alger story.

    A.   The hero performs a brave deed and is rewarded.

    B.   A lucky break puts the hero in contact with a
benefactor who can help him become independent of
a mean stepfather.

    C.   Falsely accused of wrongdoing, the hero proves
his honesty, and the villain is exposed.

4   Each major division of the outline (indicated by Roman numerals) is related to the thesis statement, and each subdivision under a particular major division is related to that major division. Hence, section III.F.2. concerning Alger's wordiness and redundancies is related to his padding (F), which illustrates his typically bad writing (III) and which is noted in the thesis.

ii

D. The hero's virtue is rewarded with material

success, which he uses to help others.

III. The quality of Alger's writing in <u>Digging for Gold</u> is

poor and typical of his work.

A. His use of exposition is mechanical.

B. His action scenes are dull.

C. He sometimes forgets what his characters have

done.

D. He sometimes forgets what he has named a

character.

E. He uses words that are too formal for their

context.

F. He pads his writing to fill up a page.

1. He uses a long unnecessary quotation.

$\boxed{4}$ 2. He uses wordy constructions and redundancies.

IV. When his books were popular at the turn of the cen-

tury, Alger's readers were concerned with the lessons

to be learned from his novels, not their style.

A. The books were inspirational to the sons of

immigrant parents.

B. The books appealed to America's faith in upward

mobility and a prosperous future.

5 Neither conclusions nor introductions are labeled in outlines.

iii

C. The books demonstrated the value of self-reliant
individualism.

D. The books accounted for why some people succeeded
while others failed.

1. Alger was not an apologist for social
Darwinism.

2. Alger had a social consciousness.

5   V. Alger's novels seem irrelevant to most Americans
today.

A. The contemporary response to Alger may reveal
something about contemporary America.

B. Alger's heroes are no longer believable but they
are still remembered.

6 | Number all pages, including the first page of the paper. Center the title two inches from the top of the page and begin the text four spaces below the title. Matthews's title is clearly related to his thesis and serves as a useful way to prepare the reader for the subject matter of this introductory paragraph. Double space the text.

7 | No source is indicated for the date of Alger's death or the "common expression," because such information is regarded as common knowledge.

8 | Matthews uses a raised number to indicate an endnote that both cites the source of his information and provides a qualification of it.

9 | Matthews quotes only a portion of a passage and leads into it smoothly.

10 | The source is named in the text in order to emphasize its recognized authority.

11 | Since the reference is to an unsigned article in a work arranged alphabetically, it is cited by a shortened form of the title and no page number is given.

1

6

Alger's Novels: Remembered but Not Read

7   Although Horatio Alger, Jr. died in 1899, his name

lives on in the twentieth century, because he created in his

novels characters who rose from rags to riches. The "Hora-

tio Alger hero" is a common expression in our language that

has become synonymous with the self-made American who

achieves success through ambition, hard work, perserverence,

intelligence, and virtue. Alger was as persistent as his

heroes. In more than 100 novels he told the same basic

story of a young boy who overcomes whatever obstacles are in

8 his way on the road to getting ahead.[1] His novels were

eagerly bought by thousands of readers even though his

9 "prose is often laughable" (Scharnhorst 73). The New

10 Encyclopaedia Britannica describes Alger as the "most

popular author in the U.S. in the last 30 years of the 19th

century and perhaps the most influential writer of his gen-

11 eration" ("Alger"). Estimates of the total sales of Alger's

novels since their publication range from 15 million to 300

million, with the greatest concentration of sales occurring

12   Matthews's name is placed before the page number to prevent confusion in case the pages become separated.

13   Matthews states his thesis in the paragraph's last three sentences, which elaborate on the thesis statement at the beginning of the outline instead of merely repeating the thesis. Although this introductory paragraph is a little longer than most, it is unified, coherent, and, therefore, effective.

14   This paragraph corresponds to section I of the outline. In the introductory paragraph Matthews briefly touched on what a typical novel consists of, but here it is discussed in more detail. A lot of ground is covered by incorporating a number of Alger's titles into this description to make the generalizations convincing.

15   Notice that the note numbers run consecutively throughout the text; they are not renumbered for each page nor is the same number used again when a source is cited more than once. Because Matthews refers to "nearly all" critics in the text, he cites several representative ones in note 2 at the end of the paper.

12

13

from approximately 1900 to 1910 (Falk 151). Despite the

predictable plots and bad writing that characterize his

novels, Alger's books were read more than those of the

great novelists contemporary to him such as Mark Twain,

Henry James, or Stephen Crane. Today, however, Alger's

work has been reduced to an allusion in the American mind;

he is invoked rather than read. Alger's popularity has

declined, because the world he created in his books no

longer seems possible to Americans.

14

   What is a typical Alger novel? Fortunately, Alger's

limitations as a writer make this question easier to answer

than if he had been a subtle and complex novelist. Though

he wrote scores of novels, the essential plot of each veri-

fies what nearly all his critics point out: "If you've

15

read one Alger novel you've read them all."[2] Many of his

titles suggest the conflicts that his heroes encounter and

the virtues that allow the heroes to overcome those con-

flicts. The typical Alger plot can be told almost entirely

through the use of his titles: With The Odds Against Him,

but The World Before Him, a Brave and Bold poor boy, Shift-

ing for Himself, sets out to Strive and Succeed by Forging

Ahead. Though his father is dead, he is a Child of Fortune

16 Here is a note card with information that Matthews did not incorporate into the paper, but he did use indirectly one of the ideas from it, and so it is acknowledged in note 3.

Heroes/virtues of   *Curti   629*

Alger composed an autograph for one of his readers by stringing together titles from his novels:

"*Strive* and *Succeed*, the world's temptations flee—
Be *Brave* and *Bold*, and *Strong* and *Steady* be.
Go *Slow* and *Sure*, and prosper then you must —
With *Fame* and *Fortune*, while you *Try* and *Trust*."

---

17 Matthews provides a smooth transition from the typical Alger plot to the particular novel he discusses (section II of the outline). Notice that his choice of the first person avoids awkward constructions such as "This writer's reading. . . ." If his instructor preferred that the first person not be used in the paper, Matthews could have written something like: "A reading of . . . confirms this basic formula."

Matthews 3

because his faithful mother has taught him to Wait and Hope.

Knowing he must Sink or Swim, his Do and Dare, as well as

his Luck and Pluck, help him in Making His Way. Seeking His

Fortune, this Strong and Steady lad moves Up the Ladder

because he is not afraid to Try and Trust. Unlike his

rivals who smoke, drink, or gamble, the hero is Bound to

Rise because he lives clean and neither cheats nor lies;

instead he rescues a rich man's daughter or returns a rich

man's wallet, thus Making His Mark. Thereafter, though his

progress may be Slow and Sure, he knows that he can Wait

and Win. By Helping Himself he is, by the end of the story,

inevitably Risen from the Ranks.[3]

16

My own reading of Alger's Digging for Gold: A Story of

California confirms this basic formula. The hero, sixteen-

17

year-old Grant Colburn, saves a train from a disastrous

wreck. The reward money he receives for this brave deed

allows him to leave his stepfather's tyrannical rule for

the wide-open spaces and the opportunities awaiting him in

California. As he travels from Iowa to California in his

new twenty-dollar suit, he endures starvation and encoun-

ters cheats and savages, but equipped with his forthright

values and aided by a fatherly benefactor he meets in the

18 Matthews wisely quotes an appropriate line from the novel to rein-force and summarize the points he makes about the basic Alger formula. Since the author's name (and in this case the title) are mentioned in the text, only the page number is included in the parenthetical reference.

19 Though Matthews summarizes instead of quoting his source here, a parenthetical reference documenting the information is nonetheless necessary.

wilderness, he makes it to the promised land. Happy in

California, Grant works hard, avoids whiskey and gambling,

and manages to clear himself of charges that he stole some

money. Once the real thief is exposed, Grant strikes it

rich on a claim given to him by yet another benefactor.

Soon after he establishes himself, he hears of his mother's

financial problems back in Iowa. He returns just in time

to save her farm from being foreclosed. The pompous and

haughty characters are punished while the virtuous are

rewarded. As Grant's mother says in the concluding lines

of the novel: Grant "had good habits and the qualities that

18 insure success" (197). Although, as John Seelye points out

in his introduction, this novel lacks the "realistic,

detailed reporting of New York City life which is asso-

ciated with Alger's most famous books" (xvii), Digging for

Gold is typical of Alger's work in its plot, characters,

and style.

    Many commentators have been awed by the amount of

writing Alger produced, but no one seems to have been

impressed by the quality of his prose. He wrote fast and

often, rarely revising and sometimes working on several

19 stories at the same time (Gardner 335-36). This method of

20 │ For a discussion of the note card Matthews wrote that includes this quotation, see pages 64–68.

21 │ This paragraph corresponds to section III.A. of the outline and begins the evidence Matthews uses to support his assertion that the quality of Alger's prose is poor.

22 │ Matthews provides a context that prepares for the long quotation, and he uses a colon to introduce it.

23 │ Quotations of more than four lines are set off from the text of the paper. Indent ten spaces from the left-hand margin; triple space before and after the quotation so that it is set off from the text; double space the quotation. Notice that quotation marks are used in this instance only because the quoted passage is dialog. The parenthetical reference comes at the end of the passage; the period is placed inside the quotation and before the parentheses, with no punctuation following the closing parentheses.

Matthews 5

20 composition resulted in his creating what one critic has
described as "a monument to bad taste" (Fink 16), a widely

shared assessment that has gone undisputed. Readers of

Alger's boy novels were not bothered by his writing--he

wrote, after all, for boys rather than critics--but even

inexperienced readers must have noticed some of his many

mistakes. Digging for Gold yields enough writing problems

to flunk a good-sized creative writing class for an entire

semester's work.

21 Alger's use of exposition--the background information

necessary for introducing the characters and their circum-

stances--is often mechanical and painfully obvious.

Digging for Gold begins on Grant's sixteenth birthday. The

reader hears sturdy Grant and his widowed mother discussing

how their lives have changed since she married Mr. Tarbox

four years earlier. She had hoped Mr. Tarbox would provide

them with a "comfortable home," but instead he turned out

22 to be stingy and, as Grant tells us, a mean stepfather:

23   "A comfortable home!" repeated Grant. "We had

        enough to eat, it is true, but you never worked

        so hard in your life, and I can say the same for

        myself. I was barely fourteen when Mr. Tarbox

24 A new paragraph does not follow the quotation because Matthews's comments here are directly related to the quotation.

25 Brackets are used to show that Matthews added words to clarify the quotation.

26 For brief quotations not set apart from the text, the parenthetical reference is followed by a period.

took me away from school and since then I have

had to work early and late. At five o'clock,

winter and summer, I have to turn out of bed,

and work all day, so that when night comes I

am dead tired." (2)

24 This background information is useful for the reader, but

it is hardly credible that Grant's mother needs to be told

what her son's daily schedule has been for the past two

years.

Action scenes are also a problem for Alger. Perhaps

the most violent episode in Digging for Gold occurs when

Grant and his friends are attacked by Indians on their way

to California. Grant's brave companion, Tom Cooper,

remains calm even though their party is outnumbered two to

one by the Indians: "He raised his rifle, and aiming at

the foremost Indian, fired deliberately. The redskin fell,

pierced to the heart." In the next sentence Alger informs

25
26 his reader that "This appeared to strike his [the Indian's]

companions with dismay" (54). The wording of this sentence

makes it seem as if the Indian were slighted by an insult

rather than shot to death. Instead of being exciting for

the reader, the scene is eminently forgettable, which

27 Here is a portion of Matthews's draft of this paragraph and the corrections he made that led to the final version:

---

(135), and no one seems to mind--or notice. ~ *new ¶* Alger's

~*conscious*
choices are sometimes as much of a problem as his

absent-mindedness
~forgetting.~ His descriptive passages are ~sometimes~ *occasionally*

curious because of   chooses
~hilarious owing to~ the words he ~uses.~ Here he is de-

scribing thirsty travelers: "Now the oxen, and the horse,

as well as themselves, were allowed to drink ad libitum"

(61). ~Unnecessary words as well as inappropriate words~

                                                      e
~make their way into Alger's novels.~ The inappropriatness

         diction   *his*
of this ~word~ is less obvious than ~Alger's~ description of a
                              which he calls
device used for sifting gold, ~called~ a "long tom," *however,*
                        a "long tom"
*W*hen a character asks what ~it~ is, Alger steps in with:

Matthews uses triple spacing (though he missed one line) to leave room for revisions.

seems to have been Alger's response to the battle also.

Twenty-four chapters later he describes Grant as "strongly

impressed" by witnessing the shooting of a robber, because

he had never "seen a death by violence before" (166). Alger

was no stickler for consistency. He also has a minor

character call his wife "Martha" (130) and then "Rebecca"

in the next chapter (135), and no one seems to mind--or

notice.

27

Alger's conscious choices are sometimes as much of a

problem as his absent-mindedness. His descriptive passages

are occasionally curious because of the words he chooses.

Here he is describing thirsty travelers: "Now the oxen, and

the horse, as well as themselves, were allowed to drink ad

libitum" (61). The inappropriateness of this diction is

less obvious, however, than his description of a device used

for sifting gold, which he calls a "long tom." When a char-

acter asks Tom Cooper what a "long tom" is, Alger steps in

with: "I won't give Tom's answer, but quote a more accurate

description from an English book published in 1857 . . ."

(114). Alger's direct quotation of a textbook definition

goes on for some 200 words and has the virtue of being not

only accurate but also a convenient way to fill up a page.

28 Several representative examples constitute convincing evidence that Alger frequently pads his work. Ellipses are used to indicate that the passages are not quoted in their entirety. Four periods serve to mark the omission and the end of each sentence.

29 The parenthetical reference documents the information that precedes it, beginning with "Russel B. Nye offers. . . ." This framing allows the reader to see precisely what Matthews borrowed from Nye and what Matthews supplies himself.

30 The final sentence of the preceding paragraph effectively leads into the discussion of the advertisement that emphasizes the content of Alger's books over their style. This paragraph begins section IV of the outline.

If Alger's juvenile books had been edited for concise-
ness, they might have been more nearly the length of short

stories instead of novels. His characters are never simply

hungry; instead they feel "a perpetual craving for food"

(61). Alger's wordiness is related to his need to fill up

the space on a page. Russel B. Nye offers several examples

of padding from other novels that are particularly inter-

esting, because most readers probably overlook them as they

are reading. The padding is obvious, however, when the

lines are reread in isolation. Here is Alger introducing

28 a character: "Tom Thatcher, for such was his name. . . ."

And here is how he indicates the passage of time: "Five

years have passed. Walter, now older. . . ." That Alger

left little to his reader's imagination is evident in his

description of two characters pulled from a river, "both

29 dripping with water" (qtd. in Nye 69). His careless

writing and inflated style offer enduring evidence that

his readers were more concerned with what he had to say

than how he said it.

30 An advertisement for Alger's works published in 1911

emphasizes the educational value of the books without

ever mentioning their style:

31 See Matthews's interesting aside for note 4 in the endnotes.

32 The repetition of "wholesome lessons" from the quotation signals its importance in Matthews's discussion. Notice how Matthews uses "lesson" in the first sentence of each of the next three paragraphs. This repetition makes it easy for the reader to follow the discussion.

33 The ellipsis indicates words were omitted from Meehan's sentence because Matthews did not regard them as essential to his point. The information from Meehan could easily have been summarized instead of quoted; the wording is not especially vivid or important. The same point could have been made, for example, this way:

Thomas Meehan suggests that Alger's novels encouraged the sons of recently arrived immigrants to believe that their expectations for success would almost certainly be fulfilled (23).

Matthews 9

Alger's books go to the right spot every time.
Their high moral character, clean, manly tone,
and the wholesome lessons they teach make Alger
books as acceptable to the parents as to the boys.

31 His characters are living boys who do things.[4]

32 This advertisement appeared when Alger's books were at the
height of their popularity. The "wholesome lessons" they
taught were very much related to the changes that were
taking place in the United States around the turn of the
century.

One of those lessons seems to have been aimed at the
many immigrants who poured into America with the hope of
achieving success. Thomas Meehan suggests that Alger's

33 novels "assured first-generation American boys of immigrant
parents that this was not only possible but . . . highly
probable (23). Such faith in upward mobility was attractive
to all Americans—not just the sons of immigrants—who
wanted to believe that the self-made heroes Alger created
affirmed the promise of America as a land of limitless
possibility and growth (Coyle viii). Alger's characters
are made over by their successes; they wear new clothes,

34 | By referring to *Digging for Gold* at the end of the paragraph, Matthews anchors a fairly general discussion to a specific example.

35 | Matthews's discussion of Alger's concern with "self-reform rather than social reform" needs to be developed more. The topic is hurriedly dispatched without any examples. Like Grant's stepfather, Matthews is too stingy here. If the discussion had been developed more, then the sentence following the cited information would begin a new paragraph; it too, however, seems undeveloped. This section is the weakest link in the paper.

sport new expensive watches, and see themselves having new

34 futures.   In Digging for Gold, Grant Colburn even seems to

have a new body at the end of the story—he's grown taller

by three inches (191).

Besides presenting America as a land of economic and

social opportunity, another important lesson that Alger's

novels teach is that individuals can rise above their own

circumstances.   The reality of America was that big cities

and big business dwarfed the individual, who seemed to be

shrinking in importance, but Alger's books, according to

Nye, showed that self-reliance was still rewarded in

America, even at a time when "a swiftly developing mass

society" seemed to be indifferent to individual efforts

(63).   By emphasizing individualism, Alger also pro-

vided an explanation of why some people did not succeed.

The characters in his books who fail usually have some

personal flaw, such as drinking, that makes them per-

sonally responsible for their misery.   Alger seems pri-

35 marily concerned with self-reform rather than social

reform (Coyle viii).   This primary focus on individualism

should not be seen, however, as a way to transform Alger

into a spokesman for the Robber Barons or the social

36 This parenthetical reference includes a joint reference. It would have been more effective to have included this joint reference in a note indicating that Fink and Scharnhorst discuss Alger's social consciousness.

37 This lengthy quotation is worth having because it provides a helpful summary for section IV in the outline and because it is so concise that it would be difficult to unpack economically. Matthews uses long quotations sparingly in the paper (there are only three), and he does not string together quoted passages to avoid having to write his own prose.

38 Matthews's discussion following the Cawelti quotation serves as a transition to section V, the final part of the paper in which he argues that contemporary Americans find Alger's lessons "quaint" rather than inspirational.

36 Darwinists. He was too much of a moralist to endorse a
dog-eat-dog world (Fink 21-26; Scharnhorst 43, 117). In
Digging for Gold, Grant is eager to make his fortune, but
money is not an end in itself: "If I am rich," says Grant,
"I can help others. That will make me happy" (71).

The lessons that appear in Alger's novels are best
summarized by John Cawelti:

37
> Alger is a teacher of traditional manners and
> morals rather than an exponent of free enter-
> prise. His fictions embody the values that
> middle-class Americans have been taught to
> revere: honesty, hard work, familial loyalty;
> good manners, cleanliness, and neatness of
> appearance; kindness and generosity to the
> less fortunate; loyalty and deference on the
> part of employees, and consideration and per-
> sonal interest on the part of employers. (121)

38 For readers of the 1980s, this summary may help to explain
why Alger's writing has been described as "a major pump
station on the pipe line that carried the American dream"
(Fink 30), but it may also make Alger's novels seem some-
what quaint and innocent.

39   Technically, Matthews is quoting out of context here, but his humor is too obvious for his reader to mistake his intentions. The quotation is clearly used for ironic purposes; there is no attempt to suggest that Alger found his own values hard to believe.

40   This paragraph and the following concluding paragraph speculate on how most Americans must feel after finding Alger's world unbelievable and his values inoperative. The purpose of these two paragraphs is, then, to discuss the significance of the thesis presented in the introductory paragraph.

Matthews 12

It is not difficult to understand why the sales of

Alger's books crashed along with the stock market in 1929

(Scharnhorst 141). Since the Depression, his novels have

offered the few Americans who have read them more a sense

of nostalgia rather than hope. Inflation, unemployment,

interest rates, multi-national corporations, and the world's

economy make Alger's assumptions and values seem terribly

vulnerable. As Grant's friend Tom says in Digging for Gold:

39 "This seems like a fairy tale" (123). For Alger's readers--

both young and old--the real world had a fabulous potential

some seventy or eighty years ago, but, according to one

important recent social critic, many Americans today feel

a sense of diminished expectations rather than a sense of

nearly limitless opportunities and possibilities (Lasch

52-53).

40 It is easy to laugh at Alger's bad writing, his wooden

characters, and the melodramatic episodes that fall flat,

but if we also laugh at his basic values, the joke may be

on us too. If Alger's heroes seem unbelievable to us, his

villains sound familiar enough. Cawelti reminds us that

they are the ones who "are disloyal to their families and

often try to cheat their relatives; they are avaricious,

41 Matthews has established the validity of his thesis that Alger's heroes are only a vague memory for most Americans, but he concludes with a slight qualification that challenges his own thesis by pointing out that a President of the United States was, in a sense, a typical Horatio Alger hero. (Matthews relies on Reagan's background as common knowledge.) The paper ends with an especially vivid detail — what Mark Twain used to call a "snapper." Matthews's conclusion is not designed to settle definitively the issues he raises; instead it is organized so that it ends on a provocative note.

miserly, and usurious; and they lack integrity and are

unscrupulous in business affairs" (Cawelti 121). We can

laugh at Alger's prose, but there is no fun in realizing

that his villains now seem to thrive while his heroes

appear a little silly.

41

Alger's stories are no longer widely read or believ-

able, but his heroes are still remembered--even if the

kind of success they represent does not seem to be avail-

able to most Americans today. There is, however, at

least one bit of striking evidence that the Alger hero has

not completely disappeared. Since 1947 the American

Schools and Colleges Association has sponsored an annual

Horatio Alger Award for individuals whose achievements are

based on ambition, hard work, luck, and pluck. The recip-

ients have been mostly conservative businessmen, religious

leaders, politicians, and entertainers. Depending on one's

own politics, this information may be cause for rejoicing

or dismay, but it is interesting, nevertheless, that one

recipient of the Horatio Alger Award was none other than

Ronald Reagan (Scharnhorst 144).

Number the first page of the Notes section as a continuation of the text. Center the heading one inch from the top of the page and begin the first note two spaces below. Indent the first line of each note five spaces and use a raised number that matches the number used in the text. When proofreading, check carefully to make certain that the numbers match.

Note 1. This information is identified as coming from the preface, because the pages of the preface are unnumbered. Additional information concerning the number of novels Alger wrote is provided in the note rather than in the text of the paper, because, though it is useful information, it is not directly related to a discussion of Alger's popularity.

Note 2. When citing more than one source in a note, separate the sources with a semicolon.

Note 3. Matthews acknowledges in this explanatory note that he has borrowed an idea and used it for his own purposes. Although he has not used any facts or actual wording from the source, he has used the strategy of the source, and so it must be acknowledged.

Note 4. The additional information in this note would not have been relevant to the discussion in the text, but Matthews apparently felt that it was too interesting and surprising to omit.

Matthews 14

Notes

[1]Scharnhorst, preface n.p. Estimates vary concerning the number of juvenile novels Alger wrote. For example, Hart refers to "nearly 130 popular books for boys" (19), but Scharnhorst, who has studied the question more recently and more carefully than anyone else, indicates that Alger wrote 103 juvenile novels.

[2]See, for example, Huber 44; Henderson 32; and Zuckerman, 191.

[3]I have adapted the idea of using titles to describe the virtues of Alger's heroes from a four-line autograph Alger wrote for an admiring reader in which he strung together a half dozen titles from his novels; the auto-graph is quoted in Curti 629. I am also indebted to Scharnhorst's description of the typical Alger plot (67-68).

[4]The advertisement appears on an unnumbered page at the end of another boy's book by Oliver Optic. The "clean, manly tone" of these novels would have been called into question if the parents of these boy readers

For information on placing notes at the foot of the page rather than at the end of the paper, see pages 157–159.

Thought, 3rd ed. (New York: Harper, 1964) 629. I am also

indebted to Scharnhorst's description of the typical Alger

plot (67-68).

[4]The advertisement appears at the end of another boy's

book: Oliver Optic [William T. Adams], Rich and Humble: A

Story for Young People (New York: New York Book, 1911) n.p.

The "clean, manly tone" of these novels would have been

called into question if the parents of these boy readers

had been aware that Alger was dismissed in 1866 as a pastor

of a Massachusetts church for having homosexual relation-

ships with young boys in the church. This episode is

discussed in Hoyt 4-6.

Number the first page of the Works Cited section as a continuation of the text. Center the heading one inch from the top of the page and begin the text two spaces below the heading. Double space within and between the entries. The first line of each entry begins at the left margin. Any additional lines for each entry are indented five spaces. Alphabetize the entries. Include all the sources cited in your paper and notes.

Alger: The author of the novel is cited first instead of the author of the introduction. Compare with Coyle, Fink, and Seelye below.

"Alger": Unsigned articles are alphabetized by title.

Cawelti: Book entry.

Coyle: Here the author of the introduction is cited rather than the author of the novel.

Curti: Entry for a book in more than one edition.

Falk: Entry for a journal article.

Fink: Same as Coyle above.

Gardner: Note the comma in place of the usual colon before the subtitle.

Works Cited

Alger, Horatio, Jr. Digging for Gold: A Story of Cali-

fornia. Intro. John Seelye. New York: Collier, 1968.

"Alger, Horatio (, Jr.)." New Encyclopaedia Britannica:

Micropaedia, 1979 ed.

Cawelti, John G. Apostles of the Self-Made Man. Chicago:

U of Chicago P, 1965.

Coyle, William. Introduction. Adrift in New York and the

World Before Him. By Horatio Alger, Jr. New York:

Odyssey, 1966. v-xvii.

Curti, Merle. The Growth of American Thought. 3rd ed.

New York: Harper, 1964.

Falk, Robert. "Notes on the 'Higher Criticism' of Horatio

Alger, Jr." Arizona Quarterly 19 (1963): 151-67.

Fink, Rychard. Introduction. Ragged Dick and Mark, the

Match Boy. By Horatio Alger, Jr. New York: Collier,

1962. 5-31.

Gardner, Ralph D. Horatio Alger, or the American Hero

Era. Medota: Wayside, 1964.

Hart, James D. The Oxford Companion to American Literature.

4th ed. New York: Oxford UP, 1965.

Hart: Same as Curti above.
Henderson: Entry for an article in a weekly magazine.
Hoyt: Book entry.
Huber: Book entry.
Lasch: Book entry. All subtitles must appear in the works cited.
Meehan: Entry for a signed article in a newspaper.
Nye: Book entry.
Optic: Entry for a pseudonymous author.
Scharnhorst: Entry for a book in a series.
Seelye. Same as Fink above.
Zuckerman: Entry for a journal article.

Henderson, William. "A Few Words about Horatio Alger, Jr."

   Publisher's Weekly 23 Apr. 1973: 32-33.

Hoyt, Edwin P. Horatio's Boys: The Life and Works of

   Horatio Alger, Jr. Radnor: Chilton, 1974.

Huber, Richard M. The American Idea of Success. New York:

   McGraw, 1971.

Lasch, Christopher. The Culture of Narcissism: American

   Life in an Age of Diminishing Expectations. New York:

   Norton, 1978.

Meehan, Thomas. "A Forgettable Centenary--Horatio Alger's,"

   New York Times 28 June 1964, sec. 6, 22+.

Nye, Russel B. The Unembarrassed Muse: The Popular Arts in

   America. New York: Dial, 1979.

Optic, Oliver [William T. Adams]. Rich and Humble: A Story

   for Young People. New York: New York Book, 1911.

Scharnhorst, Gary. Horatio Alger, Jr. Twayne's United

   States Author Series 363. Boston: Twayne, 1980.

Seelye, John. Introduction. Digging for Gold: A Story of

   California. By Horatio Alger, Jr. New York: Collier,

   1968. vii-xx.

Zuckerman, Michael. "The Nursery Tales of Horatio Alger."

   American Quarterly 24 (1972): 191-209.

10 Specialized Reference Sources

This chapter lists useful, selected reference sources for specific academic disciplines. The books and journals in each section are briefly annotated when a title is not self-explanatory. The following disciplines are covered:

Architecture	Philosophy
Art	Political Science
Business	Psychology
Economics	Religion
Education	Science
English	Sociology
Film	Theater
History	Women's Studies
Music	

USING THE LISTS

Once you have chosen a subject, you can scan the books and journals listed under a particular discipline for relevant sources. The books consist of a variety of materials including handbooks, encyclopedias, and dictionaries, as well as bibliographies, indexes, and abstracts. These reference works can save time by leading you to specific sources related to your subject area, and they can help you to define and sharpen your topic so that it is manageable. Moreover, by using these materials, you can quickly determine if your library contains enough sources on a topic to write an adequate research paper.

In addition to the books, the lists also include journals relevant to particular disciplines. Some of these titles are highly specialized academic publications while others are designed for nonspecialists; the latter group can be a potential source of topics if you take the time to browse through them (*American Heritage* is a good example for history topics).

These lists are not complete for each discipline, nor are all disciplines included. The lists do, however, represent areas for which college students frequently write research papers, and the items within each list offer an efficient and reliable way to gather information. If you do not find what you need, remember that your reference librarian and your instructor are sources for suggestions and leads. You should also be aware of two guides to sources that are far more complete and detailed than the selected lists in this chapter:

Sheehy, Eugene P. *Guide to Reference Books.* 9th ed. Chicago: ALA, 1976. See also the Supplement to the 9th edition, published in 1980.

This guide lists and briefly describes reference works for all academic disciplines. Though used primarily by librarians for selecting reference works for library collections, the *Guide to Reference Books* is also extremely valuable for researchers. There are reference works available for nearly every subject imaginable, and this is where you'll find them — even, for example, the *World Wide Space Law Bibliography*, a reference source that runs for 700 pages.

Another important guide used by librarians and helpful to researchers lists periodicals:

Katz, Bill, and Berry G. Richards. *Magazines for Libraries.* 3rd ed. New York: Bowker, 1978.

This book consists of an annotated list of some 6,500 periodicals (about 10 percent of the periodicals available) arranged by subject. The listings include academic as well as popular periodicals, and the subjects range from academic disciplines to special interests such as "Hobbies." By scanning a subject area you can quickly determine which periodicals specifically cover your interests. This guide tells you not only about the kinds of articles that appear in *Environmental Science and Technology* but also what you will find in *Pigeon Racing News and Gazette.* Indeed, it is the kind of reference work that is a delight to browse through because of the surprising and often interesting discoveries to be made.

One final word: When you use a reference source, take the time to figure out how to use it. Be sure you know what the scope of the work is (a bibliography on American history will yield nothing about the Civil War if the source is limited to events after 1900); check to see if it has an index that lists your topic or some related subject; and determine if it is up-to-date. The most efficient way to find information in a library is to first discover what the reference area has to offer.

ARCHITECTURE

Books

Architectural Periodicals Index. London: British Architectural Library, 1972 to date. A subject index to foreign journals.

Branch, Melville C. *Comprehensive Urban Planning: A Selective Annotated Bibliography with Related Materials.* Beverly Hills: Sage, 1970.

Briggs, Martin S. *Everyman's Concise Encyclopaedia of Architecture.* New York: Dutton, 1959.

Cowan, Henry J. *Dictionary of Architectural Science*. New York: Wiley, 1973. Definitions of technical terms.

Ehresmann, Donald L. *Fine Arts: A Bibliographic Guide to Basic Reference Works, Histories & Handbooks*. 2nd ed. Littleton: Libraries Unlimited, 1979.

Fletcher, Sir Banister. *A History of Architecture*. 18th ed. New York: Scribner's, 1975. A well-illustrated history from ancient times to the twentieth century.

Hamlin, Talbot F. *Architecture Through the Ages*. New York: Putnam, 1953. A social history of architecture.

Housing and Planning References. Washington: GPO, 1965 to date. Indexes to more than 1,000 international periodicals received by the U.S. Dept. of Housing and Urban Development.

Pevsner, Mikolaus. *The Sources of Modern Architecture & Design*. New York: Oxford UP, 1977.

Phillips, Margaret. *Guide to Architectural Information*. Lansdale: Design Data Center, 1971. A guide to reference materials such as bibliographies, indexes, and directories; subject index.

Riseboro, Bill. *The Story of Western Architecture*. New York: Scribner's, 1979.

Sokol, David M. *American Architecture and Art: A Guide to Information Sources*. Detroit: Gale, 1976. Annotated lists of periodicals, books, and catalogs by subject; includes author, title, and subject indexes.

Stierlin, H. *Encyclopedia of World Architecture*. 2 vols. New York: Facts on File, 1979.

Sturgis, Russell. *Dictionary of Architecture and Building, Biographical, Historical, and Descriptive*. 1902; rpt. Detroit: Gale, 1966. Still important despite its original publication date.

Vance, Mary. *Architecture Books Arranged by Style & Periods: A Selected Bibliography*. Monticello: Vance Bibliographies, 1979.

Whiffen, Marcus. *American Architecture Since 1780: A Guide to the Styles*. Cambridge: M.I.T. P, 1969.

Wodehouse, Laurence. *American Architects from the Civil War to the First World War: A Guide to Information Sources*. Detroit: Gale, 1976. Supplements Roos, Frank J., above; see also next entry.

———. *American Architects from the First World War to the Present*. Detroit: Gale, 1977.

———. *Indigenous Architecture World Wide: A Guide to Information Sources*. Detroit: Gale, 1980.

Journals

Architectural Design. Each issue usually focuses on a single topic.

Architectural Digest. Mostly interior design.

Architectural History: Journal of the Society of Architectural Historians of Great Britain.

Architectural Record. Well-illustrated articles on design and technology.

The Architectural Review. Emphasis on international modern design.

Historic Preservation. An important journal concerning the preservation of historic landmarks.

House and Home. A business-trade magazine.

Journal of Architectural Education. Historical and conceptual articles.

Journal of the Society of Architectural Historians. Scholarly treatments of international topics.

Landscape Architecture

Oppositions. Articles on controversial issues in architecture.
Progressive Architecture. Emphasis on new trends.
Urban Design

ART

Books

Adeline, Jules. *The Adeline Art Dictionary.* New York: Ungar, 1966
American Art Directory. New York: Bowker, 1899 to date. Information on schools, museums, and organizations.
Art Index. New York: Wilson, 1929 to date. International indexes to archaeology, architecture, art history, arts and crafts, fine arts, industrial and landscape design, photography and films, and related areas.
ARTbibliographies: Current Titles. Santa Barbara: ABC-Clio, 1973 to date. Indexes about 250 art and design journals.
ARTbibliographies: Modern. Santa Barbara: ABC-Clio, 1973 to date. Abstracts of selected books, periodicals, and catalogs on modern art.
Avery Index to Architectural Periodicals. 2nd ed. 15 vols. Boston: Hall, 1973. Indexes all the arts, not only architecture; annual supplements.
Britannica Encyclopedia of American Art. Chicago: Encyclopedia Britannica, 1973. Short, illustrated articles on all fields with bibliographies, glossary of terms, and information on museums.
Canaday, John. *Lives of the Painters.* 4 vols. New York: Norton, 1969. A lively history of European and American painting.
Chamberlin, Mary. *Guide to Art Reference Books.* Chicago: ALA, 1959. Annotations for over 2,500 titles. See also Ehresmann, Donald L., below.
Cheney, Sheldon. *Sculpture of the World: A History.* New York: Viking, 1968.
Clapp, Jane. *Art Censorship: A Chronology of Proscribed and Prescribed Art.* Metuchen: Scarecrow, 1972.
Creswell, Keppel A. C. *A Bibliography of the Architecture, Arts, and Crafts of Islam.* Cairo: American U at Cairo P, 1961. See also the Supplement, 1973.
Cummings, Paul. *Dictionary of Contemporary American Artists.* 3rd ed. New York: St. Martin's, 1977.
Daniel, Howard. *Encyclopedia of Themes and Subjects in Painting: Mythological, Biblical, Historical, Literary, Allegorical and Topical.* New York: Abrams, 1971.
Ehresmann, Donald L. *Applied and Decorative Arts: A Bibliographic Guide to Basic Reference Works, Histories and Handbooks.* Littleton: Libraries Unlimited, 1977. Annotates more than 1,200 books on everything from armor to toys; subject index.
———. *Fine Arts: A Bibliographic Guide to Basic Reference Works, Histories and Handbooks.* Littleton: Libraries Unlimited, 1975. Supplements Chamberlin (see entry above) to 1973.
Ekdahl, Janis. *American Sculpture: A Guide to Information Services.* Detroit: Gale, 1977. Annotated with author, title, and subject indexes.
Encyclopaedia of World Art. 15 vols. New York: McGraw, 1959–68. Comprehensive coverage of periods, countries, and types of art.
Fleming, John, and Hugh Honour. *Dictionary of the Decorative Arts.* New York: Harper,

1977. On the furniture and furnishings of Europe since the Middle Ages and North America since the Colonial Period.

Gardner, Helen. *Art Through the Ages.* 6th ed. New York: Harcourt, 1975.

Goldman, Bernard. *Reading and Writing in the Arts: A Handbook.* Rev. ed. Detroit: Wayne State UP, 1978.

Janson, Horst W., and Dora J. Janson. *History of Art: A Survey of the Major Visual Arts from the Dawn of History to the Present Day.* Englewood Cliffs: Prentice, 1969.

Jones, Lois S. *Art Research Methods and Resources: A Guide to Finding Art Information.* Dubuque: Kendall, 1978.

Karpel, Bernard, ed. *Arts in America: A Bibliography.* 3 vols. Washington: Smithsonian Institution P, 1979.

Keaveney, Sydney S. *American Painting: A Guide to Information Services.* Detroit: Gale, 1974. Annotations of selected journals, catalogs, and books.

Lucas, Edna L. *Art Books: A Basic Bibliography on the Fine Arts.* Greenwich: New York Graphic Soc., 1968.

Monro, Isabel S., and Kate M. Monro. *Index to Reproductions of American Paintings.* New York: Wilson, 1948. Supplement, 1964. Use this and the following entry to locate a reproduction when the artist, title, or subject is known.

———. *Index to Reproductions of European Paintings.* New York: Wilson, 1956.

Osborne, Harold, ed. *The Oxford Companion to Art.* New York: Oxford UP, 1970. A particularly useful introduction to the fine arts for students.

———. *The Oxford Companion to the Decorative Arts.* New York: Oxford UP, 1975. Articles on such crafts as glass making, jewelry, embroidery, etc.

Praeger Encyclopedia of Art. 5 vols. New York: Praeger, 1971. Comprehensive.

Reisner, Robert G. *Fakes and Forgeries in the Fine Arts: A Bibliography.* New York: Special Libraries Assn., 1950.

Rowland, Benjamin. *The Harvard Outline and Reading Lists for Oriental Art.* 3rd ed. Cambridge: Harvard UP, 1967.

Sill, Gertrude Grace. *A Handbook of Symbols in Christian Art.* New York: Macmillan, 1975.

Visual Dictionary of Art. Greenwich: New York Graphic Soc., 1974. Emphasis on painters and sculptors.

Walker, John Albert. *Glossary of Art, Architecture and Design since 1945.* 2nd ed. Hamden: Shoe String, 1977. Terms and labels used by artists and critics to describe styles and movements.

Western, Dominique C. *A Bibliography of the Arts of Africa.* Waltham: African Studies Assn., 1975.

Journals

American Art Journal. Illustrated articles by scholars; pre-twentieth-century emphasis.

American Artist. A wide range of topics for both general and academic readers.

Apollo. A finely illustrated magazine of international art and antiques.

Art Bulletin. Scholarly articles on art history.

Art Direction. Features all aspects of advertising art.

Art Education. Focuses on the teaching of art.

Art in America. An excellent general magazine richly illustrated.

Art International. Informed articles for general readers; well illustrated.

Art Journal. Articles on the history and criticism of art.

Artforum. Features important new trends.
Arts Magazine. Scholarly articles on modern and avant-garde art.
Costume. Illustrated articles on the history and art of costume.
Design Quarterly. Each issue centers on a particular theme.
Feminist Art Journal. Articles on the arts from feminist perspectives.
Furniture History
Industrial Design. Brief, illustrated articles on commercial design.
Interior Design. Includes residential and commercial interiors.
Journal of Aesthetics and Art Criticism
Oriental Art. Scholarly articles on all forms of art.
Shuttle, Spindle and Dyepot. A journal for weavers.
Studies in Art Education. Articles on issues and research in art education.
Studio Potter

BUSINESS

Books

Accountant's Index. New York: AICPA, 1920 to date. Indexes pamphlets, books, and government publications.
Bakewell, K. G. B. *Management Principles and Practices: A Guide to Information Sources.* Detroit: Gale, 1977. Annotated lists of books, periodicals, and audiovisual materials.
Business Books and Serials in Print. New York: Bowker, 1977 to date. Lists U.S. books by author, title, and subject.
Business Periodicals Index. New York: Wilson, 1958 to date. Indexes by subject and company name.
Business Services and Information: The Guide to the Federal Government. New York: Wiley, 1978. A bibliography and directory to government publications and agencies.
Daniells, Lorna M. *Business Information Sources.* Berkeley: U of California P, 1976. An important annotated list of business reference sources; well indexed.
Dow-Jones Business Almanac. Homewood: Dow Jones–Irwin, 1977 to date. A quick source of information on a variety of business topics ranging from advertising to investment.
Encyclopedia of Accounting Systems. 3 vols. Rev. and enl. ed. Englewood Cliffs: Prentice, 1976. Overviews by specialists on specific types of accounting for particular industries.
Encyclopedia of Business Information Sources. 3rd. ed. Detroit: Gale, 1976. Lists source-books, periodicals, organizations, handbooks, and bibliographies on business topics.
F & S Index of Corporations and Industries. Detroit: Funk, 1960 to date. Weekly issues indexing periodicals and reports on U.S. companies and products.
Gothie, Daniel L. *A Selected Bibliography of Applied Ethics in the Professions, 1950–1970.* Charlottesville: UP of Virginia, 1973. See also Jones, Donald G., below.
Jones, Donald G. *Business Ethics Bibliography, 1971–1975.* Charlottesville: UP of Virginia, 1977. Annotated listings of works on the social responsibilities of business.
Kohler, Eric L. *A Dictionary for Accountants.* 5th ed. Englewood Cliffs: Prentice, 1975.
Lipstein, Benjamin, and William J. McGuire. *Evaluating Advertising: A Bibliography of the Communications Process.* New York: Advertising Research, 1978.
Lovett, R. W., ed. *American Economic Business History: Information Sources.* Detroit: Gale, 1971.

The Modern Accountant's Handbook. Homewood: Dow Jones–Irwin, 1976.

Moffat, Donald W. *Economics Dictionary.* New York: Elsevier, 1976. See also the sources listed under "Economics" below.

Moore, Norman D. *Dictionary of Business, Finance and Investment.* Dayton: Investor's Systems, 1975.

Munn, Glenn G. *Encyclopedia of Banking and Finance.* Ed. Ferdinand L. Garcia. 7th ed. Boston: Bankers, 1973.

Standard & Poor's Register of Corporations, Directors and Executives. New York: Standard, 1928 to date. Information on U.S., Canadian, and major international corporations.

Urdang, Lawrence, ed. *Dictionary of Advertising Terms.* Chicago: Tatham, 1977.

Van Fleet, David D. *An Historical Bibliography of Administration, Business & Management.* Monticello: Vance, 1978.

Wall Street Journal Index. New York: Dow, 1958 to date. Indexes corporate news by company name and general news about products, etc.

Wasserman, Paul, and Jean Morgan. *Consumer Sourcebook: A Directory and Guide to Government Organizations; Associations, Centers and Institutions; Media Services; Company and Trademark Information; and Bibliographic Material Relating to Consumer Topics, Sources of Recourse and Advisory Information.* 2 vols. Detroit: Gale, 1978.

Wyckoff, Peter. *The Language of Wall Street.* New York: Hopkinson, 1973. A primer of terms.

Journals

Accountant's Digest. Condensed articles from journals in the field.

Accounting Review

Barron's: National Business and Financial Weekly. A widely read review of business and investing.

Black Enterprise. Focuses on blacks in the business world.

Business and Society Review. Articles on socially responsible business practices and management.

Business History Review. Scholarly articles and review essays on current books.

Business Week. A well-written, concise magazine for general readers as well as specialists.

CPA Journal

Dollars & Sense. A socialist perspective on business and economics.

Forbes. A general magazine providing investment and business information.

Fortune. A general magazine that examines business topics in the context of world affairs, economics, and politics.

Harvard Business Review. Scholarly analyses of business trends.

Journal of Accountancy

Journal of Accounting Research

Journal of Advertising

Journal of Business. Technical, academic articles on business topics, past and present.

Journal of Finance

Journal of Marketing

Journal of Retailing

Magazine of Wall Street. Analyses of business trends.

Management Review. Condensed magazine articles on current management topics.

Nation's Business. Published by the Chamber of Commerce of the U.S.; presents its perspective.

Quarterly Review of Economics and Business. Many interdisciplinary articles.
Personnel
Public Relations Quarterly
Sloan Management Review
Taxes: The Tax Magazine
University of Michigan Business Review
Wall Street Journal
Wharton Magazine. Academic and general articles on topics related to management.

ECONOMICS

Books

Ammer, Christine, and Dean S. Ammer. *Dictionary of Business and Economics.* New York: Free P, 1977. Provides definitions of terms as well as explanations of major economic theories.
Amstutz, Mark R. *Economics and Foreign Policy: A Guide to Information Sources.* Detroit: Gale, 1977. An annotated bibliography of books and articles.
Bibliographic Guide to Business and Economics. Boston: Hall, 1975 to date.
Business Periodicals Index. New York: Wilson, 1958 to date.
Economic Titles/Abstracts. The Hague: Nijhoff, 1974 to date. Indexes books, reports, and some 2,000 journals.
Field, Barry C., and Cleve E. Willis, eds. *Environmental Economics: A Guide to Information Sources.* Detroit: Gale, 1979. An annotated bibliography of books and articles.
Fletcher, John, ed. *The Use of Economics Literature.* Hamden: Archon, 1971. A valuable guide for students to sources for various fields in economics.
Gagala, Kenneth L. *The Economics of Minorities: A Guide to Information Sources.* Detroit: Gale, 1976. An annotated bibliography on the economic status of nonwhites in the United States.
Helppie, Charles E., James R. Gibbons, and Donald W. Pearson. *Research Guide in Economics.* Morristown: General Learning, 1974. Valuable information about sources, methods, and formats for beginning students.
Hutchinson, William K. *History of Economic Analysis: A Guide to Information Sources.* Detroit: Gale, 1976. An international survey for beginners from 1600 to 1940.
Oxford Economic Atlas of the World. 4th ed. London: Oxford UP, 1972. Useful for quick overviews of a region or country.
Rock, James M. *Money, Banking, and Macroeconomics: A Guide to Information Sources.* Detroit: Gale, 1977. An annotated bibliography of books and articles.
Skrapek, Wayne et al. *Mathematical Dictionary for Economics and Business Administration.* Boston: Allyn, 1976. Definitions of more than 2,000 mathematical terms.
Sources of European Economic Information. New York: Bowker, 1974.

Journals

American Economic Review. Important academic articles.
American Journal of Economics and Sociology

Brookings Papers on Economic Activity. Each issue focuses on a current topic.
Business Economics
Challenge. Well-written nontechnical articles on a variety of economic topics.
Economic Development and Cultural Change. Interdisciplinary.
Economic History Review. Academic articles linking economics and history.
Economist. A British news magazine with a world perspective on economics.
International Economic Review. Academic, quantitative articles.
Journal of Economic History. From the Industrial Revolution to the present.
Journal of Economic Issues
Journal of Economic Literature. A valuable review of current publications in all fields of economics.
Journal of Political Economy
Quarterly Journal of Economics. Academic articles on all topics in the field.
Review of Economics and Statistics. Emphasis on quantitative methodology.
Southern Economic Journal. Emphasis goes beyond regional concerns.

EDUCATION

Books

Altbach, Philip G. *Comparative Higher Education Abroad: Bibliography and Analysis.* New York: Praeger, 1976.
Arnold, Darlene B., and Kenneth O. Doyle. *Education/Psychology Journals: A Scholar's Guide.* Metuchen: Scarecrow, 1975. Descriptions of journals in the two fields.
Beach, Mark. *A Bibliographic Guide to American Colleges and Universities from Colonial Times to the Present.* Westport: Greenwood, 1975.
Berry, Dorothea M. *A Bibliographical Guide to Educational Research.* Metuchen: Scarecrow, 1975. A guide to library resources for students researching education topics.
Burnett, Jacquetta H. *Anthropology and Education: An Annotated Bibliographic Guide.* New Haven: HRAF, 1974.
Camp, William L., and Bryan L. Schwark. *Guide to Periodicals in Education and Its Academic Disciplines.* 2nd ed. Metuchen: Scarecrow, 1975.
Cordasco, Francesco, and William W. Brickman, eds. *A Bibliography of American Educational History: An Annotated and Classified Guide.* New York: AMS, 1975.
Current Index to Journals in Education. New York: Macmillan, 1969 to date. Indexes more than 700 journals.
Education Index. New York: Wilson, 1929 to date. An author/subject index to selected periodicals.
Encyclopedia of Education. New York: Macmillan, 1971. A guide to topics in education (e.g., history, philosophy, theory, etc.).
Good, Carter V., ed. *Dictionary of Education.* 3rd ed. New York: McGraw, 1973. Scholarly definitions of terms.
———. *Essentials of Educational Research.* 2nd ed. New York: Appleton, 1972. A good place to begin.
International Encyclopedia of Higher Education. 10 vols. San Francisco: Jossey, 1977.
Resources in Education (ERIC). Washington: GPO, 1966 to date. Abstracts indexed by subject and author.

Richmond, W. Kenneth. *The Literature of Education: A Critical Bibliography, 1945–1970*. London: Methuen, 1972. Evaluations of works published in a variety of educational areas.
Standard Education Almanac, Los Angeles: Academic Media, 1968 to date. A compilation of facts and statistics.
UNESCO. *World Guide to Higher Education: A Comparative Survey of Systems, Degrees, and Qualifications*. New York: Bowker, 1976.
Woodbury, Marda. *A Guide to Sources of Educational Information*. Washington: Information Resources, 1976. Annotated.

Journals

American Education. Nontechnical; general in approach.
Change. Current topics in higher education.
Childhood Education. Accessible articles on topics ranging from infancy to adolescence.
Chronicle of Higher Education. News, opinions, reviews, meetings, statistics, and other up-to-date information.
Comparative Education. International in scope.
Educational Forum. Articles covering topics from elementary grades to university education.
Educational Studies: A Journal of Book Reviews in the Foundations of Education
Elementary School Journal
Harvard Educational Review. Scholarly articles that often place educational topics in the context of larger social issues.
Journal of Educational Psychology
Journal of Educational Research
Journal of Experimental Education
Journal of Higher Education
Journal of Moral Education
Journal of Negro Education
Journal of Special Education. Focuses on handicapped children.
Phi Delta Kappan. General articles for broad interests.
Review of Educational Research
Teachers College Record: A Professional Journal of Ideas, Research and Informed Opinion
Today's Education: NEA Journal. Articles on elementary and secondary education from both practical and theoretical points of view.

ENGLISH

Books

Abstracts of English Studies. Urbana: NCTE, 1958 to date. Summarizes articles from scholarly journals covering American, English, and world literature; a valuable research tool.

Adelman, Irving, and Rita Dworkin. *The Contemporary Novel: A Checklist of Critical Literature on the British and American Novel Since 1945.* Metuchen: Scarecrow, 1972.

American Literary Scholarship. Durham: Duke UP, 1963 to date. Annual bibliographic essays evaluating the work done in all areas of American literature; very useful.

Author Biographies Master Index. 2 vols. Detroit: Gale, 1978. Indexes major biographical dictionaries of authors.

Baker, Nancy L. *A Research Guide for Undergraduate Students: English and American Literature.* New York: MLA, 1982.

Bryer, Jackson, ed. *Sixteen Modern American Authors: A Survey of Research and Criticism.* New York: Norton, 1973. Lengthy bibliographic essays on Anderson, Cather, H. Crane, Dreiser, Eliot, Faulkner, Fitzgerald, Frost, Hemingway, O'Neill, Pound, Robinson, Steinbeck, Stevens, Williams, and Wolfe.

Buchanan-Brown, John, ed. *Cassell's Encyclopedia of World Literature.* 3 vols. Rev. ed. New York: Morrow, 1973.

Cassis, A. F. *The Twentieth-Century English Novel: An Annotated Bibliography of General Criticism.* New York: Garland, 1977.

Coan, Otis W., and Richard G. Lillard. *America in Fiction: An Annotated List of Novels that Interpret Aspects of Life in the United States, Canada, and Mexico.* 5th ed. Palo Alto: Pacific, 1967. A useful source for paper topics.

Columbia Dictionary of Modern European Literature. New York: Columbia, 1947. Coverage since about 1870.

Contemporary Authors: A Bio-Bibliographical Guide to Current Authors and Their Works. Detroit: Gale, 1962 to date. Devoted exclusively to American authors.

Cook, Dorothy E., and Isabel S. Monro. *Short Story Index.* New York: Wilson, 1953. Indexes by author, title, and subject stories published before 1949; five supplements cover the period from 1950 to 1974.

Corse, Larry B., and Sandra B. Corse. *Articles on American and British Literature: An Index to Selected Periodicals 1950–1977.* Athens: Swallow, 1981. Designed specifically for undergraduates who have access to a limited, small college library.

Cowart, David, ed. *Twentieth-Century American Science Fiction Writers,* 2 vols. Dictionary of Literary Biography Series 8. Detroit: Gale, 1981. Illustrated biographical entries.

DeBary, William T., and Ainslee T. Embree, eds. *A Guide to Oriental Classics.* 2nd ed. New York: Columbia UP, 1975. Includes Islamic, Indian, Chinese, and Japanese literature.

De Laura, David J. *Victorian Prose: A Guide to Research.* New York: MLA, 1973. A summary of the scholarship in the field.

Drescher, Horst W., and Bernd Kahrmann. *The Contemporary English Novel: An Annotated Bibliography of Secondary Sources.* New York: International Publications Service, 1973.

Encyclopedia of World Literature in the Twentieth Century. 3 vols. New York: Ungar, 1967–71. Surveys authors and topics in various countries.

Faverty, Frederic E. *The Victorian Poets: A Guide to Research.* 2nd ed. Cambridge: Harvard UP, 1968. A summary of the scholarship in the field.

Ford, George H., ed. *Victorian Fiction: A Second Guide to Research.* New York: MLA, 1978. Scholarly work published from 1963 through 1974. A valuable summary. See also Stevenson, Lionel, below.

Freeman, William. *Dictionary of Fictional Characters.* Rev. ed. Boston: Writer, 1974. Lists are drawn from novels, short stories, plays, and poems by British and American writers.

Gazdar, Gerald, et al. *A Bibliography of Contemporary Linguistic Research.* New York: Garland, 1978. Lists scholarship since 1970; subject indexes.

Glenn, Robert W. *Black Rhetoric: A Guide to Afro-American Communication.* Metuchen: Scarecrow, 1976. A guide to information on Afro-American speeches and essays.

Gohdes, Clarence, L. F. *Bibliographical Guide to the Study of the Literature of the U.S.A.* 4th ed. Durham: Duke UP, 1976. An annotated guide to American studies topics; regarded as standard.

Granger's Index to Poetry. 6th ed. New York: Columbia UP, 1973. Indexes anthologies of poetry by author, first line of poem, and subject indexes.

Greiner, Donald J., ed. *American Poets Since World War II.* 2 vols. Dictionary of Literary Biography Series 5. Detroit: Gale, 1980. Illustrated biographical entries.

Hackett, Alice P. *80 Years of Best Sellers, 1895–1975.* New York: Bowker, 1977. Charts a history of American tastes and values.

Hart, James D., ed. *The Oxford Companion to American Literature.* 4th ed. New York: Oxford UP, 1965. An alphabetized listing of topics for easy reference.

Harvey, Paul, and Dorothy Eagle, eds. *The Oxford Companion to English Literature.* 4th ed. New York: Oxford UP, 1967.

Helterman, Jeffrey, and Richard Layman, eds. *American Novelists Since World War II.* Dictionary of Literary Biography Series 2. Detroit: Gale, 1978. Illustrated biographical entries. Volume 6 of this series continues additional entries for novelists since WW II.

Heninger, S. K. *English Prose, Prose Fiction, and Criticism to 1660: A Guide to Information Sources.* Detroit: Gale, 1975.

Holman, C. Hugh. *A Handbook to Literature.* 4th ed. Indianapolis: Bobbs, 1980. A valuable dictionary of literary terms as well as a concise source of information for literary periods and movements.

Humanities Index. New York: Wilson, 1974 to date. Lists articles on literary topics to be found in periodicals; a useful supplement to *Reader's Guide to Periodical Literature.*

Kearny, E. I., and L. S. Fitzgerald. *The Continental Novel: A Checklist of Criticism in English, 1900–1966.* Metuchen: Scarecrow, 1968.

Kirby, David K. *American Fiction to 1900: A Guide to Information Sources.* Detroit: Gale, 1975. Annotated bibliographies.

Leach, Maria, ed. *Funk & Wagnall's Standard Dictionary of Folklore, Mythology and Legend.* New York: Funk, 1972.

Leary, Lewis. *American Literature: A Study and Research Guide.* New York: St. Martin's, 1976. Bibliographic essays on types of sources such as literary histories, criticism, and biographical guides; emphasizes scholarship done since about 1940.

———. *Articles on American Literature, 1900–1950.* Durham: Duke UP, 1954. This, along with the next two entries, provides a quick way to determine what kinds of articles have been published on a given author or topic.

———. *Articles on American Literature, 1950–1967.* Durham: Duke UP, 1970.

———, with John Auchard. *Articles on American Literature, 1967–1975.* Durham: Duke UP, 1979.

MacNicholas, John, ed. *Twentieth-Century American Dramatists.* 2 vols. Dictionary of Literary Biography Series 7. Detroit: Gale, 1980. Illustrated biographical entries.

Magill, Frank N. *Masterplots.* 12 vols. New York: Salem, 1976. Summarizes the contents of important literary works; see also annual volumes.

MLA International Bibliography of Books and Articles on Modern Language and Literature. New York: MLA, 1921 to date. Lists books and articles; a major bibliographical source in the field.

Myerson, Joel, ed. *American Renaissance in New England*. Dictionary of Literary Biography Series 1. Detroit: Gale, 1978. Illustrated biographical entries; for mid-nineteenth-century writers.

———. *Antebellum Writers in New York and the South*. Dictionary of Literary Biography Series 3. Detroit: Gale, 1979. See description in preceding entry; covers from about 1820 to 1860.

———. *The Transcendentalists: A Review of Research and Criticism*. New York: Modern Lang., 1984. Bibliographic essays on writers associated with the American transcendentalists of the nineteenth century such as Emerson and Thoreau.

The New Cambridge Bibliography of English Literature. 5 vols. Cambridge: Cambridge UP, 1969–77. A major source covering the period from 600 to 1950.

Nilon, Charles H. *Bibliography of Bibliographies in American Literature*. New York: Bowker, 1970. Lists for authors, genres, and various topics.

Oxford Companion to Classical Literature. Oxford: Clarendon, 1937. Allusions, authors, works, and other topics related to Greek and Roman culture.

Oxford History of English Literature. 12 vols. Oxford: Oxford UP, 1945–in progress. The most comprehensive history of English literature.

Patterson, Margaret C. *Literary Research Guide*. 2nd ed. New York: MLA, 1983. An annotated bibliography of selected reference sources for British and American literature; subject index.

The Penguin Companion to World Literature. 4 vols. New York: McGraw, 1969–71. Separate volumes on American; classical, Oriental, and African; English; and European literature.

Preminger, Alex, ed. *Princeton Encyclopedia of Poetry and Poetics*. Princeton: Princeton UP, 1975.

Rees, Robert, and Earl N. Harbert. *Fifteen American Authors Before 1900: Bibliographic Essays on Research and Criticism*. Madison: U of Wisconsin P, 1971. Lengthy essays on H. Adams, Bryant, Cooper, S. Crane, Dickinson, Edwards, Franklin, Holmes, Howells, Irving, Longfellow, Lowell, Norris, Taylor, and Whittier, as well as essays on literature of the Old and New South.

Rood, Karen L., ed. *American Writers in Paris, 1920–1939*. Dictionary of Literary Biography Series 4. Detroit: Gale, 1980. Illustrated biographical entries on American expatriates, the so-called "Lost Generation."

Rubin, Louis D. *A Bibliographical Guide to the Study of Southern Literature*. Baton Rouge: Louisiana State UP, 1969. Bibliographical essays of periods, schools, and types of literature; supplemented by: Society for the Study of Southern Literature. *Southern Literature, 1968–1975*. Boston: Hall, 1978.

Rush, Theressa G. et al. *Black American Writers, Past and Present: A Biographical and Bibliographical Dictionary*. 2 vols. Metuchen: Scarecrow, 1975. Coverage from the early eighteenth century.

Schwartz, Narda L. *Articles on Women Writers: A Bibliography*. Santa Barbara: ABC-Clio, 1977. Covers articles published from 1960 to 1975.

Schweik, Robert C., and Dieter Riesner. *Reference Sources in English and American Literature: An Annotated Bibliography*. New York: Norton, 1977. A useful guide to sources including biographical, historical, critical, and bibliographical material.

Spiller, Robert E., et al. *Literary History of the United States*. 4th ed. 2 vols. New York: Macmillan, 1974. A standard history; from colonial times to the 1960s.

Stevenson, Lionel, et al. *Victorian Fiction: A Guide to Research*. Cambridge: Harvard UP, 1964. Provides a summary and evaluation of work done in the field up to the early 1960s. See also Ford, George H. above.

Walker, Warren S. *Twentieth-Century Short Story Explication*. 3rd ed. Hamden: Shoe

String, 1977. A bibliography of criticism written between 1900 and 1975 on short stories written since 1800.

Whitlow, Roger. *Black American Literature: A Critical History.* Chicago: Nelson, 1973.

Woodress, James L. *American Fiction, 1900–1950: A Guide to Information Sources.* Detroit: Gale, 1974. Annotated bibliographies.

———, ed. *Eight American Authors: A Review of Research and Criticism.* Rev. ed. New York: Norton, 1971. Lengthy bibliographic essays on Poe, Emerson, Hawthorne, Thoreau, Melville, Whitman, Twain, and James.

Journals

American Literature. An important journal of literary history, criticism, and bibliography.

American Quarterly. Includes articles on literature and related cultural topics.

American Scholar. Interesting general articles often related to literary topics.

American Speech. Emphasis on the history, structure, and use of language.

American Studies. Interdisciplinary articles on society and culture.

Boundary 2: A Journal of Postmodern Literature. Articles on recent literature.

CLA Journal. Emphasis on black American literature.

College Composition and Communication

College English. Emphasis on literary criticism and the teaching of literature.

Comparative Literature. International topics.

Contemporary Poetry: A Journal of Criticism. Articles written for nonspecialists.

Criticism: A Quarterly for Literature and the Arts. Includes articles on literature and the fine arts.

Critique: Studies in Modern Fiction. Covers world literature.

Early American Literature. Covers up through 1820.

ELH. Focuses on English and American literary history.

ESQ: A Journal of the American Renaissance. Articles on nineteenth-century authors and topics.

Explicator. Brief notes on American, Continental, and British poetry and prose.

Journal of American Folklore. Covers world folklore as well as American.

Journal of American Studies. Literary topics and related areas.

Journal of Modern Literature. World literature from about 1885 to 1950.

Language in Society. Articles and book reviews on international topics.

Literature and Psychology. Psychological interpretations of literature.

Modern Fiction Studies. Articles on British, American, and European fiction since about 1880.

Modern Philology. Articles on the literature of Britain, America, and to a lesser degree, Continental literature.

New England Quarterly. Articles on New England life and literature.

New York Review of Books. Lengthy reviews of recent books.

Nineteenth Century Fiction. British and American.

Partisan Review. Concerned with making connections between literature and politics.

Philological Quarterly. Articles on classical and modern languages and literature.

PMLA. Academic articles on a wide variety of topics; sponsored by the Modern Language Association.

Resources for American Literary Study. Strong on bibliographical information.

Studies in American Humor

Studies in Romanticism. Covers a variety of topics related to Romanticism.

Studies in Short Fiction. Emphasizes articles on short stories.
Studies in the Novel. Articles on all aspects of the novel.
Studies in 20th Century Literature. Focuses on European literature.
Victorian Studies. Articles on the humanities, arts, and sciences of the period.
Virginia Quarterly Review. Includes articles on literary topics of broad interest.
World Literature Today. Especially useful for keeping up with writers abroad.
Yale Review. Interesting, accessible articles on a variety of literary topics.

FILM

Books

Bawden, Liz-Anne, ed. *The Oxford Companion to Film.* New York: Oxford UP, 1976.
  A useful handbook that answers questions about individual films, actors, terms, etc.
Bukalski, Peter J. *Film Research: A Critical Bibliography with Annotations and Essays.*
  Boston: Hall, 1972.
Cowie, Peter. *Concise History of the Cinema.* 2 vols. New York: Barnes, 1971.
Dyment, Alan R. *The Literature of the Film: A Bibliographical Guide to the Film as Art
  and Entertainment, 1936–1970.* London: White Lion, 1975. Annotations for English-
  language books.
Film Literature Index. Albany: Filmdex, 1973 to date. An international subject/author
  index to more than 300 periodicals on film.
Garbicz, Adam, and Jacek Klinowski. *Cinema, the Magic Vehicle: A Guide to Its Achieve-
  ment.* Metuchen: Scarecrow, 1975. A film-by-film history to 1949.
Geduld, Harry M., and Ronald Gottesman. *An Illustrated Glossary of Film Terms.* New
  York: Holt, 1973. Especially useful for students; nontechnical.
Halliwell, Leslie. *The Filmgoer's Companion.* 6th ed. New York: Hill, 1977. An alpha-
  betical listing of films, actors, producers, directors, and film topics.
International Encyclopedia of Film. New York: Crown, 1972.
International Index to Film Periodicals. New York: Bowker, 1972 to date. Covers about
  sixty periodicals.
International Motion Picture Almanac. New York: Quigley, 1929 to date.
MacCann, Richard D., and Edward S. Perry. *The New Film Index: A Bibliography of
  Magazine Articles in English, 1930–1970.* New York: Dutton, 1975.
Manchel, Frank. *Film Study: A Resource Guide.* Rutherford: Fairleigh Dickinson UP,
  1973. Particularly helpful for beginning students.
The New York Times Film Reviews. 6 vols. New York: New York Times Book and Arno,
  1970. Reprints *The New York Times* film reviews from 1913 to 1968. See also the
  supplements to these volumes.
Powers, Anne. *Blacks in American Movies: A Selected Bibliography.* Metuchen: Scare-
  crow, 1974.
Sklar, Robert. *Movie Made America: A Cultural History of American Movies.* New York:
  Random, 1975.

Journals

American Film. Retrospective articles as well as information on current films.
Cineaste. Offers a political perspective on film.

Film Comment. A fine general magazine.
Film Culture. Focuses on alternative films rather than Hollywood productions.
Film Literature Quarterly. On films made from literature.
Film Quarterly. Scholarly articles on international film; also lengthy film and book reviews.
Film Review Digest. Excerpts of film reviews appearing in magazines and newspapers; format similar to *Book Review Digest.*
Journal of Popular Film. Academic but accessible articles on film topics.
Quarterly Review of Film Studies. Scholarly articles as well as book reviews.
Sight and Sound. Solid articles on international film; includes interviews with filmmakers.
Take One. Informed and highly readable articles on international film.

HISTORY

Books

America: History and Life. Santa Barbara: ABC-Clio, 1964 to date. Abstracts of articles about North America, past and present; also includes book reviews and extensive bibliographies. This, along with *Historical Abstracts,* is a standard bibliographical source.
American Historical Association. *Guide to Historical Literature,* New York: Macmillan, 1961. A basic bibliographical guide for historical researchers.
Auty, Robert, and Dimitri Obolensky, eds. *An Introduction to Russian History.* Cambridge: Cambridge UP, 1976. An excellent source for students.
Bibliography of British History. 3 vols. Oxford: Clarendon, 1928–1970. Coverage from 1485–1789. A standard source; for other periods see the next entry, as well as the Brown, Hanham, and Havighurst entries below.
Binder, Leonard, ed. *The Study of the Middle East: Research and Scholarship in the Humanities and the Social Sciences.* New York: Wiley, 1976. Bibliographic essays, including one on the history of the region.
Brown, Lucy M., and Ian R. Christie. *Bibliography of British History, 1789–1851.* Oxford: Clarendon, 1977.
Calmann, John. *Western Europe: A Handbook.* New York: Praeger, 1967.
Cambridge Ancient History. 12 vols. New York: Macmillan, 1923–39. History from Egypt to the fall of Rome; revisions in progress.
Cambridge History of China. Cambridge: Cambridge UP, 1978. The first published volume of this projected fourteen-volume work is vol. 10: covering Late Ch'ing, 1800–1870.
Cambridge Medieval History. 8 vols. New York: Macmillan, 1911–36. Revisions in progress.
Cassara, Ernest. *History of the United States of America: A Guide to Information Sources.* Detroit: Gale, 1977. The place to begin for annotated sources for U.S. history.
Day, Alan E. *History: A Reference Handbook.* Hamden: Linnet, 1977. A valuable guide to bibliographies, handbooks, dictionaries, and other sources.
Delpar, Helen, ed. *Encyclopedia of Latin America.* New York: McGraw, 1974. Includes some bibliographic information.

DeVore, Ronald M. *The Arab-Israeli Conflict: A Historical, Political, Social, and Military Bibliography*. Santa Barbara: ABC-Clio, 1976.

Dictionary of American History. Rev. ed. 8 vols. New York: Scribner's, 1976. A useful quick source of information for almost any topic.

Facts on File Yearbook. New York: Facts on File, 1940 to date. Weekly summaries of world news indexed by subject.

Freeman, Grenville, and S. P. Greville. *Chronology of World History: A Calendar of Principal Events from 3000 BC to AD 1973*. Totowa: Rowman, 1975. This provides a cross-section of people, places, and events for any given period.

Freidel, Frank, ed. *Harvard Guide to American History*. Rev. ed. 2 vols. Cambridge: Harvard UP, 1974. An important standard bibliographic source to articles and books for all of American history.

Graves, Edgar B., ed. *A Bibliography of English History to 1485*. Oxford: Clarendon, 1975. The best bibliographic source for the period.

Hanham, Harold J. *Bibliography of British History, 1851–1914*. Oxford: Clarendon, 1976.

Harper Encyclopedia of the Modern World. New York: Harper, 1970. Covers from 1760 to late 1960s.

Havighurst, Alfred F. *Modern England, 1901–1970*. Cambridge: Cambridge UP, 1976. A handbook to bibliographic sources.

Historical Abstracts. Santa Barbara: ABC-Clio, 1955 to date. Abstracts of articles in selected periodicals throughout the world from 1775 to 1945; includes subject indexes. Since 1964 North American history is excluded; see *America: History and Life* for coverage of articles published after 1964.

Illustrated Encyclopaedia of the Classical World. New York: Harper, 1975. Information includes Greek and Roman history, mythology, art, and other topics.

Index to Book Reviews in Historical Periodicals. Metuchen: Scarecrow, 1972 to date.

Langer, William L. *The New Illustrated Encyclopedia of World History*. 2 vols. New York: Abrams, 1975.

Morrison, Donald G., et al. *Black Africa: A Comparative Handbook*. New York: Free, 1972. Information on independent black African countries.

New Cambridge Modern History. 14 vols. Cambridge: Cambridge UP, 1957–1970. Coverage from the Renaissance through the World Wars.

Nunn, Godfrey R. *Asia: A Selected and Annotated Guide to Reference Works*. Cambridge: M.I.T. P, 1971. Organized by country.

Panofsky, Hans E. *A Bibliography of Africana*. Westport: Greenwood, 1975. A guide to information sources on Africa.

Poulton, Helen J., and Marguerite S. Howland. *The Historian's Handbook*. Norman: U of Oklahoma P, 1977. A descriptive guide to reference sources for students; a good place to start.

Powell, James M., ed. *Medieval Studies: An Introduction*. Syracuse: Syracuse UP, 1976. An interdisciplinary guide with bibliographic information.

Prucha, Francis P. *A Bibliographical Guide to the History of Indian-White Relations in the United States*. Chicago: U of Chicago P, 1977. Subject and author index.

Recently Published Articles. Washington: American Historical Association, 1976 to date. A bibliography of articles organized by topic; especially useful for finding up-to-date research.

Schöpflin, George, ed. *Soviet and Eastern Europe; A Handbook*. New York: Praeger, 1970. Information on political, economic, and social life; each section written by a specialist.

Simon, Reeva, S. *The Modern Middle East: A Guide to Research Tools in the Social*

Sciences. Boulder: Westview, 1978. Annotated entries; coverage for the study of the Middle East in the nineteenth and twentieth centuries.

Smith, Dwight L. *Afro-American History: A Bibliography*. Santa Barbara: ABC-Clio, 1974. Abstracts covering all aspects of Afro-American history; organized by subject.

Steinberg's Dictionary of British History. 2nd ed. New York: St. Martin's, 1971.

Stephens, Lester D. *Historiography: A Bibliography*. Metuchen: Scarecrow, 1975. Indexed, annotated entries on reference works as well as methods and theories of history.

Wager, W. Warren. *Books in World History: A Guide for Teachers and Students*. Bloomington: Indiana UP, 1973.

Woods, Richard D. *Reference Materials on Mexican Americans: An Annotated Bibliography*. Metuchen: Scarecrow, 1976. A guide to dictionaries, bibliographies, and biographical materials.

Journals

Africa. Academic articles on African studies.

American Heritage. A readable, popular magazine with authoritative, illustrated articles; a good starting point for finding topics.

American Historical Review. Academic articles and many book reviews.

American History Illustrated. Accessible articles on a wide range of topics.

American Quarterly. Interdisciplinary articles on art, history, literature, and other American studies topics.

Asian Affairs. Articles on cultural, economic, and political topics, past and present.

Black Scholar: A Journal of Black Studies and Research

British History Illustrated. A magazine for general readers; illustrated articles on topics from the beginnings of British history to the present.

China Quarterly. Articles on contemporary China.

Clio: An Interdisciplinary Journal of Literature, History, and the Philosophy of History. Sometimes difficult but rewarding articles.

Comparative Studies in Society and History. Interdisciplinary articles connecting history to issues in other fields such as psychology.

Diplomatic History. American foreign relations.

English Historical Review. Articles on British topics, past and present; many book reviews.

European Studies Review. Interdisciplinary articles.

Harvard Journal of Asiatic Studies

History: Reviews of New Books. A useful source of reviews of books on all aspects of history.

History Today. Illustrated articles on international topics for general readers.

International Journal of Middle East Studies. Academic articles and book reviews.

Journal of African History. Emphasizes perspectives on the entire continent instead of single countries.

Journal of American History. Important articles and many book reviews.

Journal of Asian Studies. Academic articles and extensive book reviews.

Journal of Economic History. Articles and book reviews on how economics affects history.

Journal of Modern African Studies. Emphasizes the twentieth century.

Journal of Modern History. Primary coverage is European history since the Renaissance.

Journal of Negro History. Articles on black history; book reviews.

Journal of Psychohistory. People and events examined from the point of view of psychological theories; controversial but interesting.

Journal of the History of Ideas. Emphasizes the ideas that have shaped cultural and intellectual history.

New England Quarterly. Although the focus is on New England life, history, and literature, the articles and reviews have more than regional interest.

Reviews in American History. Consists entirely of lengthy essay reviews of recent books.

Speculum. Articles on medieval studies.

William and Mary Quarterly. Focuses on early American history and related history abroad.

MUSIC

Books

Anderson, Ruth. *Contemporary American Composers: A Biographical Dictionary.* Boston: Hall, 1976. Includes only those composers born since 1870.

Annual Index to Popular Music Record Reviews. Metuchen: Scarecrow, 1972 to date.

Apel, Willi. *Harvard Dictionary of Music.* 2nd rev. ed. Cambridge: Harvard UP, 1969. Especially strong on history and theory.

Claghorn, Charles E. *Biographical Dictionary of American Music.* West Nyack: Parker, 1973.

Cumulated Index of Record Reviews. Washington: Music Library Assn., 1950 to date. Locates reviews of mostly classical recordings.

Drone, Jeanette M. *Index to Opera, Operetta, and Musical Comedy Synopses in Collections and Periodicals.* Metuchen: Scarecrow, 1978.

Duckles, Vincent H. *Music Reference and Research Materials.* 3rd ed. New York: Free, 1974. An important annotated list of resources for the study of music.

Fink, Robert, and Robert Ricci. *Language of Twentieth Century Music: A Dictionary of Terms.* New York: Schirmer, 1975. Definitions of terms used in jazz, electronic music, rock, multimedia, etc.

Fuld, James J. *Book of World-Famous Music: Classical, Folk, and Popular.* Rev. ed. New York: Crown, 1971.

Grount, Donald J. *A History of Western Music.* Rev. ed. New York: Norton, 1973.

Grove, Sir George. *Dictionary of Music and Musicians.* 5th ed. 10 vols. New York: St. Martin's, 1955; Supplement 1961. A standard, comprehensive source.

Havlice, Patricia P. *Popular Song Index.* Metuchen: Scarecrow, 1975. Indexes some 300 song books published between 1940 and 1972.

Horn, David. *The Literature of American Music in Books and Folk Music Collections: A Fully Annotated Bibliography.* Metuchen: Scarecrow 1977. The index provides ready access to the wide variety of topics covered.

Jackson, Richard. *U.S. Music: Sources of Bibliography and Collective Biography.* Brooklyn: Inst. for Studies in American Music, 1973. Annotated.

Kinkle, Roger D. *The Complete Encyclopedia of Popular Music and Jazz, 1900–1950.* 4 vols. New Rochelle: Arlington, 1974.

Kobbé, Gustav. *The New Kobbé's Complete Opera Book.* Rev. ed. New York: Putnam's, 1976. A guide to opera, including summaries of plots.

Meggett, Joan M. *Musical Periodical Literature: An Annotated Bibliography of Indexes and Bibliographies.* Metuchen: Scarecrow, 1978. Indexed by subject, titles, authors, editors, and compilers.

Music Index. Detroit: Information Service, 1950 to date. Indexes articles, book reviews, and performance reviews in about 300 periodicals.

Picerno, Vincent J. *Dictionary of Musical Terms*. Brooklyn: Haskell, 1976. Definitions written for students.

Popular Music: An Annotated Index of American Popular Songs. 6 vols. New York: Adrian, 1973.

RILM Abstracts of Music Literature. New York: International RILM Center, City U, 1968 to date. Abstracts include books, articles, and reviews in international periodicals.

Sandburg, Larry, and Dick Weissman. *The Folk Music Sourcebook*. New York: Knopf, 1976. Focuses on North American folk music.

Scholes, Percy A. *The Oxford Companion to Music*. 10th ed. New York: Oxford UP, 1970.

Stambler, Irwin. *Encyclopedia of Pop, Rock, and Soul*. New York: St. Martin's, 1975.

Thompson, Kenneth. *A Dictionary of Twentieth-Century Composers (1911–1971)*. New York: St. Martin's, 1973.

Thompson, Oscar. *International Cyclopedia of Music and Musicians*. 10th rev. ed. New York: Dodd, 1975. Authoritative brief articles on composers, music history, and related topics.

Journals

American Music Teacher
Billboard. A magazine that stays abreast of contemporary popular music.
The Black Perspective in Music
Down Beat. An interesting and widely read jazz magazine; reviews of books, recordings, and performances.
Ethnomusicology. International coverage of primitive and folk music.
High Fidelity. Excellent reviews of popular and classical recordings.
Jazz Journal
Journal of Jazz Studies
Journal of Music Theory
Journal of Music Therapy
Journal of Renaissance and Baroque Music
Music Journal. Emphasizes contemporary music.
Music Quarterly. Important articles, book reviews, and record reviews.
Opera News. For opera enthusiasts.
Rolling Stone. Articles on popular music and related topics.
Stereo Review. Includes general articles on music and informed reviews of recordings.

PHILOSOPHY

Books

Bertman, Martin A. *Research Guide to Philosophy*. Morristown: General Learning, 1974. Information on sources, research methods, and terms that beginning students will find valuable.

Borchardt, D. H. *How to Find Out in Philosophy and Psychology*. Oxford: Pergamon, 1968. Basic reference sources for students.

Copleston, Frederick. *A History of Philosophy*. 9 vols. Garden City: Doubleday, 1977.

Dictionary of the History of Ideas: Studies of Selected Pivotal Ideas. 5 vols. New York: Scribner's, 1973–74. Interdisciplinary essays on the history of ideas in fields such as religion, philosophy, mathematics, linguistics, etc.

Encyclopedia of Philosophy. 8 vols. New York: Macmillan, 1967. A comprehensive treatment of Eastern and Western philosophy from ancient times to the present.

Guerry, Herbert. *A Bibliography of Philosophical Bibliographies*. Westport: Greenwood, 1977. Lists bibliographies on particular philosophers and bibliographies by subject.

Lineback, Richard H. *Ethics: A Bibliography*. New York: Garland, 1976.

Lucey, Alan R. *A Dictionary of Philosophy*. London: Routledge, 1976. Definitions of terms for students.

Magill, Frank H. *Masterpieces of World Philosophy in Summary Form*. New York: Harper, 1961. Summarizes important Western philosophic works.

Philosopher's Index: An International Index to Philosophical Periodicals. Bowling Green: Bowling Green U, 1967 to date. For additional indexing for earlier articles and books, see *Philosopher's Index: A Retrospective Index to U.S. Publications from 1940*. 3 vols. Bowling Green: Philosophy Documentation Center, 1978.

Journals

British Journal of Aesthetics. Articles on the theoretical study of the arts.

Ethics. Focuses on social, political, and legal philosophy.

Journal of Aesthetics and Art Criticism

Journal of Philosophy. Includes historical articles as well as those on linguistics, logic, and philosophy of science.

Journal of Symbolic Logic

Journal of the History of Ideas. Specializes in cultural and intellectual history, including the history of philosophy.

Journal of the History of Philosophy

Metaphilosophy. Articles on philosophy as a method and a discipline.

Monist. Each issue devoted to a single topic; accessible to informed general readers.

Philosophical Books. Consists of reviews of selected recent books in philosophy.

Philosophical Forum. Articles on a variety of topics for general readers.

Philosophical Quarterly. Emphasis on political philosophy, ethics, and philosophy of linguistics.

Philosophical Review. Academic articles on a wide variety of topics.

Philosophy. Includes book reviews and review articles.

Philosophy and Rhetoric

Philosophy East and West. Comparative studies of Oriental and Western philosophies.

Philosophy of Science

Philosophy of Social Sciences

Review of Metaphysics. Includes abstracts of recent periodical articles.

POLITICAL SCIENCE

Books

ABC Pol. Sci. Santa Barbara: ABC-Clio, 1969 to date. Reprints the table of contents pages of some 300 current journals; author/subject indexes; a useful source for recent articles.

Blackey, Robert. *Modern Revolutions and Revolutionists.* Santa Barbara: ABC-Clio, 1976. Lists books and articles by subjects (e.g., counterrevolution) and by region or country.

Blackstock, Paul W., and Frank L. Schaf. *Intelligence, Espionage, Counterespionage, and Covert Operations: A Guide to Information Sources.* Detroit: Gale, 1978. An annotated bibliography emphasizing the post–WW II period.

Brock, Clifton. *The Literature of Political Science: A Guide for Students, Librarians, and Teachers.* New York: Bowker, 1969.

Cook, Chris, and John Paxton. *European Political Facts, 1918–73.* New York: St. Martin's, 1975.

Gallup, George H. *The Gallup Poll: Public Opinion, 1935–1971.* 3 vols. New York: Random, 1972. A chronological listing of reports on American social and political opinions; subject index. See also next item.

———. *The Gallup Poll: Public Opinion, 1972–1977.* 2 vols. Wilmington: Scholarly Resources, 1978.

Greenstein, Fred I., and Nelson W. Polsby. *Handbook of Political Science.* 9 vols. Reading: Addison, 1975. Bibliographical essays by experts on important areas of study.

Harmon, Robert B. *Political Science Bibliographies.* 2 vols. Metuchen: Scarecrow, 1973, 1976. A bibliography of bibliographies.

Hawley, Willis D., and James H. Svara. *The Study of Community Power: A Bibliographic Review.* Santa Barbara: ABC-Clio, 1972.

Holler, Frederick L. *The Information Sources of Political Science.* 2nd ed. 5 vols. Santa Barbara: ABC-Clio, 1975. Annotated lists of general reference sources as well as sources on specific areas such as federal, state, and local governments; international relations; and political theory.

LaBarr, Dorothy F., and Joel D. Singer. *The Study of International Politics; A Guide to the Sources for the Student, Teacher and Researcher.* Santa Barbara: ABC-Clio, 1976.

Laqueur, Walter Z., ed. *A Dictionary of Politics.* Rev. ed. New York: Free, 1974.

Leif, Irving P. *Community Power and Decision-Making: An International Handbook.* Metuchen: Scarecrow, 1974.

Manheim, Jarol B., and Melanie Wallace. *Political Violence in the United States, 1875–1974: A Bibliography.* New York: Garland, 1975.

Menendez, Albert J. *Church-State Relations: An Annotated Bibliography.* New York: Garland, 1976.

Mikolus, Edward F. *Annotated Bibliography on Transnational and International Terrorism.* Washington: U.S. Central Intelligence Agency, 1976.

Pfaltzgraff, Robert L. *The Study of International Relations: A Guide to Information Sources.* Detroit: Gale, 1977. Annotated lists of significant journals in the field and books on theory and method since WW II.

Political Handbook of the World. New York: McGraw, 1975 to date. Annual information on governments, parties, etc. From 1927 to 1974 the title was *Political Handbook and Atlas of the World.*

Vose, Clement E. *A Guide to Library Sources in Political Science: American Government.* Washington: American Political Science Assn., 1975. Valuable information for students on available resources.

Journals

American Academy of Political and Social Science. Annals. Each issue develops a single topic from a variety of points of view.
American Journal of Political Science. Articles on all areas of the discipline.
American Political Science Review. Published by the American Political Science Association; important articles and reviews.
American Politics Quarterly
Atlantic Community Quarterly. Focuses on nations on both sides of the North Atlantic.
Comparative Political Studies. Interdisciplinary articles on international topics.
Comparative Politics. International emphasis.
Congressional Digest. Articles on current issues in the U.S. Congress.
Congressional Quarterly Weekly Report. Summarizes congressional activity.
Congressional Record. The daily workings of the Congress.
Current History. Each monthly issue takes up a single world affairs topic.
European Journal of Political Research
Foreign Affairs. Important articles by experts on American foreign policy.
Foreign Policy. Like *Foreign Affairs*, an important journal on international topics.
International Affairs
International Studies Quarterly. Published by the International Studies Association; interdisciplinary.
Journal of Politics. Articles and lengthy book review essays.
Political Science Quarterly. International coverage but emphasis on American topics.
Politics and Society. Offers nontraditional, radical perspectives on society.
Public Opinion Quarterly. Articles on how opinions are shaped by the media.
Science and Society. A wide variety of topics from a Marxist perspective.
Studies in Comparative Communism
U.N. Monthly Chronicle. A record of deliberations and actions of the United Nations.
World Affairs. Articles on international topics and issues.
World Politics. Articles on historical and contemporary international topics.

PSYCHOLOGY

Books

Alexander, Franz G., and Sheldon T. Selesnick. *The History of Psychiatry: An Evaluation of Psychiatric Thought and Practice from Prehistoric Times to the Present.* New York: Harper, 1966.
Annual Review of Psychology. Palo Alto: Annual Reviews, 1950 to date. Evaluates current work.
Arieti, Silvano, ed. *American Handbook of Psychiatry.* 2nd ed. 6 vols. New York: Basic, 1975. A complete overview of psychiatry.
Bell, James E. *A Guide to Library Research in Psychology.* Dubuque: Brown, 1971. Geared for undergraduates writing research papers.

Chaplin, James P. *Dictionary of Psychology*. New rev. ed. New York: Dell, 1975.
Dunnette, Marvin D., ed. *Handbook of Industrial and Organizational Psychology*. Chicago: Rand, 1976.
Eysenck, Hans J., ed. *Handbook of Abnormal Psychology*. 2nd ed. San Diego: Knapp, 1973.
Eysenck, H. J., et al. *Encyclopedia of Psychology*. 3 vols. New York: Herder, 1972. An important overview with bibliographies.
Harvard List of Books in Psychology. 4th ed. Cambridge: Harvard UP, 1971. An annotated guide to important books.
International Encyclopedia of Psychiatry, Psychology, Psychoanalysis, and Neurology. New York: Van Nostrand, 1977.
Kiell, Norman, ed. *Psychiatry and Psychology in the Visual Arts and Aesthetics: A Bibliography*. Madison: U of Wisconsin P, 1965.
———, *Psychoanalysis, Psychology, and Literature: A Bibliography*. Madison: U of Wisconsin P, 1963.
Nordby, Vernon. *A Guide to Psychologists and Their Concepts*. San Francisco: Freeman, 1974. An introduction for the general reader.
Psychological Abstracts, 1927 to date. Lancaster: APA. Abstracts new books, articles, and reports; author-subject index. See also *Cumulated Subject Index to Psychological Abstracts, 1927–1960*. 2 vols. Boston: Hall, 1966; and its supplements.
Psychological Index, 1894–1935. 42 vols. Princeton: Psychological Review, 1895–1935. For more current listings see *Psychological Abstracts*.
Wilkening, Howard E. *The Psychology Almanac: A Handbook for Students*. Monterey: Brooks, 1973.
Wolman, Benjamin B., ed. *Dictionary of Behavioral Science*. New York: Van Nostrand, 1974. Includes psychology and related fields.
———, *Handbook of Parapsychology*. New York: Van Nostrand, 1977. Information on psychic phenomena such as clairvoyance, extrasensory perception, and telepathy.

Journals

American Imago: A Psychoanalytic Journal for Culture, Science and the Arts. Applies psychoanalytic interpretations to various aspects of culture.
American Journal of Psychiatry
American Journal of Psychoanalysis
American Journal of Psychology
American Journal of Psychotherapy
Behavior Modification
Behavioral Science
Contemporary Psychology: A Journal of Reviews. Lengthy reviews of current books, articles, and media on psychology.
Human Behavior. Aimed at a general audience interested in analyses of behavior.
International Journal of Aging and Human Development
Journal of Applied Psychology
Journal of Black Psychology
Journal of Humanistic Psychology. Philosophical approaches to psychological issues.
Journal of Psychology
Journal of Thanatology. On death and dying.
Omega: The Journal of Death and Dying
Personnel Psychology

Psychology of Women Quarterly
Psychology Today. Illustrated, clearly written articles for a general audience on all phases of psychology.

RELIGION

Books

Adams, Charles J., ed. *A Reader's Guide to the Great Religions*. 2nd ed. New York: Free, 1977. Bibliographical essays written by specialists.

Attwater, Donald, ed. *A Catholic Dictionary*. 3rd ed. New York: Macmillan, 1958. Explains Roman Catholic Church terminology.

Bowden, Henry W. *Dictionary of American Religious Biography*. Westport: Greenwood, 1977. Includes significant persons of all denominations who had an impact on American religion.

Brandon, Samuel G. F., ed. *A Dictionary of Comparative Religion*. New York: Scribner's, 1970.

Buttrick, George A., and Keith R. Crim. *The Interpreter's Dictionary of the Bible*. 5 vols. Nashville: Abingdon, 1976. An illustrated encyclopedia of names, terms, and subjects.

Capps, Donald R., and Paul Ransohoff. *Psychology of Religion: A Guide to Information Sources*. Detroit: Gale, 1976.

Cross, F. L., and Elizabeth A. Livingstone. *The Oxford Dictionary of the Christian Church*. New York: Oxford UP, 1974. Many bibliographies are appended to the more than 6,000 articles included.

Encyclopaedia Judaica. 16 vols. New York: Macmillan, 1972.

Gaustad, Edwin S. *Historical Atlas of Religion in America*. Rev. ed. New York: Harper, 1976. Shows growth of various denominations since 1650.

Kennedy, James R. *Library Research Guide to Religion and Theology*. Ann Arbor: Pierian, 1974. A guide for writing undergraduate research papers in religion and theology.

May, Herbert G., et al., eds. *Oxford Bible Atlas*. New York: Oxford UP, 1974. Maps and history related to the Bible.

Mead, Frank S. *Encyclopedia of Religious Quotations*. New York: Pillar, 1976.

———. *Handbook of Denominations in the United States*. 6th ed. Nashville: Abingdon, 1975. Describes more than 300 groups.

Mitros, Joseph F. *Religions: A Select Classified Bibliography*. New York: Learned, 1973. Written for students preparing a research paper.

Regazzi, John J., and Theodore C. Hines. *A Guide to Indexed Periodicals in Religion*. Metuchen: Scarecrow, 1975. An alphabetical listing of about 2,700 periodicals and where they are indexed.

Religion Index One: Periodicals. Chicago: American Theological Library Assn., 1977 to date. A subject and author index to periodical literature with abstracts; includes a book review index. This is the new title for *Index to Religious Periodical Literature*.

Religion Index Two: Multi-author Works. Chicago: American Theological Library Assn., 1976 to date. A subject-author index to works written by more than one author.

Rice, Edward. *Eastern Definitions: A Short Encyclopedia of Religions of the Orient*. Garden City: Doubleday, 1978.

Stevenson, Burton E., ed. *The Home Book of Bible Quotations.* New York: Harper, 1949. Includes a subject index.

Strong, James. *Exhaustive Concordance of the Bible.* Nashville: Abingdon, 1977. A listing of principal words in context of the King James version.

Wigoder, Geoffrey, ed. *The New Standard Jewish Encyclopedia.* 5th ed. Garden City: Doubleday, 1977.

Williams, Ethel L., and Clifton F. Brown. *The Howard University Bibliography of African and Afro-American Religious Studies.* Wilmington: Scholarly Resources, 1977.

Yoo, Yushin. *Books on Buddhism: An Annotated Subject Guide.* Metuchen: Scarecrow, 1976.

Journals

America. A national Catholic weekly.
Biblical Research
Christian Century. A nondenominational Protestant weekly.
Christianity and Crisis: A Christian Journal of Opinion
Church History
Commentary. Essays on contemporary issues; sponsored by the American Jewish Committee.
Commonweal. A national Catholic weekly.
Ecumenist
Friends Journal. Contemporary Quaker life and thought.
Harvard Theological Review
Journal for the Scientific Study of Religion
Journal of Biblical Literature
Journal of Church and State
Journal of Ecumenical Studies
Journal of Religion
Judaism: A Quarterly Journal of Jewish Life and Thought
The Muslim World
Religion in Life: A Christian Quarterly of Opinion and Discussion
Religious Studies
Religious Studies in Review. Extensive reviews of important books.
Theology Today. An ecumenical approach to issues.

SCIENCE

Books

Annual Review of Information Science and Technology. Washington: American Soc. for Information Science, 1966 to date. Annual bibliographic updates.

Applied Science and Technology Index. New York: Wilson, 1913 to date. Subject indexes to periodicals covering fields such as chemistry, earth sciences, space research, engineering, physics, etc. From 1913 to 1957 this was entitled *Industrial Arts Index.*

Asimov, Isaac. *Asimov's Biographical Encyclopedia of Science and Technology.* Rev. ed.

Garden City: Doubleday, 1972. A chronological treatment of the work of nearly 1,200 great scientists since ancient times.

Burke, John G., and Jill S. Reddig. *Guide to Ecology Information and Organizations.* New York: Wilson, 1976. Includes information on indexes, periodicals, reference works, government publications, and organizations.

Caldwell, Lynton K., et al. *Science Technology and Public Policy: A Selected and Annotated Bibliography.* 3 vols. Bloomington: Indiana U, 1968–72. An annotated list of books, documents, and articles published since 1945 that relates science and technology to social issues.

Dictionary of Scientific Biography. 15 vols. New York: Scribner's, 1978. Articles on individual scientists throughout the world who have made important contributions.

Ferguson, Eugene S. *Bibliography of the History of Technology.* Cambridge: M.I.T. P, 1968. Annotated books, articles, and bibliographies.

Gardner, Martin. *Fads and Fallacies in the Name of Science.* Rev. ed. New York: Dover, 1957. Some potentially interesting paper topics here.

General Science Index. New York: Wilson, 1978 to date. A subject index to general science periodicals.

Grogan, Denis Joseph. *Science and Technology: An Introduction to the Literature.* 3rd ed. Hamden: Shoe String, 1976. A valuable guide to finding information in scientific publications; includes sections on dictionaries, encyclopedias, handbooks, microforms, and computerized sources.

Index to Scientific and Technical Proceedings. Philadelphia: Inst. for Scientific Information, 1978 to date. Includes subject indexes to important published conference proceedings.

Lasworth, Earl J. *Reference Sources in Science and Technology.* Metuchen: Scarecrow, 1972. A guide to finding literature in scientific fields; includes information on locating and using reference sources.

Malinowsky, Harold R., et al. *Science and Engineering Literature: A Guide to Current Reference Sources.* 3rd ed. Littleton: Libraries Unlimited, 1980. Annotated lists of reference works in various scientific fields.

McGraw-Hill Dictionary of Scientific and Technical Terms. 2nd ed. New York: McGraw, 1978. Clear definitions for quick reference.

McGraw-Hill Encyclopedia of Science and Technology. 4th ed. 15 vols. New York: McGraw, 1977. Entries covering all branches of science and technology; entries are for the nonspecialist; an excellent starting point for developing a science topic. Updated information is published annually in the *McGraw-Hill Yearbook of Science and Technology.*

Mitcham, Carl, and Robert Mackey. *Bibliography of the Philosophy of Technology.* Chicago: U of Chicago P, 1973. Lists works that reflect on the philosophical, ethical, political, and religious meanings of technology.

Owen, Dolores B., and Marguerite Hanchey. *Abstracts and Indexes in Science and Technology: A Descriptive Guide.* Metuchen: Scarecrow, 1974. Provides detailed information of more than 100 abstracts and indexes listed by subject.

Rider, Kenneth J. *History of Science and Technology: A Select Bibliography for Students.* 2nd ed. New York: International Publications Service, 1970.

Science Citation Index. Philadelphia: Inst. for Scientific Information, 1961 to date. Indexed articles from nearly 3,000 journals on science and technology.

Technical Book Review Index. New York: Special Libraries Assn., 1935 to date. Brief excerpts from reviews appearing in scientific and technical periodicals.

Van Nostrand's Scientific Encyclopedia. 5th ed. New York: Van Nostrand, 1976. Entries of varying length for terms used in nearly all branches of science.

Journals

American Philosophical Society Proceedings. Includes articles on issues related to science.
American Scientist. General articles on all facets of science; excellent book reviews.
British Journal for the History of Science. International in scope.
Endeavour. Brief, illustrated articles covering timely topics.
Ethics in Science and Medicine. Emphasizes moral and social issues.
Frontiers: A Magazine of Natural History. For general readers particularly interested in environmental topics.
Impact of Science on Society. International in scope.
Natural History. Accessible, illustrated articles to a broad spectrum of topics related to nature.
Nature. A weekly devoted to news, articles, and reviews of current scientific topics around the world.
New Scientist. Scientific news in nontechnical prose for general readers.
New York Academy of Sciences. Annals. Solid academic articles on a variety of topics.
Philosophy of Science. Philosophical perspectives on science.
Science. Provides articles and news reflecting current developments in various branches of science.
Science and Public Policy. Emphasizes science and society.
Science Progress. Articles and book reviews for nonspecialists.
Scientific American. An excellent starting point for research topics of current interest.
Technology and Culture. Focuses on the history of technology from ancient times to the present; articles on the social, political, and economic impact of technology on people.
Technology Review. Surveys technological changes and their impact on society.

SOCIOLOGY

Books

Bart, Pauline, and Linda Frankel. *The Student Sociologist's Handbook.* 2nd ed. Morristown: General Learning, 1976. A guide to writing a research paper; information on sources, terms, etc.
Encyclopedia of Social Work. New York: National Assn. of Social Workers, 1965 to date.
Encyclopedia of Sociology. Guilford: Dushkin, 1974. Descriptions of terms, theories, and important theorists.
Mark, Charles. *Sociology of America: A Guide to Information Sources.* Detroit: Gale, 1976. Annotated lists of books, periodicals, and reference works.
Rzepecki, Arnold. *Book Review Index to Social Science Periodicals.* Ann Arbor: Pierian, 1978 to date.
Sills, D. E., ed. *International Encyclopedia of the Social Sciences.* 17 vols. New York: Macmillan, 1968.
Social Sciences Citation Index. Indexes about 2,000 journals; hence, a valuable research tool.
Social Sciences Index. New York: Wilson, 1965 to date. Before 1974 entitled *Social Sciences and Humanities Index.*
Social Work Research and Abstracts. New York: National Assn. of Social Workers, 1965

to date. Prior to 1977 known as *Abstracts for Social Workers;* international coverage of articles on social work and related areas.

Sociological Abstracts. New York: Sociological Abstracts, 1952 to date. Especially useful for surveying recent research on a topic.

Journals

American Journal of Sociology. Research in sociology and social psychology; book reviews and lists of recently published books.
American Sociological Review. The publication of the American Sociological Association, field studies as well as theoretical articles.
Contemporary Sociology. Consists of reviews of recent books; many are lengthy essay reviews as well as surveys of work done on a particular topic.
Environment and Behavior. Studies of how environment affects people.
Insurgent Sociologist. Socialist and radical perspectives.
International Journal of Comparative Sociology
Journal of Applied Social Psychology
Journal of Marriage and the Family
Journal of Political and Military Sociology. Interdisciplinary and comparative approaches.
Journal of Social Issues. Interdisciplinary, nontechnical articles on contemporary issues.
Journal of Youth and Adolescence. Interdisciplinary approaches to varied topics.
Rural Sociology. International in scope.
Single Parent. Informed articles for nonprofessionals interested in issues facing single parents.
Social Problems. Lucid, interesting, and accessible articles.
Society. Articles on race, politics, education, housing, etc. for general readers.
Sociological Inquiry. Interesting articles on varied topics.
Sociological Quarterly
Sociological Review
Urban Life and Culture. Focuses on contemporary social phenomena.

THEATER

Books

Adelman, Irving, and Rita Dworkin. *Modern Drama: A Checklist of Critical Literature on 20th Century Plays.* Metuchen: Scarecrow, 1967.
Bowman, Walter P., and Robert H. Ball. *Theatre Language: A Dictionary of Terms in English of the Drama and Stage from Medieval to Modern Times.* New York: Theatre Arts, 1961.
Breed, Paul F., and Florence M. Sniderman. *Dramatic Criticism Index: A Bibliography of Commentaries on Playwrights from Ibsen to the Avant-Garde.* Detroit: Gale, 1972.
Cheshire, David F. *Theatre: History, Criticism and Reference.* Hamden: Archon, 1967. An overview of books about theater.
Chicorel Theater Index to Drama Literature. Vol. 21. New York: Chicorel, 1975.
Crowell's Handbook of Contemporary Drama. New York: Crowell, 1971. American and European drama since WW II.

Cumulated Dramatic Index, 1909–1949. 2 vols. Boston: Hall, 1965. Subject indexes to a wide variety of theater topics.

The Encyclopedia of World Theater. New York: Scribner's, 1977. Short entries on all aspects of theater.

Fordyce, Rachel. *Children's Theatre and Creative Dramatics: An Annotated Bibliography of Critical Works.* Boston: Hall, 1975.

Hartnoll, Phillis. *The Oxford Companion to Theatre.* 3rd ed. London: Oxford UP, 1967. Emphasizes popular theater over the classics; international.

Hatch, James. *Black Image on the American Stage: A Bibliography of Plays and Musicals, 1770–1970.* New York: DBS, 1970.

Humanities Index. New York: Wilson, 1974 to date. Includes indexing to periodicals related to theater.

The New York Times Theater Reviews, 1920–1970. 10 vols. New York Times Book, 1971. Reprints *Times* reviews; titles and names indexed.

Palmer, Helen H. *European Drama Criticism, 1900–1975.* 2nd ed. Hamden: Shoe String, 1977.

Salem, James M. *A Guide to Critical Reviews.* 5 vols. Metuchen: Scarecrow, 1966–71. Reviews of plays and films in popular periodicals.

Samples, Gordon. *How to Locate Reviews of Plays and Films. A Bibliography of Criticism from the Beginnings to the Present.* Metuchen: Scarecrow, 1976.

Schoolcraft, Ralph N. *Performing Arts Books in Print: An Annotated Bibliography.* New York: Drama Book Specialists, 1973.

Sprinchorn, Evert, ed. *20th-Century Plays in Synopsis.* New York: Crowell, 1966. Includes American, British, and Continental plays.

Theatre/Drama Abstracts. Pleasant Hill: Theatre/Drama & Speech Communication Information Center, 1974 to date. Abstracts and indexes to articles, and reviews of performances and books.

Whalon, Marion K. *Performing Arts Research: A Guide to Information Sources.* Detroit: Gale, 1976. Annotated lists of reference sources such as bibliographies, indexes, dictionaries, and encyclopedias.

Young, William C. *Famous Actors and Actresses on the American Stage.* 2 vols. New York: Bowker, 1975. Biographical information and critical assessments on more than 200 actors and actresses.

Journals

Comparative Drama. Scholarly articles; international in scope and occasionally interdisciplinary in method.

Drama Review. International in scope; emphasis on developments in contemporary avant-garde theater.

Educational Theatre Journal. Especially aimed at college theater; articles on theory, history, special single topics, etc.

Modern Drama. Interviews as well as articles; international coverage.

Modern International Drama. Features contemporary international drama in translation.

New York Theatre Critics Review. A compilation of reviews from important New York newspapers, national magazines, and network television; offers a quick way to compare the views of critics about a production.

Nineteenth Century Theater Research. International in scope.

Performing Arts Journal. Articles, reviews, and interviews on theater as well as other performing arts.

Theater Design and Technology
Theatre Quarterly. Emphasizes modern drama; includes strong bibliographies as well as articles and interviews.
Theatre Survey. Focuses on the history of theater; international in scope.
Variety. A newspaper important to nearly everyone in the business of entertainment.

WOMEN'S STUDIES

Books

Ballou, Patricia K. *Women: A Bibliography of Bibliographies*. Boston: Hall, 1980.
The Book of Women's Achievements. New York: Stein, 1976.
Equal Rights Amendment Project. *The Equal Rights Amendment: A Bibliographical Study*. Westport: Greenwood, 1976.
Goodwater, Leanna. *Women in Antiquity: An Annotated Bibliography*. Metuchen: Scarecrow, 1975.
Haber, Barbara. *Women in America: A Guide to Books*. Boston: Hall, 1978. Annotations of recent literature on women's issues.
Hinding, Andrea, and Clarke A. Chambers. *Women's History Sources*. 2 vols. New York: Bowker, 1980.
Hughes, Marija M. *The Sexual Barrier: Legal, Medical, Economic and Social Aspects of Sex Discrimination*. Washington: Hughes, 1977.
Krichmar, Albert, et al. *The Women's Movement in the Seventies: An International English-Language Bibliography*. Metuchen: Scarecrow, 1977. Arranged geographically with subject indexes and many annotations.
Krichmar, Albert. *The Women's Rights Movement in the United States, 1848–1970: A Bibliography and Sourcebook*. Metuchen: Scarecrow, 1972.
Lerner, Gerda. *Black Women in White America*. New York: Pantheon, 1972.
Rosenberg, Marie, and Leonard Bergstrom. *Women and Society: A Critical Review of the Literature with a Selected Annotated Bibliography*. Beverly Hills: Sage, 1975. This is supplemented by Een, JoAnn Delores, and Marie B. Rosenberg-Dishman. *Women and Society, Citations 3601–6000: An Annotated Bibliography*. Beverly Hills: Sage, 1978.
Schlachter, Gail. *A Guide to the Reference Literature on Women in the Social Sciences, Humanities, and Sciences*. Santa Barbara: ABC-Clio, 1981.
Williams, Ora. *American Black Women in the Arts and Social Sciences: A Bibliographic Survey*. Rev. ed. Metuchen: Scarecrow, 1978.
Woman's Almanac. Philadelphia: Lippincott, 1976.
The Women's Rights Almanac. Bethesda: Stanton, 1974 to date. International statistics on women.
Women's Studies Abstracts. Rush, New York: Women Studies, 1972 to date. Published quarterly with an annual index. Abstracts from periodicals, some books, and pamphlets.
Women's Work and Women's Studies. New York: Barnard College, 1972 to date. An interdisciplinary bibliography published annually.

Journals

Aphra. A quarterly journal of literature and social criticism.
Feminist Studies. Scholarly; emphasizing history and the social sciences.
Ms. A feminist popular magazine.
Psychology of Women Quarterly. Professional articles on women's psychology and behavior.
Quest: A Feminist Quarterly. Each issue devoted to a special topic.
Signs: Journal of Women in Culture and Society. Scholarly articles and review essays.
Spare Rib. A very popular feminist periodical in Great Britain.
Women: A Journal of Liberation. Each issue devoted to a specific theme.
Women and Literature. Focuses on women writers and the image of women in literature.
Women's Studies. Includes all fields but emphasizes literature and the arts.

Index